FRINGE

FRINGE

Seeing it, doing it, surviving it –
A complete guide to the
Edinburgh Fringe

James Aylett and James Lark

FRIDAY
BOOKS

First published in Great Britain in 2006 by Friday Books
An imprint of The Friday Project Limited
83 Victoria Street, London SW1H 0HW

www.thefridayproject.co.uk
www.fridaybooks.co.uk

ISBN – 10: 0 9548318 9 6
ISBN – 13: 978 0 9548318 9 9

British Library Cataloguing in Publication Data

A catalogue record for this book is available
from the British Library

Designed by Amina Dudhia
West 8 Design Ltd

Produced by Staziker Jones
www.stazikerjones.co.uk

Index compiled by Indexing Specialists (UK) Limited

The Publisher's policy is to use paper manufactured
from sustainable sources

Contents

Acknowledgements

Many thanks to those who have contributed material to this book; Andrew McClelland, Matt Green, John Finnemore, Alex Horne, Robin Strapp and Becky Moore. Also to those who didn't contribute actual words but did say nice things to us all the same, including David Jarman, Mark Watson, Kate Copstick, David Tickner, Stewart Lee, The Mighty Gareth, Elizabeth Park, Marianne Levy, David Mitchell, Delyth Jones, Jon Croker and James Mackenzie.

Thanks also to Leroy Harris, Anthony Alderson, Christopher Richardson, Carola Stewart, James Casey, Lydia Aers, Neil Hewitt, Frog Stone, Liz Aylett, Katharine Aylett, the Cambridgeshire Constabulary, the General Register Office for Scotland, ScotsGay, Baillie Gifford and Tartan Silk, all of whom gave us information, tea or kangaroo butties when they were required. Peter and Frances Lark sent their son a nice card and he was touched. Also to the press offices of Pleasance, Gilded Balloon, Underbelly and Stand Comedy Club, who didn't send either of us cards but helped us get into shows without paying too much. To the Red Bull for continued and quality sustenance, and to James Booth for not firing James Aylett. Also to Luke Staiano, who did nothing at all to aid us in writing this book but did promise us money if we mentioned him.

We are also grateful to all those who have been involved with and supported the Uncertainty Division over the years, for their company and shared suffering in the Fringe experience. Those who didn't go to the Fringe still suffered on occasions, so hello to you as well.

Our knowledge of the Fringe, the Cambridge Footlights, and all life in general, was much enriched by Dr Harry Porter, who is fondly remembered and much missed. We are sorry that the book doesn't have enough songs in it.

Special thanks to Mary Chester-Kadwell. Thanks in abundance to Paul and Clare for letting us write a book; to Heather for organising Paul and Clare while we wrote a book; to the other Clare who looks like Angelina Jolie for shepherding us through the process, and indeed for just shepherding us when we had erred and strayed like lost sheep; and to Lorna for caring for the words and the jokes.

Finally to the many Fringe-goers who were helpful, supportive or indeed abusive throughout our searches for information about the Fringe experience. If the helpful ones aren't always acknowledged in the text, the abusive ones almost certainly are.

Introduction: Fookin' Fringe

Imagine the scene: it is warm and sunny. The vista of a cobbled, Scottish street, walled on each side by historic buildings, stretches out before you, the bright blue of the sea glistening on the horizon. Wherever you look you see people dressed as Shakespearean characters, or animals, aliens, famous people, dead people, completely naked people... and all of them dancing, singing and acting their hearts out, clambering over any available bollards, bins or podiums to make themselves seen.

They serenade you with their performances; they attend to you, showering you with flyers, special offers and gifts, spreading their joy and happiness without repression or resentment. A few metres away Henry V is addressing the masses, a group with a guitar sing a song about the podium they are standing on and a stall is giving away free samples of a chocolate liqueur.

You realise you have entered a fairyland.

Two weeks later you are living in a nightmare.

It is raining. The Shakespearean characters, animals, aliens et al. continue to serenade you with soundbites and slogans which you have now heard a million times. The naked people are getting increasingly daring and you just wish they would put some clothes on. And you can't move anywhere because they're all in the way.

You have enough flyers, special offers and gifts to sink a ship. Whilst the people showering them upon you still radiate happiness you have learned to see through this superficial sheen; you know that they hate you, and they hate you more each time you politely try to turn down their flyers.

Henry V is still giving the same speech (with the same mistakes) and the groups clambering over bollards are regularly getting injured. The bins have long since become a health hazard as they fill to overflowing with discarded flyers and the occasional dead body (which usually tries give you a flyer at the last minute). The group with the guitar are still singing about the podium they are standing on, and have been doing so without rest for two whole weeks – you are now considering garrotting the guitarist with his own E string. And you have figured out just why the chocolate liqueur needs to be given away free – but it is the only way of coping, so you have carried on drinking it anyway.

To cap it all, you haven't seen a single decent show since you arrived…

The curse of the Fringe

That, at least, is one experience of the Edinburgh Fringe. The Fringe is a genuinely unique event, taking place in the rarefied atmosphere generated by a million thespians on Scottish soil, and coping with the contradictions it throws up – let alone enjoying it all – is a tricky task. It is at once a month-long party and a prison sentence. It manages to combine the best and most creative theatre and comedy in the world with the shoddiest, most lacklustre of productions. People love the Fringe, and they hate it – the same people.

Our friend Andrew is a case in point. Andrew has been taking shows to the Edinburgh Fringe for most of his life, and he hates it. Every year he vows never to do the Fringe again. He contacts all of his friends and instructs them to remind him the next year round that he is never to do the Fringe again. And each year he goes back with another show, finds himself hating the Fringe again and spends a whole month stomping up and down the Royal Mile and muttering to himself 'fookin' fringe...'

We had been performing with Andrew in an improvisation group called The Uncertainty Division for about a year and a half before the subject of taking a show to Edinburgh was broached. When we reached that point there was never really any question about whether or not to do it: we were a locally successful group, we wanted to reach a bigger audience and Edinburgh was the obvious place to find one.

So it began: finding a venue, arranging accommodation, investigating train fares and chatting excitedly about poster designs and show descriptions. Oh, apart from Andrew. He had agreed at an early stage to take part in the show, but during the preparations he wore a look of impending doom, making practical comments but pausing every now and then to mutter under his breath 'fookin' fringe'.

We did our show in a small, new venue that was slightly too far from the centre of Edinburgh to attract sizeable audiences, and for a month we struggled to do the best show we could to extremely unpredictable numbers. We struggled to get reviews, we struggled to maintain the quality of what we were doing and we struggled to maintain some semblance of sanity. But we made it to the end of the festival with the whole cast more or less intact and a show that we knew some people at least had enjoyed – some had even come to see it more than once. And on the day we returned homewards, we received a very flattering notice in The Guardian. Although there were definite undercurrents of 'never again' from some quarters, we felt as though we had achieved something rather special. Everyone who does the Fringe ought to feel a similar sense of achievement, Guardian review or not.

We went back the next year as well. It seemed the obvious way to build on our success and we had several ideas about improving what we'd done before. We presumed Andrew would not want to come. He did.

So it was that we found ourselves once again finding a venue, arranging accommodation, investigating train fares and chatting excitedly about poster designs and show descriptions, with the obligatory 'fookin' fringe' muttered at regular intervals. This time we got a slot in a bigger, better-known venue and our accommodation was in the pink district rather than the red light area, we didn't all take the train but hired a car to more efficiently transport our equipment and our producer, and we had a more distinctive idea for a poster and snappier descriptions for our show.

This time, being at a bigger venue and having a reputation already half-cemented from the previous year, our audiences were generally large; we had a larger company and flyering was better organised, and we'd learned enough from the year before not to repeat certain mistakes, with the net result that many of us were happier and the show was certainly better. On the other hand, when we finished there were still relieved mutterings of 'never again'.

We're going to go back, though. Whether or not those who declared 'never again' will join us is hard to predict, but stranger things have happened. It's like a drug; there is something about the Fringe that you can't keep away from. It's awful, it's absurd, it's brilliant, and it is THE place to take shows.

Why Edinburgh?

Why not hire a London Fringe theatre for three weeks? It would be closer, cheaper and more convenient all round, with considerably less competition and arguably more chance of pulling in a few agents and casting directors (on account of their filofaxes not being entirely full of a million Edinburgh shows). What makes Edinburgh special?

This is what this book is about. There's no simple explanation for Edinburgh's importance as the premier place for all sorts of performers to get experience and get seen. In an increasingly competitive and professional atmosphere, the Fringe is not an easy ride for anyone. In fact, as far as performing goes, it's up there with the most difficult work artists ever endure.

For this reason, it acts as an invaluable training ground for budding performers of all varieties – if you can cope with the Fringe, you can cope with pretty much anything – which is why so many known actors, writers, musicians and comedians cite the Fringe as a great stepping-stone in their careers.

But there's more to it than that. There must be, because people continue to do the Fringe even after they have seen considerable success. Okay, Hollywood stars don't play the Fringe in the same way as they play the West End, but West End stars have certainly played the Fringe, and recent years have seen bigger and bigger names going up north to star in their own shows. Some television personalities who you'd have thought could be earning a lot more elsewhere can't seem to keep away.

Perhaps the biggest appeal of the Fringe, then, is simply that it has a creative atmosphere that nowhere else can match. It is three weeks of unbelievably sustained artistic activity, and because it is essentially subsidised by the performers it is not only self-sufficient but run by people with a significant stake in what they're doing. There is an element of competitiveness, but also a healthy sense of camaraderie (perhaps brought on by a joint sense of suffering) amongst a huge number of people who really care about what they're doing. The shows are of variable quality, but there are more risks taken and ideas tried out than in any of the big funded arts festivals.

In fact, comparing the offerings of the little-known Edinburgh International Festival to the things we have seen at the Fringe, we've started to wonder if a lack of arts funding is actually rather conducive to bold and inventive theatre. Sure, it's a pity that several hundred people have to go bankrupt for the Fringe to happen, but there's no chance that it will ever get boring. That is why more and more people flock to Edinburgh every year.

The problem is, because of the rather *ad hoc* way in which the

Fringe has developed, its scale and the complexity of its organisation, nobody really knows best how to handle it. It's hardly surprising that it becomes a nightmare for so many of the people involved in it, but equally it is hard for visitors to the Fringe to know where to begin and how to get the most out of such a large, labyrinthine world.

That, too, is the purpose of this book. In 'How Edinburgh became a festival' we look at the history of the Fringe and the way it is run to explain exactly why it is like it is, offering a way for newcomers to understand its confused and difficult nature. In 'Where do shows come from?' we look at the way shows are developed – essential information if you're thinking of taking something to the Fringe, but also a vital insight if you're wondering how the *Macbeth* you've just seen turned out quite so wrong.

'Lots and lots of shows' is about the Fringe itself, what happens there, the best way to enjoy it and how it all works. In 'It's not just shows' we point out some of the other aspects of Edinburgh you might like to experience when you're up there, and how they might be affected by the Fringe. Finally, in 'Where do shows go?' we look at life after Edinburgh (we still believe there is one, although some jaded Fringe performers will tell you otherwise).

Whether you are intent on conquering Edinburgh with your own show, or experiencing the best of other people's, this book will allow you to venture into Scotland without fear, full of knowledge and ready for the trip of a lifetime. It's an experience you need to have, if only once. But you never do experience it only once, because anyone who has experienced it once goes back.

What you need to read this book

1 This book

2 A bottle of whisky

3 A pen

4 A telephone

5 A bottle of gin

6 About 3 hours' uninterrupted time

7 A map of Edinburgh

8 A meal (if hungry)

9 A copy of *Macbeth*

10 Five reams of paper and an idea for a chain letter

11 Photoshop

12 A copy of The Guardian

13 A bottle of absinthe

14 Microsoft Excel

15 A mobile phone camera

16 A fish

17 Membership of a gym

18 A photograph of Paul Daniels (or, if you can't find one, Debbie McGee)

19 Rat poison

20 A Pink Floyd CD (Genesis will do)

21 A Kylie Minogue CD (Jason Donovan will do)

22 An Andrew Lloyd Webber CD ('Any Dream Will Do')

23 A really big bottle of whisky, and possibly by this stage a mixer

24 A small plastic keyboard

25 A flip chart

26 Chalk

27 An indomitable will

or:

28 None of the above

How Edinburgh became a festival

It's a beautiful city

The first time you get to Edinburgh, no matter what you do, don't get off the train, lump your bags to a taxi, zip off to wherever you're staying and start thumbing through the Fringe guide. You may have come to Scotland's capital solely to watch shows, 24 hours a day, at the world's biggest arts festival. You may be performing, or producing, you might be a street artist or a drag queen, a techie on contract to the

Pleasance or a starlet hoping to make it big. You might have a wall chart of your stay to ensure you don't miss a show; you might be planning on sitting in the Spiegeltent until they throw you out. You might be an acrobat, a priest, a student or a computer programmer with a dark artistic streak. You might even be Paul Daniels. We don't care. When you get to Edinburgh, for the love of God look up (or, if you're Paul Daniels, more up).

Edinburgh is a beautiful city (don't worry, this isn't a guide book, we'll get on to the comedy and booze and burlesque strippers soon enough) and, for all its foolishness in trying to cram seven festivals into one month*, it deserves some recognition for that beauty. You wouldn't go to London's clubbing hotspots without first pointing up at Big Ben and saying 'Ooh, it is big, isn't it!' and you wouldn't go and see a cricket match in Australia without first visiting its famous Ramsey Street to see the place where Todd was fatally knocked down by a van. So don't abuse Edinburgh just because there are burlesque strippers to see (okay, okay, we're going to get to that bit soon).

Not only is the city itself beautiful, but the people are great too. Forget that bit in Trainspotting where they glower at the American tourists, it's not true (and anyway, they were American). Spend a bit of time away from the Fringe venues, the sandwich shops and central bars that everyone goes to – climb Arthur's seat, go swimming, go shopping, go to the sea at Leith. One year, we popped into a stationer's to get some letter paper and envelopes and had a very friendly conversation with the proprietor about the decline of cursive writing as an art form. Of course, you'll bump into rude bastards too – but no more than in Soho or Ramsey Street.

The truth that so many people fail to grasp is that Edinburgh is not just a festival venue. This isn't Chichester. You really have to visit outside Fringe time to get the full measure of the place, but even during August, with the Fringe sparkling like some festal boil on the skin of the city, there's stuff to see and do and enjoy that has nothing to do with the festival at all. That a fairly small city – a population of half a million (the size of Wiltshire, or of a popular bath tub in Tokyo) – should open its arms every year to let the great and the good and the

*Actually, no one can agree on how many festivals there are. The numbers seem to vary between five and about twelve, with more appearing every year.

tiny and the awful and Paul Daniels trample across it, get drunk in it, fall over and vomit into it, is something of a mystery, but we should be eternally grateful that it does. Their inconvenience is the gain of the one million people who enjoy it every year. Can you imagine having something similar in Guildford? We thought not.*

Getting perspective

If you arrive in Edinburgh by train, be sure to take a moment to stop outside the station and admire the view from the bridge down to the railway. Wait for a train to come along, and instantly you will realise a truth about Edinburgh: it's a model train set.

If you're just visiting for the Fringe, perhaps for a weekend, you might not have time to do much more than stroll briskly through Princes Street Gardens on your way to see a new piece of physical theatre, but if you're there for a month – 'doing the Fringe' – then having escape exits helps keep you sane. We'll come back to keeping you sane, probably quite a lot, because it's difficult and you need all the help you can get. Even if you're not in danger of going mad (which you are, you just don't know it yet) and think you're too busy for anything non-Fringe related, wandering away from the centre can bring unexpected benefits. Some of the best fried food shops are a little further out (make sure you ask

---

*At least, 'footfall' is reckoned to be around one million, which we're assuming means one million people. Naturally, most people have two feet, so if footfall actually measures the feet that fall on Edinburgh then the number of visitors may be more like 500,000. That's still a lot and we still can't imagine it happening in Guildford.

for sauce) and so are some of the more interesting venues. There are also some great street names, if you like that sort of thing.

If nothing else, you'll look pretty stupid when Aunty Fiona asks you what you saw in Edinburgh and the only thing you can remember is a tedious stand-up comedy show and an experimental version of *Macbeth* using animal masks. That may be what you're in Edinburgh for, but your relatives might at least want reassuring that the castle that used to be there in the 1940s is still standing. It's a good castle, too – better than Aberystwyth, better than Rochester, and on a par with Harlech. If you don't like castles, or if the Edinburgh dungeons sound like too much work, you're surely going to find the Scotch whisky heritage centre interesting. That's the other thing about Edinburgh – if all else fails, you can always relax and have a drink.

Okay, we're done. Bring on the strippers.

The history of the Fringe

The late 1940s saw the world recovering from six years of war-enforced belt tightening and misery. Rationing and xenophobia were still firmly entrenched in the mind of the British government, but in the arts world people were seeing opportunities for a new, vibrant post-war creativity which could lift the nation out of its depression. Just as music, theatre, film and those broadcasts from the ever-reliable BBC had played an essential part in maintaining morale during the war, so they would be a vital part of the reconstruction process. Vaughan Williams knocked out symphony after symphony to the delight of highbrow music lovers, the British film industry blossomed as directors such as Charles Crichton, Alberto Cavalcanti and Michael Balcon led it towards a golden era and the BBC continued its ever-reliable broadcasts on both radio and television. All a little bit like things are now, really, except better (and Vaughan Williams' output has dipped significantly in recent years).

Scottish people, although known for keeping themselves to themselves, had mucked in and helped out in the war too, putting the fear of God into the Hun with their ferocious tartan skirts and bagpipe playing on the beaches of France. Once they were no longer needed on the beaches of France (the French no doubt begging the pipers to go back to their families as quickly as possible for compassion's sake) the Scots returned to their homeland, taking their pipes with them, ready to play an equal part in the artistic rejuvenation of the British Isles. So it was that in 1947 Edinburgh decided to stage an arts festival, something they hoped would demonstrate the new, vibrant artsy life of the country and which would engage both audience and performers alike.

Well, they succeeded but just not quite in the way they expected. From the first year, when eight groups turned up unannounced, through the creation of the Fringe Society, the founding of Pleasance, Assembly Rooms and Gilded Balloon, to the present day, the Fringe – not the International Festival that spawned it – has grown to be the largest and most vibrant arts festival in the world. Audiences and performers flock from around the world to be there, and its success has caused various tensions between it and the International Festival over the years, from outright hostility to today's sniping comments in The Guardian*. The Festival Fringe is Luke Skywalker to the International Festival's Obi Wan Kenobi: the International Festival is serious, weighty, with a track record of great works, while the Fringe is edgy, skittish, heroic, whining, a backwater kid with a bold idea, and an idiot. On average, it's not very good, but its moments of genius are not as few or far between as you might think.

Festival adjuncts: the beginning

In retrospect, it all makes a great deal of sense; if you can't be arsed to start up your own festival properly, just hitch a ride on somebody else's and something will emerge. So it was in 1947, when the (mostly local) productions that made up what would become known as the Fringe had no co-ordinated organisation, no programme and no community to help them – indeed, it's unlikely there was much communication between the groups involved at all. But they got good audiences and good reviews, and in 1948 they got a name: 'Fringe', coined (unknowingly) by playwright Robert Kemp in an article for the Evening News which made an offhand

___
*Okay, so 'outright hostility' means fighting with weapons, and we're not sure that's ever happened. But people get really shirty.

reference to the goings-on 'round the fringe of the official Festival…' This replaced clumsy references to the Festival's 'Semi-Official' elements, or the horrific term 'Festival Adjuncts' that had been employed in the first year. Given some sort of identity, groups started to help each other. Denied facilities or assistance from the Festival Society, the Fringe performers instead had a reception centre run by Edinburgh University students, providing cheap meals and accommodation, and from 1955 a central box-office and café. A single programme started to appear and, by 1959, when the new Fringe Society took over some of these functions, the Fringe had grown to 19 groups, including professionals, students and amateurs. What's more, there was now interest being shown from further afield than Glasgow – good news for audiences who couldn't quite understand what the Glaswegians were saying.

From the beginning, one of the most important aspects of the Fringe was its openness. Anyone could come and perform, provided that they could arrange a theatre, find accommodation and stay within the law. The idea that groups might submit to central selection and programming – as would have happened if the Fringe had sought a formal relationship with the Festival Society (although opposition to that idea existed on both sides) – ran contrary to what was making the Fringe successful. Professional groups with professional shows – including, in 1952, *After The Show*, the Fringe's first revue – mingled with student groups, productions of drama by Scots and for Scots, and what some members of the press characterised as 'propaganda thinly disguised as experimental drama' (the practice of politics within theatre having fallen a little out of fashion and yet to work its way back into full acceptance).

It was precisely this freedom to experiment, and indeed the freedom to go off the rails, out into the wilderness, and perhaps to fail utterly, that made the Fringe so appealing, not only to performers, but to audiences, reviewers and even the Festival Society, whose Director in 1951 welcomed the enthusiasm and talent the Fringe encouraged – although he distanced himself from the scantily-clad actresses promoting the London Theatre Club Group's second late-night revue, two years later. Clearly, freedom of expression was only welcome if it didn't involve scantily clad actresses (almost the exact opposite is true today.)

Too intellectual an element: growth

It was perhaps this sort of show – unashamedly light-hearted and unashamedly using sex to sell – which, combined with a mistrust of political, activist theatre, led many critics to believe that the essence of the Fringe was more frivolous than not, even at the same time as they praised some increasingly inventive theatre. Larger numbers of revue shows, with student productions involving Ned Sherrin, Dudley Moore, Ken Loach and Alan Bennett, cemented this staple of the Fringe some time before the Festival proper hit back with 1960's *Beyond the Fringe* (although most people these days still think it was a Fringe show, despite and possibly because of the title). The lack of selection or censorship beyond what was proscribed by law enabled all sorts of ideas to thrive, so when the Fringe Society was founded in 1958 the independence of performers to do what the hell they liked was enshrined as a guiding principle. The Society would publish a single programme, run a box office for all groups, and provide information and assistance, but would keep its nose out of programming itself. It also took over running a club for those involved in the Fringe, which was often the liveliest place in Edinburgh, with entertainment being put on by the same groups that were relaxing there.

The downside of lack of central programming was lack of quality control. As the balance started to shift from professional to amateur and university groups, so the average standard dropped. While critics had initially taken into account the difficulties groups faced in bringing shows to the Fringe, as the field widened and some groups demonstrated brilliant works despite these hardships, reviewers began the gradual shift towards treating Fringe shows as if they were all professional productions. While a daunting prospect, this has been at least partly responsible for the Fringe's reputation of launching careers; although the number of careers actually launched is small next to the number of performers who have struggled their way through the Fringe process, the confidence given to a young performer or writer by a favourable review is great, and certainly can dispose them (and perhaps their doubting parents) to the idea of a career in acting. One example of a great acting career launched by the Fringe is that of Anna Quayle*.

The university groups, though strictly amateur, were garnering their share of good reviews – the Oxford Theatre Group began to make a name for itself with UK and world premières of plays, alongside the Oxford Revue with up-and-coming comic talents such as Willie Rushton and Richard Ingrams. In 1963 Cambridge University got in on the act, with the Cambridge University Theatre Company bringing up *Brand* by Henrik Ibsen, directed by Trevor Nunn, and the Cambridge Footlights show *Double Take*, featuring Tim Brooke-Taylor, Graham Chapman and John Cleese. The Footlights show the following year, the unwisely titled *A Clump of Plinths*, was the first of many to transfer to the West End (albeit with a marginally better name). Sheffield, Cardiff, London… more and more universities saw their student productions coming to the Fringe to show their wares, with an expected spread of both quality and success. It was not long before some people were going to university more for the dramatic opportunities it presented than for the chance to further their education.

Perhaps it was this rise in student shows that prompted Gerard Slevin, directing a 1961 play for Scottish professional company Mercat Theatre Trust, to attack the Fringe for being too big and containing too 'intellectual' an element**. If this sprung from a resentment of the solid competition that the student element of the Fringe was introducing, then Slevin would have been horrified by the competition that would arise over more time – over the next 40 years the Fringe would grow from under 50 groups in 1963 to over 1000, and far from being discouraged by his outburst, the non-professional side of the Fringe would continue to thrive, and indeed some professional companies would appear that modelled themselves on Fringe productions.

15

*Are you thinking, 'who on earth is Anna Quayle'? You heartless, heartless beast. Anna Quayle has done more for you than you could ever possibly imagine, and you're sitting there questioning who she is. Even the least educated amongst you will have seen her playing the Baroness in *Chitty Chitty Bang Bang,* and many of you will have grown up terrified of her superlative Mrs Monroe in *Grange Hill.* But for the connoisseur there are also her appearances in *Carry On Up the Chastity Belt, Casino Royale* (in which she dies), *A Hard Day's Night* and *Brideshead Revisited.* Hardcore followers will also have seen her in *Mistress Pamela.* A great woman through and through, and our biography of her (featuring rare colour photographs from Mistress Pamela) ought to be coming out soon.
**If recent evidence is to be believed, the intellectuals are still at the forefront of the Fringe. An experiment by the *Scotsman* put eleven Fringe comedians through an IQ test invigilated by Mensa officials, and apart from the person who spoiled his paper by drawing a pair of breasts on it, they all gained scores which put them in the top quarter of the population. More than half were in the top 3%, the chances of which are statistically very low indeed, at least as far as the Mensa officials were concerned. Not that it stopped them offering membership to several of the participants on the spot.

Bookshops and art galleries: diversification

The 1960s established many of the strong elements of the Fringe that survive today: student revues, children's theatre and the structure of the Fringe itself, with the Fringe Society restructuring as a limited company and being granted charitable status in 1969. It also saw the beginnings of one company that grew directly out of the Fringe, namely the Traverse Theatre Club. Formed after two successful previous productions in the chairman's bookshop, the club, to avoid the tedious necessity of seeking approval for public performances through the office of the Lord Chamberlain, opened in January 1963 in a one-time brothel called 'Kelly's Paradise' (why they didn't keep the name as well remains a mystery). In fact, the venue had previously housed a temporary and successful club called the Sphinx run by the Cambridge Footlights, showing how student groups were taking the lead in Fringe developments. On the other hand, student groups evidently did not have the continuity or organisation to sustain such ideas, whereas the Traverse has a successful track record which has lasted to this day. In 1969 it moved to new premises in the Grassmarket and more recently became a public theatre next to the Usher Hall, where it continues to have praise lavished on it from several quarters.

The 'Kelly's Paradise' venue had seating for 60 people close up to a tiny stage (at least as a theatre; we don't know how many people it sat as a brothel). Jim Haynes, the Traverse's founding chairman, believed in drama that involved the audience – previous plays in his bookshop, on theological issues, had ended with a discussion between audience and actors over the issues raised. Its first artistic directors, Terry Lane and John Malcolm, set about producing a programme that was varied and generally well-received. Twenty-two plays in its first year, including work from throughout Europe, Japan and the States, established the Traverse (named after its arrangement of blocks of seating either side of the stage) as an important new part of British theatre. Most importantly, it moved Fringe-like risk-taking into the open all year round and showed how a small, even cramped, space could be used to create great theatre. (The way the Fringe has developed since then, you would imagine that cramped spaces were a prerequisite for great theatre...)

Perhaps inspired by this, groups started performing further out and in any spaces they could reasonably turn into a theatre. The 1960s saw shows in a church hall in Portobello, a Masonic lodge in Morningside, and even stranger places – the Royal College of Art Theatre Group turned up one year with a circus tent, so probably ought to take some responsibility for the now regular visits from the marquee containing the Ladyboys of Bangkok. There were few professional groups at this stage, but no one seemed to mind too much – perhaps unsurprisingly, as 1964 saw Cambridge and Oxford offer up consistently inventive revues which between them involved Graeme Garden, Michael Palin, Terry Jones and Eric Idle. 1965 also saw Theatre Workshop open its doors as an arts and drama centre for children.

The Fringe was also becoming more diverse: from 1963, Richard Demarco had run art exhibitions at Traverse, moving on later to other places in the city under the same banner. In 1966 he founded the Richard Demarco gallery, in which he established a reputation for new, inventive artistic ideas, for example introducing Edinburgh to Eastern European art in the 1970s. The legacy of this foresight can be seen to this day in the numerous exhibitions which form a small but significant part of the Fringe.

1966 also saw the appearance of Tom Stoppard's *Rosencrantz and Guildenstern are Dead* at the Fringe. Somebody is said to have asked Stoppard what it was about, to which he accurately responded, 'it's about to make me rich'. Despite negative reviews from several directions and the cast's complaints about the script, the play eventually found a favourable notice in The Observer, and neither it nor Stoppard looked back. He wasn't the only one, since it played alongside the Oxford Revue with future actress Diana Quick and future BBC Chief Political Correspondent John Sergeant among the cast. How much easier things might have been if Quick and Sergeant had been cast as Rosencrantz and Guildenstern.

Salacious details: pushing boundaries

The 1960s also saw the first of what is now a large volume of Fringe shows from the States. The University of Southern California School of

Performing Arts Drama Department Festival Theatre (USCSPADDFT for short – they perhaps should have thought of that) appeared in 1966 with a range of plays by American writers and were successful enough to be able to return regularly. The following year, La Mama Experimental Theatre Company brought the professional side of US drama to Auld Reekie – albeit with a similar Fringe-like approach as their hosts, the ever-innovative Traverse. With six years' experience, and a successful European tour just completed, they also brought – not for the first time, and certainly not for the last – the sensation of scandal to the Fringe. (We mean that it wasn't the last time the Fringe experienced scandal, though it's equally true to say that it was not the last time our American cousins brought the sensation of scandal with a visit to the British Isles.)

These days it's nothing new for something pushing boundaries on television to be condemned from all sides, often by people who haven't seen the show in question – recent years have seen viewers scandalised by Chris Morris's *Brass Eye*, Stewart Lee and Richard Thomas' *Jerry Springer – The Opera* and Andrew Gilligan's report on the Iraq dossier, though, admittedly, the damage to the broadcasters is greater when said scandalised viewers happen to be running the Government. So it was in 1967 with La Mama Theatre Company's *Futz*, an avant-garde play about bestiality. The play portrays an idyllic love affair between Farmer Futz and a pig, besides which the Scottish Daily Express reported that an actress 'bares her bosom before her mentally defective son who has just murdered a girl' (why do playwrights always have to spoil lovely stories about idyllic bestial love affairs with bosoms and murder?). It got good reviews from some quarters, but from others came calls for it to be banned, with second-hand reports of salacious details (such as the outraged views of the Scottish Daily Express) being bandied about to support the demands. The people running the Government were obviously quite happy with avant-garde bestiality, however, as the play continued to thrive amidst the adverse publicity.

These days, calls of horror come no less frequently – shows are sometimes moved on from a venue uncomfortable with the attention to one more prepared to deal with it – and in general it does little more than create publicity for the show in question (certainly bigger venues are always delighted to help out when a controversial show is ejected from another place on the grounds of taste). With blasphemy still on the statute books in Scotland, however, groups may wish to be cautious*. Since many venues are converted churches, Quaker meeting houses and other assorted religious buildings, potentially dangerous and subversive shows can give them cold feet – performers of such theatre are better off finding a former brothel to stage their show in (or even just a brothel).

None of this is really new, though, and the Fringe struggles on still blaspheming, shocking and denigrating its way through the few remaining respectable folk in Edinburgh (most of whom support it anyway). In the end, August is a prime month for the British media to run with any story, no matter how small, simply because there is so little actual news. It certainly did no harm to La Mama. Neither did it put off other American groups from coming to the Fringe, with initiatives such as the American High School Theatre Festival giving hundreds of US school kids the chance to experience Edinburgh, in addition to the many professional, amateur and university groups that appear to this day.

When the Fringe Office reformed itself as a charity in 1969, it was an acknowledgement that the Fringe had grown beyond the limits of a volunteer organisation to manage even the modest aims it had. Accordingly, within a year of the new structure, the new Board of Directors were able to appoint a professional, albeit part-time, administrator. In John Milligan, they found someone capable of setting the Fringe firmly on the road of continuous expansion. There had been a risk that, with an increasingly diverse set of groups and productions, the differing voices and opinions might fracture the Fringe into smaller festivals, each focused around their own thing; with an impartial, professional centre, this seemed much less likely. Although to this day there are rumblings of subversive counter-counter-festivals, be they to improve the inclusion of local Edinburgh artists and residents, to fight the growing commercialism of the Fringe or simply to give Edinburgh another much-needed festival, nothing has come close to threatening the size or supremacy of the Fringe, and it continues to involve people from all over.

---

*Because of blasphemy laws, Scottish religious groups have recently instigated investigations into the BBC for their broadcast of the aforementioned *Jerry Springer – The Opera* on televisions north of the border, so it isn't just Fringe performers who need to be careful… although they can take heart from the fact that the last prosecution for blasphemy in Scotland was in 1843 when bookseller Thomas Paterson was sentenced at Edinburgh High Court to 15 months in prison for selling blasphemous books.

Newbury Youth Theatre
Robin Strapp

Much has changed since I first brought Gloucestershire Youth Theatre to the Fringe in the late 1970s – back then you could run your own venue, as we did for 4 years at St Serf's Hall, and the Fringe box office was based on paper tickets under the wonderful guidance of the late Mrs Tulloch and her daughter. They both knew you personally, as did the directors John Milligan and Alistair Moffat – and the programme fitted onto a double-sided A1 paper!

Nowadays it has become a highly commercial, computerised venture that is not so much a Fringe but a Festival in its own right, and for the likes of Youth Theatres it becomes more and more of a challenge to participate. There have been many successful youth theatre companies who no longer can come for one reason or another.

So what keeps me and Newbury Youth Theatre returning? Simply, it offers our youngsters (aged 14–19) a unique experience to take part in the largest arts festival in the world. They learn much about themselves as individuals having to live and work together as a company with the discipline of having to sell a show in the frenetic High Street, and to perform each day. It is an experience that they remember for ever, with many of them returning each year before moving on to higher education or jobs.

However, it is a massive undertaking with many hurdles to overcome. One of the major issues is finding a venue that you can afford and where you feel safe and supported – not an easy task for youth theatres.

It's equally important to find accommodation that is safe – and cheap. We book university self-catering flats, which are the most economical way of accommodating large numbers. Often they are already gone by January so it is vital to book early.

Having travelled by train and tried to book air group travel, the cheapest way I've found for groups is a coach – you can at least get set, props and costumes on board and can hold the whole group together and decide travel times. We also travel overnight on our return journey to save accommodation costs.

Our major concern is always raising money to afford the trip. Members pay for their travel, food and accommodation but the total sum still comes to over £10,000 for a week run so it is vital to gain sponsorship or grant aid from a whole variety of bodies. Ticket sales can help but you need to budget for a very small return – there just aren't that many audience members to go round all the shows, and it's difficult to make a big impact.

It would be encouraging if the Fringe really supported this sector with help in marketing and promotion. The likelihood of a youth theatre show gaining press recognition is fairly limited, which means that it has become increasingly difficult to build an audience for what is often new, experimental and devised work. Thankfully, Newbury Youth Theatre has gained a following from audiences wishing to take a chance on new work and many return each year, including Edinburgh locals.

It is a wonderfully rewarding adventure, perhaps summed up best by one of our company, 15-year-old Karin: 'Before joining NYT, I had never been further than Birmingham and with NYT I got the chance to not only travel to Edinburgh but perform in the biggest arts festival in the world. That is a memory that will stay with me forever'.

Despite the daunting challenges it has always been an occasion to make memories.

Robin Strapp is artistic director of Newbury Youth Theatre, which has been bringing shows to the Fringe for more than 10 years and recently celebrated its twenty-first birthday.

Fringe firsts: success

It was not only changes to the Fringe's structure that were having an effect on shows in the 1970s. The 1960s had seen a new brand of comedian, often forged at the Fringe, moving gradually through the different media of stage, print and television. Peter Cook and Dudley Moore (both Fringe performers before 1960's wildly successful *Beyond the Fringe* which, we would you remind you again, was not a Fringe show, whatever everybody thinks and thought at the time) had gone on to win over the entire country with *Not Only... But Also*, Cook also founding The Establishment Club in Soho which was for a short time the place to be seen if you were John Lennon, Barry Humphries, Frankie Howerd or any other fashionably left-of-centre celebrity. A bit like Number 10 Downing Street in the late 1990s, but more intentionally satirical. Peter Cook was also the proprietor of a new publication called *Private Eye*, launched in 1962 by Christopher Booker and Willie Rushton. David Frost, after Peter Cook (him again) turned down the opportunity, was chosen to present *That Was the Week That Was*, the first of many influential television shows fronted by Frost (culminating, of course, in the brilliant *Through the Keyhole*).

It is no coincidence that Peter Cook seems to have had fingers in pretty much all of the satire pies in the 1960s, even the ones he didn't actually eat. His success in Edinburgh had propelled him into a position of great influence, which affected the way people would see the Fringe forever. Critics were constantly looking for 'the next Peter Cook', whilst young hopefuls often set out to be 'the next Peter Cook'. (To date, 'the next Peter Cook' doesn't seem to have turned up anywhere, and people have largely stopped looking.) In fact, the most successful young hopefuls were those who didn't try to be the next Peter Cook – the 1970s saw the arrival of *Monty Python's Flying Circus* on British television screens; almost all of the participants having found their way there via student productions that had played at the Fringe. Whether or not you were actually going to be 'the next Peter Cook', the Fringe was increasingly seen as a place to go if you wanted to work in television, particularly if you were 'doing comedy'.

Meanwhile, there were once again people complaining that too much theatre was for the middle classes – or rather that there was not enough for everyone else. However, instead of just complaining, they decided to do something about it. The 7:84 Theatre Company arrived in Edinburgh in 1972, with its founder John McGrath determined to make theatre more accessible to the working class. Quite how this undertaking resulted in a play involving an apricot-scented vagina and buggery is unclear, and it's doubtful whether that made it more accessible to the working class. Still, it sounds like a laugh. Certainly the two 7:84 productions that year (*Trees in the Wind* by John McGrath and *Apricots* – the scented vagina one) were the first of many touring productions taken to village halls, technical colleges and miners' clubs in both England and Scotland for 'the people'. Efforts had been made before to expand the Fringe's 'theatre for the masses' into other areas at other times of the year, but while the work of former Traverse artistic director Jim Haynes south of the border had resulted in some Traverse-style fringe theatres springing up in London in the 1960s, the Fringe-like productions touring in the 1970s were welcomed across the country as never before.

The increased success of groups and individuals outside the Fringe were reflected by a growing expansion of the Fringe itself. By 1972 John Milligan had made his administration role full-time, as the

Fringe Society saw greater financially stability and a new Fringe Club on the Royal Mile for performers to unwind and party until the scandalously late hour of 1.30 a.m. The number of performers was also increasing, as new performance spaces continued to open. In the same year, at the bidding of the Board of Directors, he worked with The Scotsman to create 'Fringe Firsts' awards for (in the words of The Scotsman's artistic editor Allen Wright) 'enterprise and originality'. This innovation gave much-needed publicity to new plays struggling to find audiences and can take as much credit as the general growth of the Fringe for the tripling of new works between 1933 and 1977. The assistance offered to companies by the Fringe Office also increased – the first Fringe brochure appeared, which, along with other bulletins and informational pamphlets (some of which had been around since the early 1960s), set the model for much of the Fringe Office's activities to this day.

Mammoth changes: gaining pace

During a series of trips abroad in the late seventies to advise on or investigate the possibility of fringe festivals in other cities, the Fringe team realised one crucial part of Edinburgh's success. Because of the city's multilayered structure, most venues were very close to each other: one might be just round the corner from where you were, or indeed literally underneath you. In Manhattan, for example, despite plenty of the sort of artistic vigour Edinburgh enjoys, the distance between venues would make the same kind of intense experience impossible. On the other hand, Woody Allen evidently didn't find enough in Edinburgh's skyline to want to make a film out of it, so every city got what it deserved: Manhattan got Diane Keaton, Edinburgh got, well, Russell Harty. Harty presented his TV show from the Debating Hall of the Fringe Club in the mid-eighties, a decade in which media exposure became more and more a measure of success for pretty much everything.

The Fringe had been well-prepared for this garish, limelight-hogging decade through the guidance of Alistair Moffat, the new Fringe administrator from 1977. Unlike former civil servant Milligan's fastidious approach and the all-male Fringe board where everyone was addressed by their surnames, Moffat's era was more chancy and even daring, but he had a flair for the job and his skill with the media propelled the Fringe forward as it continued to grow. While there had been around 100 groups at the Fringe in 1973, by 1977 there were double that. Moffat kept the expansion going and the number was up to nearly 500 when he stepped down in 1981.

The way the venues were run was also changing; while traditionally they had been run by the group performing there, now groups started banding together to run a venue. This lowered the cost to each group but also meant that more shows were presented during the day, or late at night, starting the move to the almost round-the-clock Fringe of today. This had to some extent been initiated by the Fringe Club, as when it received a license in 1972 to open until 1.30 a.m. the pubs were still closing at 10 p.m. When later licenses were approved in 1976, Fringe venues took full advantage of this, running shows from 10 a.m. or midday right until midnight, with bars and cafés to keep the interest going when there wasn't a show to your taste.

The 1979 move of the Fringe Club to Chambers Street gave it a more 'studenty' air, and although the subsequent move to the Edinburgh student union-owned Teviot Row buildings (now the home of the Gilded Balloon) didn't entirely dispel it, the range of services from bars and cafés to, by 1984, a permanent cabaret, made the Club popular not only with performers but also with members of the general public (no doubt Russell Harty's patronage also helped pull in the crowds). By then two other mammoth changes were making themselves felt, one within the Fringe office and one without. Under the supervision of Treasurer Leslie Bennie, computerisation of first of the accounts and later the production of the programme, which was sent to the printers in 1984 on computer tape, enabled the Fringe office to keep up with a massive expansion in the number of shows (at least part of which was due to the super-venues).

In 1980, seven professional groups got together to create Circuit. Sharing a space with a bar/café, it returned for the next three years, getting larger each year. In 1982, with thirty-eight companies and spaces totalling around a thousand seats, it was one of the most significant parts of the Fringe – together with the Assembly Rooms, started in 1981 in the former Festival Club (as in International), it accounted for 24% of all Fringe ticket sales. However, Circuit still managed to lose £28,000 and, despite a better year in 1983 with five tents on the proposed site of the ill-fated Edinburgh Opera House, never returned – so not unlike a rather huge version of many individual Edinburgh shows.

The standard had been set, however, and the Fringe was gaining pace (still). Along with the founding of the Pleasance and the Gilded Balloon, now two of the leading Edinburgh Fringe venues, came the Perrier Awards. Although the first Perrier Award for comedy in 1981 only had a short-list of three (causing complaints from the many groups who hadn't been eligible), it had also grown in prominence and helped gather interest in Edinburgh. Interest was also strong from within the city, as could be seen from the growing popularity of the aptly-named Fringe Sunday, which was held on a Sunday during the Fringe. Started by Alistair Moffat in his last year before handing over to Michael Dale, it originally took place on part of the High Street, which was closed off to accommodate the festivities. After 25,000 turned up to the first compared with an expected 5000, then 40,000 the following year, both the regional council and the police expressed concerns. In 1983 the third Fringe Sunday was moved to Holyrood Park where it remained until 2001 (it currently takes place on the Meadows). Five hours of family entertainment, wacky stunts and the relentless promotion of shows has since become a staple of the Fringe, but at the time it was all new and exciting. Early sponsorship by the Alloa Brewery, who supplied lorries used as temporary stages, has long since been replaced by the ubiquitous RBS constructions, but in the open-air fun and freedom perhaps a little of that chaotic Fringe still exists.

Going back to the Fringe

A student from the University of Edinburgh who tells you they are 'going back for the Fringe' is quite possibly actually going back to re-sit their exams. The two just happen to coincide and the Fringe is felt to be marginally less embarrassing.

By the same logic, it is possible that the person who tells you they are going back to re-sit their exams is really a Fringe performer doing a shamefully bad show.

Shameful bias: spread of information

Although groups now regularly complain that publicity is impossible, they generally do know the sort of things you can do to try and draw attention to your show*. This hasn't always been the case. A pair of guitarists went to the Fringe Office in 1981 looking for advice. Their Latin style jazz guitar show was playing to audiences of one or two – what could they do? New Fringe administrator Michael Dale told them to play the Fringe Club for 30 minutes each day as a free taster. They did, and by the end of the run had capacity audiences. They were Dylan Fowler and Dominic Miller – the latter now guitarist for Sting. Many others made their names in the Fringe Club, securing careers there rather than with their main shows. Rory Bremner and John Otway, for instance, both pulled big crowds in the mid-eighties. As the Fringe grew so did the competition, and as the available standard rose, so too the pressure of knowing that the person in the wings could be much better than you. The audience came to know this as well, and the Bearpit eventually became feared by many performers. Someone who did stunningly one night could be heckled offstage after a few minutes the next. And yet they returned, night after night, looking for

---

*Those that don't should probably read this book.

that good gig that would persuade people to come and see their show.

These days there are around three times as many shows as when Fowler and Miller played the Fringe Club – it probably wouldn't be possible to provide a similar opportunity for everyone at the Fringe, even if the Club were still at Teviot Row. However, many venues now run their own stand-up/cabaret shows, although getting to perform is a little less egalitarian, with the top names from the stand-up circuit also vying for spots. Audiences perhaps are also worse off; rather than watching 10 or 20 acts in a night you now see only four or five, and although the standards are pretty high and more consistent than the Bearpit, it all lacks the unexpected discovery of something great. Not to mention the gladiatorial excitement of watching performers struggling to survive against an audience that could change from loving to rowdy in minutes.

Overall, performers probably are better off these days. The growth of the Fringe through the eighties was remarkable – from 1981, with a one-off Fringe Marathon demonstrating that not only were there enough shows, there were also people crazy enough to watch them back to back for 24 hours (the winner saw twenty), to being the vacation of choice for two characters from The Archers in 1984. The size was such that the Fringe Office had to come up with ways of making it easier to find which show you actually wanted. The first Daily Diary (now the Guide Daily) appeared in 1980, giving an hour by hour view of what was on, and in the late eighties came Fringe Find, a computerised programme search (which was all very well except that the machines, dotted around Edinburgh, were rare enough that they themselves were hard to find). Nonetheless, they predated the World Wide Web by some years, although the Fringe's own website, launched in 1995, was no slouch when it finally arrived. These days you can go to a tent full of computers, browse for shows and buy tickets on the spot.

The late 1980s saw other changes. In 1986 Michael Dale stepped down as Fringe Administrator, handing over to Mhairi Mackenzie-Robinson and so starting a period of strong female leadership. Gone already were the days of an all-male Fringe board, but at this point long-serving Fringe secretary Andrew Kerr remembers that there were simply no men who came close to the quality of female applicants, and for some time they interviewed mostly women. Towards the end of Mackenzie-Robinson's time, the entire Fringe office was staffed by women, and at one point Kerr wound up a woman who had asked about the Fringe's gender balance, going on about a shameful bias they were suffering – not revealing until the end that the missing sex in question was male.

Mackenzie-Robinson had to contend not only with moving the Fringe Office when 170 High Street was sold, but again 2 years later – although in both cases they stayed on the High Street, and now the Fringe has its home at 180. During the final work on the most recent move the office was in a hut out the back, which was set fire to by vandals, destroying records and making life even more difficult. The new box office was almost not ready for the opening of the Fringe. By then, sales before August through the Fringe box office had reached 3%; the old system of one or two volunteers taking care of tickets was gone, with the Fringe team now taking on part-time workers, many of them students, during August, although the box office itself was not fully computerised until 1992.

The last crisis of the 1980s was brought on by the NALGO (National Association of Local Government Officers) dispute. The Fringe, using so many spaces converted afresh every August, is totally reliant on temporary theatre licences, and in 1989 an unofficial strike in the offices responsible almost stopped the Fringe from happening at all. If it hadn't gone on, it might never have recovered – while the Fringe is able to support itself financially, the loss of income for a year could possibly make it fold. Fortunately, thanks to frantic last-minute talks, a deal was worked out, licences issued, and the Fringe went ahead.

Jaunty angles: independence

With continual growth comes difficulties in presenting all the information about the Fringe. The Daily Diary was going strong and the Fringe poster had, since 1980, been chosen through a competition for Scottish schoolchildren, when in 1991 the brochure cover design was handed over to a student at the Edinburgh College of Art. The programme within has remained largely the same since it was started, despite some design alterations, a contentious change to the index, and the occasional change of major sponsors, but farming the cover design out to a different student every year produced an ever-changing series of images and colours. These days the brochure cover is done by the Fringe Office themselves, although the Fringe poster is still produced by competitive school children.

In 1994 the Fringe lost its last (although only fourth) administrator. Hilary Strong, the new appointee, was titled Fringe Director, and although bringing a greater formality in some senses, nonetheless remained firmly committed to traditional Fringe ideals. The title of Director might have made some think of other, programmed, festivals, but the Fringe remained open, chaotic, random and joyous – and big, with a half million visitors in 1996. The only censorship the Fringe itself would countenance was of images in the programme: in 1997 Stewart Lee's show *King Dong vs. Moby Dick* boasted a great big penis on the poster and although the Fringe programme carried the advert there was a sticker over the offending member saying 'this section of the advert was removed at the insistence of the Fringe programme'. Lee got his own back by quoting the letter written to explain the problem to promoters Avalon, which described the penis as 'at an especially jaunty angle', although that couldn't have embarrassed the lawyer who wrote it, Andrew Kerr – who had after all been involved with the Fringe since 1969 and must have seen numerous penises as a result, jaunty or otherwise.

More of a public fuss was made when, in 1998, the Fringe moved its dates forward by week, and so was no longer concurrent with the International Festival. If it doesn't run at the same time as the Festival, can it really still be considered the Festival's Fringe? Really, though, that is missing the point – these days, if the Fringe is on the fringe of anything, it is simply on the fringe of everything – the International Festival, Edinburgh, Britain, life. From before it even became a registered company, the Fringe has been more than the thing scattered round the edge. Indeed, with the continuing hold of TV comedy on our lives, many

of the stars of which started on the Fringe, it's become more of a part of mainstream culture than the International Festival could ever wish.

Some television stars go back to the Fringe and many are critically panned, if for no more reason than that they're famous. Rowan Atkinson fell foul of the critics in 1980 after making his name on *Not The Nine O'Clock News*. It can't have affected him too badly, though, as he went on to even greater success with *Blackadder*, co-written with Richard Curtis whom Atkinson had met at the Fringe in 1973. Atkinson also joined the Fringe board for a couple of years – one of a great many who have recognised the importance of the Fringe in British culture and are prepared to put in the time to help it continue.

In 1999, Paul Gudgin became the Fringe's second Director, and since then the Fringe has shown no signs of slowing. In 2000 it became the first arts festival in the world to sell tickets online in real time (whatever that means – though they do seem very proud of it). The super venues are yet bigger, with the Pleasance now eclipsing the Assembly Rooms and new ones starting to appear, such as C Venues (primarily focused on student work and drama rather than the comedy slant of much of the Pleasance's or the Gilded Balloon's output) and Underbelly (where in 2005 Stewart Lee spent half the show talking about Jesus begging forgiveness from him, only weeks after the blasphemy case against the TV production *Jerry Springer – The Opera*, itself based on the 2002 Fringe phenomenon co-written by Lee and Richard Thomas, had been thrown out of court).

Come what may: the future

In December 2002 the main Gilded Balloon building was gutted by fire, losing years of memorabilia and destroying a lovely venue that had been central to Fringe comedy through the 1990s. Nonetheless, in their new home on Teviot Row (which they had started using in 2001, and concentrated on from 2003) they still thrive, and remain one of Edinburgh's most important venues. Disasters are regularly averted in preparing for each year's Fringe, and those that can't be avoided are – somehow, and often through more work that is really healthy – dealt with.

The Fringe isn't going to stop. It can't stop: too many people organise their year round it, too many companies depend on it for income, for exposure and for new talent. Come what may, there will be a Fringe.

Although, as its tangled history shows, what the future holds for the Fringe and its venues is far from easy to predict. Experience shows it will probably continue to get bigger. But what controversy and jaunty angles it may contain, what new ideas it will introduce to the world and where it will all happen is not by any means in the hands of its organisers; they are not, and never have been, 'organising' the Fringe in the same way that a big international festival might be overseen. Their job is to try and make sense of a growing and changing phenomenon so that people who come to partake of it might have some hope of understanding what's available to them from one year to the next.

Similarly, we are not in any position to predict what is going to happen to it and organise its contents into a series of easily-browsed chapters. We can only try to explain why it is like it is; the future is very much in your hands. We hope they're steady ones – you'd better have a drink.

Where do shows come from?

Each year, thousands of shows appear in Edinburgh. Think about that: four for every day of the year. Seven for every Asian lion in the wild. If you were to say just the names out loud at the rate of one every 5 seconds (to allow time for *Amor de Don Perlimpln con Belisa en su Jardn* or to work out just how to pronounce *The Translucent Frogs of Quuup*) it would take you more than 2 hours – and if you wanted to actually see them all, it would take you months. Furthermore, with each show come performers, producers, directors, technicians, designers, musicians, publicists... an enormous number of people to descend on Edinburgh and an enormous number of people working their socks off over the course of several months to get together, get ready and (at least in most cases) do everything right to put on a show.

The work all begins months before the Fringe itself. Way back in the gloomy wintry months people will be choosing plays, or coming up with the ideas that will eventually become shows. Unless they are performers from Australia, in which case there are no gloomy wintry months and they will be surfing. Back in Britain, as winter turns to spring and crocuses shyly push their heads through the soil only to be trampled on by small children playing football, the people organising Fringe shows will be gathering the necessary forces to put them on – not just performers but all the others who make up the crew and production team. There will be people who have to find the money, people looking for venues and people organising somewhere to live. In the meantime, hopefully, the show itself will be in preparation, being rehearsed and all ready to go by the opening weekend when the summer's sun finally heralds the month of August in Edinburgh's fine city. If that sounds like a ghastly, nightmarish process, that's because it is. Let us take you through the details.

33

Where do all the people come from?

Everywhere. Walk your fingers through a page of the Fringe guide and you'll find feisty American high-school students jammed up against up-and-coming British comedians, a smattering of established television and theatre stars from overseas set off with the tiniest hint of home-grown celebrity, penned in on all sides by a large number of people you've never heard of. (That's pretty much how people live during the Fringe, as well.)

An awful lot of Fringe shows are of course British. An awful lot, furthermore, are made up of schoolchildren (who have helpful adults to organise the hard bits), university students (who have parents to organise the expensive bits) and struggling writers and performers in the UK's shadowy comedy industry (who have no help, no money and no parents, but do have a fair amount of time on their hands to make up for it). There are also lots of professional performers (either slightly less struggling denizens of the comedy underworld, or proper actors) and a fair number of celebrities – both successful comedians, musicians and so forth – and people whose reason for being famous no longer comes to mind and who are trying to start a new career.

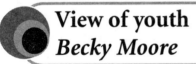

View of youth
Becky Moore

I was 13 when I went up to the Fringe to act in *Theseus*, a musical written and directed by two of the teachers at my school. It had originally been put on in the previous year, on home turf, and there hadn't been any plans to resurrect it – until one of the crew suggested taking it to Edinburgh. The school had never done anything like that before, and I'd never even heard of the Fringe, but it seemed too exciting to turn down. One thing led to another and before I knew it there we were.

The work was far harder than any of us had expected – although we only did five performances, we rehearsed every morning, performed every afternoon, and spent the evenings watching as many shows as we could. We also had to find time each day to roam the city handing out leaflets and singing loudly on street corners – this on top of an all-singing, all-dancing show! It was thrilling, exhilarating and terrifying all at once, and by the end of the week nearly every cast member had developed a sore throat.

The experience of the Fringe is something I couldn't have got anywhere else; I learned to combine fun and work, watched shows I'd never have considered and, most importantly, developed a camaraderie not only with people within my own group, whom I knew only really by name, but also with all the other performers I met. The Fringe also gives you the space to develop your art – and the incentive. Stripped of any self-consciousness, and aware of how much there was happening around me, I felt my acting skills improved with every day I was there.

The most memorable moment was our encounter with ABC, the American television network. They seemed quite intrigued by us, though I imagine it had something to do with our procession being led by two boys, one wearing only gold hotpants, the other just a furry cow-print loincloth – an image that I don't think I'll ever get rid of.

I don't intend to go into acting, but it was an invaluable experience and I learned a lot – even if only how to interest American TV producers. And if you've got a job going in the arts, I probably wouldn't say no...

Becky Moore was in her third year at Dauntsey's School when she went up to the Fringe, playing the role of 'R' in the 'Maids R Us' trio in Theseus.

Deep down, though, they are all the same. They all come to Edinburgh to do what they do in front of as many people as possible. They may claim lofty motives: we once wrote a show outline that claimed our reason for taking a show to Edinburgh was 'to raise awareness of improvisation as a way of producing serious dramatic theatre' (which looks even more deluded in hindsight, knowing that the 'serious dramatic theatre' we created included shows about petrol-guzzling pandas, furniture stores on the moon and two-headed quiz show hosts). However, there is one thing driving every Edinburgh performer. They do what they do because they must. It is what they are – it's certainly what we are and maybe is also what you are. And if you are, Edinburgh is the place for you. Without it, you are nothing – we certainly are.

Performers, then, come from all over the world to be at Edinburgh, see Edinburgh and be seen at Edinburgh. But a thousand-thousand performers alone would lead to a lot of cancelled shows, late shows, silent shows, dark shows, naked shows and money-losing shows. Fortunately, there are people for whom being seen to do their thing is less important that just getting on and doing it, so the people who make up production teams also flock to Edinburgh to learn and practice their trade slightly less ostentatiously. Even with them, a lot of shows fall into the above categories (although naked shows are usually meant to be that way).

It's this production side of Edinburgh shows that creates so much work in the months before the Fringe begins. Of course, performers like to think they're the most important thing about the show at every stage of its development, and express their importance in the pre-Edinburgh period usually by sitting around in pubs, getting very drunk and talking about putting the world to rights. Meanwhile, in the background, there are people designing and building sets, making or borrowing costumes, finding props and creating publicity materials (everything from posters and flyers to promotional clothing and freebies). Then there's all that tedious administrative stuff: making sure nobody goes bankrupt and that when everyone turns up in Edinburgh there will be more than just a field to perform in and

indeed live in. It all takes a lot of foresight so that when the cast eventually get out of the pub and rehearse they have their set, props and costumes to work with, the venues in Edinburgh get the publicity materials before the Fringe starts in order to begin distributing them, and the Fringe Office itself has all the information it needs for the Fringe guide before its April deadline. This is why everything starts so early for the production team, who may be assembled before the show is even cast; it may end equally early for some, who may not even need to be in Edinburgh for the show itself.

Most of the people who do these things are not theatre professionals – indeed, many will never have worked on an Edinburgh show before. They come from the same places as performers and go back there when they're done. Of course, different shows have different ways of organising the production side of things. In some cases, the cast and production crew are the same people, doubling up on a number of roles to make things easier and more efficient. Some productions have no need of certain crew members – naked shows don't need a costume designer and very few plays require a moth wrangler. However, there are essential departments that need to be filled for every production, each with a head and perhaps a body, tail and clawed thing on the end. In a more ideal and richer world than most Edinburgh shows inhabit, these would be dealt with by separate people, but in Edinburgh shows often a single person ends up doing an impossible number of different jobs. On some shows the responsibilities overlap so much there is no point trying to separate them anyway – if your cast is wearing moths for most of the play, why have both a costumier and a lepidopterist? However, if we artificially separate the jobs out, in a way which would leave most actual Edinburgh participants headless and with their clawed thing thrashing about hopelessly in Leith somewhere, the most obvious roles would be as outlined below.

The producer

The vast majority of shows in Edinburgh will have a producer, also known as a production manager (particularly in more professional companies). Companies that don't have a producer will almost certainly have several stressed family members mucking in to do the jobs that people in the cast have forgotten about, as even the smallest show creates an inordinate number of little jobs that need organising. Producers, or at any rate good producers, do the organising: they are responsible for everything on the production side of things, from rehearsal space and rights negotiation down to ensuring that there is enough boot black to shine the face of your little orphan boy. In other words, they are God.

Of course, being responsible for everything doesn't mean they will deal with it in person; nobody expected God to go out and pull down Jericho with his own hands – he murmured to Michael, who sent a memo to the smiting department, which assigned the message to some Seraphim delivery service which in turn told the human race to sort it out and ultimately it fell to the trumpeters to get on with the demolition itself. So it is in your ideal production team; although many Fringe groups opt for a stripped-down approach where the producers end up blacking the orphan's face themselves, production managers in their element will funnel tasks out to other people in charge of set design, publicity, lighting design and so on, who, if they're lucky enough to be part of a big production team, will have others to delegate jobs to, right on down the chain. The main difference is that in Fringe productions which actually have trumpeters, they are absolutely the least likely people to get a job done, preferring to sit in the pub until any actual playing is required, so the person who ends up doing everything may well turn out to be the orphan boy, who probably has to black his own face too.

Except that, being Edinburgh, it doesn't usually work like that. Rather than happily delegating from behind a desk, producers are more likely to be seen limping around Edinburgh, a wary smile fixed on their faces as they try to figure out what they will be asked to do next because nobody else is available. These days, some shows don't even have an orphan boy. In Edinburgh, producers also do the strangest things; for a show one of us was in years ago, the producer had to go out every couple of days to buy a vile pink milk drink that appeared at a critical moment in the show.

An orphan boy yesterday. He had to black his own face.

Another year we got ours to book haircuts for us, and it is with great shame that we admit that this wasn't because we were far too busy ourselves, but because receptionists make us nervous. (Although if a hairdresser thinks you're important enough to have a personal assistant to arrange a haircut, you have a rather pleasant time.)

The director

Most shows have a director; shows without directors might be put on by ambitious comedians who think they know it all and who are destined to receive poor reviews describing them as 'under-directed'. Or they may be put on by groups of people who know and like each other and feel that they will work perfectly well as a committee who are destined to fall out and never speak to each other again. A director of some sort is, in 99 out of a 100 cases, essential. They have overall responsibility for the creative and artistic direction of the show* –

---

*Unless the production manager has decided they want to do all this – they are God, after all.

everything from deciding that this production of *Macbeth* is going to be performed behind a big fish tank full of jelly, to ensuring that the actors can pronounce 'Dunsinane' and don't trip over the furniture (or, in the case of a show starring Lee Evans, that they do). They will set the overall feel for the show, which affects the way others on the production team will need to do their job. They are responsible for casting (if it isn't the case of 'you're all in it' – even then there is still the question of who takes which part). They also run rehearsals, which we will come to later. It sounds like a lot of work (it is!), but that needn't stop first-time directors cutting their teeth, and doing so successfully, on a Fringe show. Just don't ask either of us to direct yours.

A lot of directors are instrumental in the decision to take a show to Edinburgh having had the creative idea for the show in the first place (student groups planning to take a show to Edinburgh often ask for applications from directors with ideas, rather than foisting *Macbeth* onto somebody who'd much rather be directing *Oh! What a Lovely War*). Directors may well already be associated with the group that is performing. However, if the director is not involved in the show's initiation, it is likely that they have been hired to do the job, either by a producer, a company or probably most commonly a writer (a fair number of writers try their hands at directing their own work, and few of them turn out to be Harold Pinter). If someone has the vision for a show, but not the technical resources to get it done themselves, then the director is the person who can translate their dreams into a reality.

An area where, increasingly, directors are being hired, is comedy; the difference between a comedian with a director and a comedian without one can be palpable – the guy with comedy ears you saw last year who was quite good but nothing special without a director, might win the Perrier Award this year with one. Then again, there's only one Perrier Award to go around a lot of comedians and professional directors are not cheap. Most people will not splash out on one until they're confident they are ready – the worst thing is to bring in a director who expects you to be able to think and work at a level you haven't yet reached.

If the producer is God, the director is naturally Jesus – the one who comes along just in the nick of time and says 'actually, you're not doing that quite right…'. Some people may not believe he is as important as he claims, but ultimately everyone will grudgingly admit that what he said generally made a lot of sense. Although few casts actually crucify their director, when things go wrong the director is usually blamed and when the director finally breaks down from the pressure the others will mock him, saying 'he saved our show, but himself he could not save!' (Unless you're Jewish.)

Publicity

The design of print publicity (and perhaps website, T-shirts, badges and customised pogo sticks) is always an important aspect of any production, but even more so in the heightened competitive atmosphere of the Fringe. Some groups choose professional designers, but you can do just as well with someone who knows how to use computer graphics software. The most important part of eye-catching publicity is having an eye-catching idea, which may involve the entire company brainstorming, but thereafter it is usually best to leave one person to get on with it: hence the need for a publicity designer*. The publicity designer may also design programmes, perhaps press packs if you want to show off a little, and anything else that comes under the broad banner of 'publicity design'. Advice about doing this well can be found later in the book.

Whether or not they decide to follow this advice (and they would be foolish not to), they deliver everything to the publicity manager (often the same person, it has to be said), who needs to get the posters and flyers out. This may mean employing people to distribute it, or press-ganging members of the company to do it, or in many cases of weary publicity manager resignation, just doing it themselves. They also take responsibility for dealing with the press, the venue's publicity team, and for writing the necessary press and news releases to go with this. The Fringe Office publication *How To Sell A Show* is full of advice

41

*One of our stranger rehearsal techniques was to draw pictures as a company, a line each at a time without discussing the effect we were aiming for. Although the results were intriguing – brilliant, in a few instances – it also provided sufficient evidence that you should not design posters by committee. Surrealistic works of art, yes; posters, no.

A poster created a line at a time. We don't recommended doing this.

on how, why and when to do the myriad of things needed to efficiently publicise a show such as chasing press contacts*. The Fringe Office also run a publicity-focused workshop in the spring and provide all shows with a single list of press contacts for the Fringe, from national press down to small websites and local radio stations.

God had herald angels to do his publicity. They had the advantage of bloody great big choirs – we have cheap digital printing and the internet. Use them.

Costume design

Some shows spend very little time on costume (some sketch shows, improvisation shows and naked shows just have their cast turn up

---

*We refer to the process of phoning them to follow up on correspondence or visits from reviewers to ensure that they deliver some sort of publicity. However, actually physically chasing press contacts may be a useful last resort; if nothing else it's good exercise.

The Fringe office:
They'll be there for you

If you're taking a show to the Fringe, the people at the Fringe Office will become your new best friends. Perhaps you're a bit put off by the idea of making friends online – but these are more reliable and useful than most friends you'll pick up on a singles website, and you can guarantee that your relationship will last at least until the end of the Fringe. From the time you register, through all the planning, and during the Fringe itself, they are there to provide advice, assistance and a whole load of information. Periodic mailings keep you abreast of impending deadlines and news about the forthcoming Fringe, and they provide publications about how to go about producing and selling your show. Their website has a performers' area where you can find all the forms you'll need to fill in and all the logos you'll want to put on your posters.

If these helpful and efficient (albeit formal and slightly serious) friends are not enough for you, there are online forums where you can make even more friends and arrange flatshares, carshares, jobshares, loveshares, weddings, babysitters…hell, we've never tried it but we reckon you could probably arrange a funeral on there as well. Essentially, you could plan for the whole of the rest of your life (as long as you time it to finish roughly around the end of August).

During August itself the Fringe Club (yes, your new friends have a club – so they're posh friends as well) provides photocopying and internet facilities at reasonable prices (for "reasonable" read "cheaper than most other things in Edinburgh") and yet more people with yet more information. Plus, they actually run the festival (ye gods, important friends too! it's a wonder they manage to fit in such a fantastic social life) so they're the ones producing the brochure, running the central box office – the works. If you don't know what to do at any point, they (as well as the staff at your venue) are the people to turn to.

But they're also very busy, so don't take the friends metaphor too literally

wearing whatever they want, or less), but usually what the cast wear is an important aspect of the visual feel of the show. There are often practical considerations as well, particularly with more physical shows. Someone has to design all the costumes and hire, beg, modify or make them, even if it is only the mother of the leading actor (Sheila Hancock's first wedding dress was cleverly designed by her mother to be adaptable as a costume for rep shows after the honeymoon). Not all costume designers can actually sew (neither can all fashion designers), but it's a useful skill in any case (we can both sew) – it is also helpful to have someone who can repair clothes while up in Edinburgh, or you may suddenly discover that your brilliant visual gag doesn't work because Emma's peacock tail has fallen off. For a production with lots of costume changes you may end up with people backstage looking after costumes, and helping people get in and out of them – although in many Fringe venues there is little backstage to speak of, so the options for ten changes of dress for your leading lady are a little thin. God didn't bother with a costume designer, he just said 'let's go with robes', although he might have got Versace to make them for him.

Set designer

Once your cast are all dressed up pretty, it's time to put them onstage. That means set. No set is only really a good idea if the cast are a crack team of mime artists, or if the play takes place in an empty theatre. In professional theatre a set is often designed in miniature, sometimes quite elaborately so you get a doll's house version of the show (very creative set designers even make the dolls, though they usually stop short at little cups and saucers for them to drink out of). With more large-scale Fringe shows this is well worth doing, if only because you can see immediately if something is not going to work as well as you thought it was going to.

Some shows go for minimalist. We did one with a load of beer crates as an infinitely flexible set, using them like giant Lego blocks. Unlike Lego blocks they fell over a lot and generally looked a mess, but they were a good set for a Fringe show because they were easy to transport and store – space for sets while not in use is severely limited at the Fringe. A well-designed set that you manage to cram into whatever space is available can be stunning, however, and as it is often the first thing your audience sees it is worth getting right. Also, 'techies' love destroying sets at the end of a run, so having a big one will make them happy.

God did his own set design, although he got bored in East Anglia which is why it is so flat. He liked destroying it again, too. (Just his design in general, not East Anglia – there is precious little to destroy in East Anglia except fields and barge owners.)

Production designer

It sometimes makes sense, in the limited-personnel scenario, for the same person to design costumes and set. In this case, although the sewing load is greater (well, assuming that they make dolls for their miniature set) they earn the flashier title of production designer, and perhaps achieve a greater harmony between the stark black and white set design and the stark black and white leotards. For example.

Lighting designer

If your cast is standing, beautifully decked out, on an unlit stage, something is wrong. You either have no lighting designer, or it's a very experimental piece designed to play with the concept of sensory deprivation. Either way it's just wrong.

A lighting designer is an artist, as many will go to great lengths to make clear. And artists don't trouble themselves with pushing buttons, twiddling knobs or sliding faders – they produce a lighting plot, with colours arranged beautifully across the stage (ideally across your cast also, though some manage to get this wrong). There's an old joke that on a film set the actor should first make friends with the director of photography – we know, it's a corker, you'll be telling that to your mates in the pub later. The point is that by controlling shot position and lighting they are the people with the power to make you look like Billie Piper or Billy Bragg. In a theatre, the lighting director has the same power, so if you see a show where the lead's face is always in shadow, or bright green, you know who they crossed (or it's an experimental production).

Some argue that God did his own lighting design, but although he certainly created light there is little evidence that he bothered pointing it anywhere with much care, which explains why it is so dingy in Chicago and yet you can see everything in California. The burning bush wasn't so much a lighting effect as a trick prop that got out of hand.

Sound designer

If lighting needs designing, then so does sound – or at least it does if you have microphones, amplified instruments, or pre-recorded sound effects. Sound designers can have endless fun creating thunder effects by hitting bits of metal together, but you probably shouldn't let them because few plays actually need thunder, and the speakers in many Fringe spaces don't really do it justice.

Lucifer did all God's sound design before the Fall, but then ran off with the CD of happy sound effects, which explains why the Old Testament is so depressing.

Backstage crew

Behind every successful actor is a lonely woman. (Actually, that is a glib untruth; it being the liberated twenty-first century, behind many actors are lonely men, transsexuals and in extreme cases animals. It being real life, behind a fair number of actors are empty houses, forcing them to be essentially lonely people themselves.)

Getting back to the point, which was not to demonstrate quite how much loneliness actors cause and how, therefore, the government has made the right decision not to give any funding to the arts – so well done them, you just carry on giving money to scientists because they make bombs which are, of course, far more important than maintaining any sense of national culture; after all who'll need culture when we're all dead? And yes, strictly speaking, sport is culture, but really, it's not as if it has enough money of its own and yes, I suppose if it's a huge international event we might as well bring the whole world to London, because it's not like the tube is crowded already or anything, and please feel free to divert money from the arts to pay for all the brand spanking new shiny hurdles you've got to buy for ugly muscular women to leap over, and to make sure they can all travel home safely on public transport instead of using their shiny limousines like everyday famous people and government ministers.

Getting back to the point... also behind every actor is a stage crew, including people who operate the lights and sound (designed by the people mentioned above), scene changers, follow spot operators, fly crew, property managers, costume managers, make-up artists... the list of names is endless, and in some cases so obscure that even the people in question are not sure what they mean.

Of course, that's a theatrical generalism; we are talking about the Fringe, where there are no rules. Although most shows would be stuck without somebody to operate the lights at the very least, it's not uncommon for actors to end up doing their own sound, changing their own scenes, operating their own spotlights (or at least pointing torches at the right people from the wings), flying their own crews, managing their own property, managing (or failing to manage) their own costumes and putting on their own make-up. Quite often the person doing the lights is actually the producer. The cast and crew is usually small enough to sort things out as a kind of theatre-folk socialist collective, the principal reason being that the fewer people you have to get to Edinburgh, accommodate and feed, the cheaper it all is.

Being the Fringe, the complete opposite is sometimes true, and in productions put on by educational establishments there are sometimes far too many people doing the backstage work because of the need to involve everyone.

Many of the people who make up the backstage crew are 'techies'. 'Techies' is the disparaging term employed by actors to describe the people who can't wait to get their hands on something really boringly technical like a mixing desk, a lighting board or a book about building mechanical parrots, although for some reason they seem to really love being called techies so what is clearly intended to be an insult becomes a sort of sideways compliment. This explains why, although techies and actors are clearly of different races, they rarely have wars. They are, of course, races which can only survive by coexistence; much as they brag about how they don't need the other, with only one or the other, no play would happen. So if a techie yells at the cast to get off the stage before he kills them, or an actress remarks loudly how that sound cue has never worked in an *ad lib* in front of a full house, there aren't usually any hard feelings. Any slight tension is dissipated by the jokes they tell about each other; however, since the actors are creative performers and the techies are clever but entirely logical geeks, the actors' jokes about the techies are rather better*.

How many techies does it take to change a lightbulb? That's not the start of a joke, just a question we continue to fail to see the answer to in a slightly disbelieving way. You'd think with all that expertise one would be enough, but somehow the simplest jobs seem to take huge swathes of technical expertise to get done. If you asked a techie to change a lightbulb, there'd be at least six of them crowded around it within minutes, shaking their heads and talking about wattage and angles of elevation and the need to use a lot of gaffer tape. One of us

48

---

*Techies can only really tell jokes to each other. You see them chuckling to each other in pairs sometimes, or overhear one of them saying something like 'you know why this play is like a positive imaginary number – because if you push it about the origin it turns out to be real!' and guffawing at their wit. In the unfortunate instance that a techie is able to make a joke which is visible to the audience, generally in the form of a piece of set with a technical pun incorporated (particularly a problem in pantomimes), you get to see whole audiences squinting at the offending article in complete incomprehension.

recently did a performance involving a keyboard which wouldn't work; before long, the techie in charge was joined onstage by a second techie, casually discussing the problem without a thought for the poor performer frantically ad-libbing in front of them. Twenty minutes of ad-libbing later, there were six techies on the stage and it was in fact one of their girlfriends who discovered how to make the keyboard work, by which time it was hardly worth starting on the scripted material*.

A performance well worth looking out for is the get-out of a larger show in a venue with plenty of technical elements. Actors are sometimes involved in a minimal capacity with the simpler tasks this entails, but essentially it is the one time when the stage truly becomes the domain of the techie. They find it so exciting themselves that they often go into theatres just on the off-chance of being able to help with a get-out. What ensues is as visually entertaining as a highly choreographed piece of experimental theatre; as the stage is slowly dismantled, techies march about in hard hats, moving along what appear to be complex pre-defined routes, shouting instructions at each other like 'flying in onstage!' and 'flooring needs to be reversed!' What makes it so spectacularly entertaining is the fact that every single techie thinks they are the most important person in a get-out, creating a piece of physical theatre with a more complex series of relationships than you would get in a bedroom farce.

Alas, at the Fringe the personnel are so few in number that the cast usually have to muck in and do the get-out themselves. Actors do not like get-outs. Being actors, we can't stand them ourselves.

If the producer is God, the backstage crew are the Saints and Apostles. They are a worthy but serious bunch – though we would like to feel that the description Julie Andrews applies to the Saints and Apostles in *Mary Poppins* is also somehow true of techies:

> 'Although you can't see them, you know they are smiling
> Each time someone shows that he cares...'

---

*Techies always seem to have stunningly beautiful girlfriends, the reasons for which we can only guess at. Maybe what women really want is somebody who actually can mend the washing machine, without the help of seven or eight of his friends.

Stage manager/technical director

The Optimus Prime of the techie world is undoubtedly the stage manager*: the person with responsibility for running every performance (making sure the techies don't get out of hand, keeping the cast sober enough to perform and ensuring that no one breaks any laws). They are also responsible for the safety of the audience, which in some of the Fringe venues can weigh heavily on the mind. Just how do you get 60 members of the public out of a burning building designed in the Middle Ages for monks to store carrots?

The stage manager is in a difficult position; there is a lot to think about, and much to organise, but none of the ostentatious power-wielding that the director or producer gets. Given that a stage manager needs cooperation from absolutely everyone to do their job efficiently, patience and friendliness are essential characteristics. A stage manager who just gets on with it, quietly encouraging people and bringing out the best in them so the show runs like clockwork, may well be the most respected member of the company. Conversely, a stage manager who is bolshy and inflexible will get everyone's backs up. One of us once did a show with a stage manager in this mould and it was, for that reason alone, one of the most stressful experiences in a varied acting career. She was prone to mindlessly screaming at people when things didn't happen as they were supposed to, which is funny because it was *her* job to make things happen as they were supposed to. In the dress rehearsal one prop didn't quite work and a good-natured ad lib about 'the best-laid plans of mice and techies' was interpreted as an affront to the whole technical world, and after the screaming fit that followed many techies felt it necessary to apologise to the actor in question. The stage manager in this case was hated by everyone – even the audiences. Although audiences are not usually even aware of the stage manager's presence, in this case the actor who got the big telling off deliberately ad libbed special lines of an anti-stage managerial bent, drawing everyone's attention to what an unpleasant cow she was.

Most stage managers are not like this, and if you are a stage manager this is a perfect model for how not to do your job.

---

*Although we have yet to see one turn into a lorry.

In professional productions, there may be an entire stage management team, so no one person has to worry about everything (though most theatres have the seat of ultimate power, a desk to the side of the stage from which the whole performance can be carefully monitored and organised, and that's really what most techies covet). Conversely, in Fringe shows there may be no stage manager at all – the show's technical director takes on responsibility for all things techie, which means doing it all themselves. On our improvised shows we make the technical director do everything. To make life even more interesting we make them do it all live, with no idea what we're going to do next. We seem to have more difficulty finding techies than some shows.

If God is the producer, then the stage manager is Gabriel. He sits at God's side in meetings, worries a lot more, and only rarely has a beard. On the other hand he does get a nice pair of wings to play in.

Minimalist crew

Some shows don't bother with all that backstage and production nonsense and still get away with it. As already mentioned, it involves less housing and feeding. In a short-sighted way it also involves less organisation; why bother hunting around for a producer when you could do it yourself? (Well – because then you have to do it yourself. But there we're talking with hindsight…) Quite a lot of comedy shows work like this – or at least appear to. But don't be misled by the three smiling people at the front and no one else tucked into their flat – they may have taken on the roles of producer, publicity manager and prop mender in Edinburgh, but behind them are legions of boyfriends, girlfriends, husbands, wives, friends, relatives, slaves and fools who've probably done much of the actual work while the performers play their rehearsal games and decide how long their Shakespearean 'O!'s are going to be.

Sometimes, performers genuinely do write, organise, build and publicise everything themselves, and sometimes this goes hideously wrong. With the best intention in the world, when you're worrying about your performance and how much money you'll lose, things can slip past you. Some of them can be quite serious – for example there are various legal and safety considerations for shows, and if it turns out that your carefully-planned stunt where you fire an audience member across the stage isn't safe then it will have to go. Simon Munnery once turned up to the Fringe with a large prop bus, only to be told that it wasn't fire-safe so couldn't be used onstage*. Other shows have arrived in Edinburgh to discover that their set is too tall for the venue, or that they can't play their soundtrack because there's no minidisc player. If you're going to do everything yourself, you need to do absolutely everything yourself, which means being organised enough to remember all the little things professionals have sub-sub-sub-sub-assistant-assistants to think about for them. Going up to Edinburgh with a load of good ideas that you end up throwing away isn't the most soul destroying thing that can happen at Edinburgh – that's seeing a group of nine-year-old nuns performing *Cabaret* – but it could still be a lasting emotional trauma.

If you're taking a show up and have no techies of your own, you can usually borrow them. Many venues will arrange for a lights and sound operator (but they'll charge you for the pleasure), or there are often techies doing several shows at once (at the bigger venues, with fully automated computer-controlled lighting boards, this can be sufficiently easy that they can also read novels and write up their PhDs at the same time) and you can often find one on the Fringe website. Unless you find one through a friend, of course, you could be getting a psychopath who will sell your sound cues tape and eat your leading lady, but this doesn't happen very often.

Musicians

Musicians are required in varying amounts depending on the kind of show we're talking about. A show that has no music at all in it doesn't, in practice, require any musicians at all, though it is worth bearing in mind that musicians often try to involve themselves all the same, purely because they're a self-important bunch and can't imagine why

---

*We've no idea what has become of the bus. Presumably there's quite a big chance that it's burned down by now.

anyone would want to do a show without them. Interestingly, in a show like a musical where musicians are obviously a key part of the proceedings, they usually can't wait to get away from the show and into the pub.

That said, productions that don't use music are usually very stupid and only rarely being deliberately brave. Like ecstasy, music will almost always make things more vivid, memorable and involving; that's why people like Howard Shore are allowed to drown films in relentlessly pompous, unimaginative and mind-numbingly repetitive shopping-centre musak – it reduces the need for the once-respected actors to make any effort or the overrated director to do anything interesting with the rolling landscapes of New Zealand he's filming in. When Joss Whedon decided to do an episode of *Buffy the Vampire Slayer* without any music, it was because he likes impossible challenges and it was the next step up from doing an episode without dialogue. Unless you're Joss Whedon or Howard Shore, you'd be well-advised to do something with music.

The main musical roles that a show may want to fill are those of composer/arranger and musical director, roles which may overlap. A composer may be integrally involved in the show from an early stage, particularly if it is a new musical (in which case it is likely to be the composer's baby and God help anyone who doesn't quite do it in the way they intended). If it is an old musical, no composer is needed, unless it is by Andrew Lloyd Webber where it might well benefit from the input of a composer, or at least of a different composer.

Leaving aside its actual quality, once the music itself exists it is down to the musical director to sort it out. The level of involvement again depends on the kind of show it is. Some musical directors get all their work out of the way before the Fringe even begins, if all that is needed is a few pre-recorded tracks. Others take on the self-elected role of most-important-person-around, taking on a main instrumental and/or conducting role themselves and organising instrumentalists and cast alike in instances where there is a lot of singing, playing and all-round musician work. The musical director is one of the few people in any company who may even have authority over the stage manager.

How a musical director organises and directs rehearsals for the music very much depends on their individual methods, but the main thing to remember is that they should always look as if they're absolutely in control, even if they're completely out of their depth. Things usually work out for the best that way.

The other musical roles in productions are for instrumentalists and singers – the people performing it. They rarely find it easy to cope with the disorganised nature of the Fringe – if it's not all written on lines in black blobs they start going to pieces – and the standard way of dealing with this is for them to spend all their time in the pub. If you're in any doubt about what to do, it's never a bad idea to join them. Have a drink.

Other people at the Fringe

Of course, the people who make up the cast and crew of shows are not the only people who make the Fringe work – there are also venue staff, Fringe staff, other miscellaneous workers and oddities such as High Street performers.

All sorts of people go up to the Fringe to work. It doesn't pay very well, but depending on where you're working there can be compensations, such as getting into shows for free. If you're not working for a venue, there's the Fringe Office, who employ more than 100 people during August. If you can't manage that, there are always jobs doing leaflet distribution or handing out samples of new drinks. Free drinks wear thin a lot quicker than free shows, as we discovered to our cost the year they were handing out Tia Lusso, but it's better than a slap round the face by Paul Daniels (the absolute bottom of the barrel as far as August jobs go). Some magazines and newspapers (such as *Time Out* and *The Guardian*) have a few people selling their wares around Edinburgh during August, and presumably they get paid something. (They tend to be very attractive women and we are too shy to ask them.)

Venue staff probably have the best of these jobs, although they get worked hard and paid little (so occasionally rebel against management). They are also the most important people to make friends with. The venue publicity staff can be extra heads for ideas on getting punters into your show, and if you're particularly lucky extra hands to make it happen. The venue's admin staff should be able to help you through all sorts of organisational bumps and may have a good list of reliable suppliers. The venue techies will make the difference between your show living and dying. It's difficult to overestimate how useful a couple of friendly venue techies can be. Need a glitter ball at short notice? They'll know where to get one. Suddenly realise you need a scenic wall to hide your props behind? Ask nicely and they might even build you one. Lose the power cable for your keyboard and they'll hunt around for a kettle lead. On top of this, you have to work with them every day, doing your get-in and get-out (usually in about two minutes with sweat dripping down your arms as you try to manoeuvre a grand piano down a spiral staircase in the dark) and if you don't hit it off with them then you'll hate every moment. They also tend to know the best bars.

There are other people who frequent the Fringe – promoters, agents, journalists and of course audience – but their roles are more loosely defined and they're not so essential in making the shows work.

Useful, but not vital (otherwise some shows wouldn't get past the first week of the Fringe). For now, take a deep breath and have a drink. You've met the people who make up Fringe shows.

Except for the strippers.

Three Macbeths – again

Leafing through the Fringe brochure, the programme of all things Fringe that is launched in June, you might be forgiven for thinking that all you need for a Fringe show is a new riff on a Shakespeare play, plus a silly title – *Macbeth on Ice, Hip-hop Macbeth, Macbethany and the Girls of Edinburgh…*

Well, you'd be right. That is all you need. But that's not to say it's the best option and there are many, many others. Because you can take anything to the Fringe. Even people who think they've seen everything are constantly surprised by a new, hitherto unattemptedly weird idea at the Fringe.

Choosing what to take to Edinburgh is one of the most important decisions a group has to make. The most important decision is whether to go at all, or instead to spend the cash at the Guinness brewery in Dublin, but what show to take is nearly as vital. In many cases, the idea for the show comes before the decision to take it to Edinburgh – which is really the more logical way of doing it if you think about it. But since many groups take shows to the Fringe as a matter of course, they will spend a long time deciding what to do, and it is just as important for them to do it early. Applications to most venues start around January, and by that time people who are going to apply need to know not only what show they're doing but also what size theatre they want to do it in, what their technical needs are and, well, why people might want to see it, as no application will be considered without some kind of marketing plan.

With so many people applying, perhaps it's unsurprising that there is so much overlap. After all, experts say that there are only seven real stories (we're not sure quite how this works, but we suspect that each story 'type' corresponds to one of the Chronicles of Narnia). As a result, there may be eight productions of *Macbeth*, more than one production of even relatively obscure musicals and amongst the several brand new works being staged certain... er... similarities. We are not suggesting for a minute any sort of plagiarism, or a conspiracy theory involving a single writer hammering out all the new drama at the Fringe, but you'd be surprised by how many ways there are to explore the sexual awakening of a middle-class white girl in a big city: in fact, it's only the one, so if that's someone's brand new show they'd best be prepared for competition (and may want to consider turning it into a musical). It's a big decision. This is the show that the group will live and breathe for six to twelve months preparing it, and up to thirty days performing it. Make the wrong choice and they'll hate every minute. Make the right choice and there will still be two or three cast or crew members hating every minute; there's no pleasing some people.

Choosing the title

Under most normal circumstances, the title of any work of art is almost the last thing to be finalised. It is rare than an author decides what a book will be called then writes 90,000 words to fit the title; playwrights usually struggle to find a title that will adequately encompass their masterpiece, not the other way round; great composers didn't begin by writing a random word at the top of their manuscript paper before trying to compose music that would fit the description. That would be like naming a baby before you knew what gender it was.

At the Fringe, though, several babies are named before they're even conceived. With comedy shows in particular, the title can be the only thing that gets fixed early on – most stand-up comedians will only have the haziest idea what they might end up talking about when they start approaching venues, and many comedy groups don't really have the first idea about what they want to do, except for 'a comedy show'. This is why many comedy shows have titles like 'Greased by a Silver Spoon', 'Rattled by Goosings', 'Whiskers on Kittens' and 'Clogs'. If the

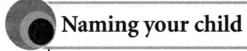

Naming your child

Actually, one of us was named before his parents knew his gender. Fortunately, they rethought the name when he turned out not to be a she. However, if you're of an impatient bent and are too lazy to go through the process of changing your mind, you might consider the following names which can work for both boys and girls: Sam, Jo, Georgie, Jamie, Tony, Kim, Tracy, Marian, Hilary, Joyce, Elvis.

Failing that, you could just do the modern parent thing and make up a name which is equally male, female or indeed transgender, such as Cabernet, Absinthe, Mozzarella or Bin.

It's only fair of us to point out that either of the lazy methods have a high risk of your child being bullied mercilessly until they finally have their head held down the toilet bowl for just a few seconds too long and you have to pay for all their brain damage treatment, and eventually their funeral bills when they leap off a tall building. Your choice.

show turns out to fit the title, so much the better.

This has never been truer than for comedy ensemble Population:3. Having scored a hit with their film parodies *Gladiatrix* and *The Wicker Woman*, the trio admitted to us that to find names they have resorted to going through all of the DVDs in HMV to find ideas for shows. Enjoyable though it was, their next show, *The Elephant Woman*, did not have the strong storyline of the others and it occurred to us that their gender-reversing titular requirements may have created an unwanted restriction. It may sound easy finding a feminine counterpart to a well-known film title, but the options are not as wide-ranging as they may initially seem. Before leaping up and suggesting *The Invisible Woman*, consider how different from an invisible man an invisible woman would actually look, and then imagine the problems creating a witty poster image.

The lovely Population:3 folk assured us that they had covered all the possibilities – 'if you can think of one, we'll have heard it already,' they claimed. Which sounded a bit like a challenge to us. Within minutes we were offering the suggestions, '*Dame*' (the feminine equivalent of *Fame*) and '*You've Got Female*', neither of which they had though of previously. There is probably a goldmine of other less obvious names that Population:3 haven't yet considered. But they're incredibly busy, so if you think of any why not pop onto their website and send them an email to save them the trouble of thinking things up themselves.

Naturally we've experienced the title-panic ourselves, and when your show is going to be made up on the spot each night it's even harder finding a title that is going to describe it. Ultimately, with our improvised shows the title has always come out of phrases from our publicity blurb, which means that even if they don't fit the show they do at least fit what we're telling people about it.

However, when the Fringe organisers are demanding a title several months before you have even written in, sometimes it frankly doesn't matter what you tell them. Comedy ensemble Fat Fat Pope used to write words on bits of paper then pull three of them out of a hat to form a title. Unless you're keen to do gender-reversal of some sort, that seems like as good a method as any.

Choosing the show

Different groups choose shows in different ways. Indeed, different groups *create* shows in different ways; be it theatrical, comedic, 'dancey' or musical in nature, options range from producing established works (the Shakespeares, the Pinters, the Tennessee Williamses and, God help us, the Lloyd Webbers), through new writing (the... oh, well there's no point in listing names, if you've heard of them it's probably too late and they'll be in the 'established works' category) to devised pieces (created as a group in rehearsal and usually pulled together by a director), fully-improvised pieces (created by a group in performance when the director hasn't a hope of pulling it together) and finally pieces that are never created at all, such as Theatre of Relativity's 2003 *Sweet F.A.*, a theatre left empty for an hour or so (unlikely as it sounds, ticket sales were good and the show

Musicals – Anything goes

If you have ever had the slightest desire to write a new musical, the Fringe is the place for it. Don't worry too much about having a fully developed idea for one, either; all you need is to take a famous person, a film, a book, a picture, a nursery rhyme, and add the magical words 'the musical' to it – and apart from the tiny business of writing songs and stuff, you're made. (N.B.: if you have delusions of grandeur, you could try adding 'the opera' instead, unless it is actually an opera, in which case I would suggest it will sell better as a musical.)

Anyone can do it. Go on, think of something that hasn't been turned into a musical yet. Sound like a great idea? (Almost certainly yes, unless you chose the holocaust or *Blankety Blank* – oh, I don't know though…) Since the songs themselves are usually the last consideration in the process (getting the poster and the costumes right is so much more important) nobody should feel restricted from joining in the musical-writing fun.

Naturally, there are copyright issues to consider. For example, wonderful though it would be to put on *Reservoir Dogs: the Musical*, you would first have to obtain permission from Quentin Tarantino and persuade our lawyers that you hadn't copied the idea from this book. If you're writing a musical about somebody who is alive and in the public eye you might also want to run it past some libel lawyers.

But don't let that put you off. There was a time when writing musical productions was the arena of the talented, trained artist – the Mozarts, the Verdis and the Wagners of the world. Thank God that the current state of the West End has changed all that and the general public will watch any old crap – finally, musical theatre is not an elitist, exclusive members' club, but a truly Marxist equality. Get stuck in, there's always room in the world for another musical.

garnered enough interest to be broadcast on the internet).

How do they decide what type of show to take, then? The groups making the decision usually have a good starting point in the reasons why the group was formed in the first place. A musical theatre group will not be flicking through *avant garde* mimed theatre from the German expressionist era, any more than a children's theatre company will be looking to adapt *Titus Andronicus**, and dance groups will not begin by devising a comedy show (at least not intentionally). Even with such boundaries already in place, several options are open. The musical theatre company clearly has a whole range of musicals to choose from, ranging from ones you can almost take seriously to most of the rest, or they might put on something new. The children's theatre company (presenting plays *for* children, not *by* a load of nine-year-old nuns) can use new writing, devised work, or improvisation to interpret popular children's books, folktales or completely new stories. The dance group can dance slowly, or fast, or somewhere in between. So the genre they are working in doesn't altogether restrict the shows that can be done or the ways they might be created.

Which is better, then, things written by dead folk, things written by live folk or things that are not so much written as born? Since all of the options come in subcategories good, boring and awful, it really depends on what you're trying to achieve.

---

*Although our ironic production *Tot-us Andronicus*, with a cast of nine-year-old nuns, should be ready in a few years.

Dead folk

Shows by dead folk have a number of advantages. First, with very few exceptions, you do not have to pay royalties (the cut-off point for copyright in Britain is 50 years after the author's death, so anything before the 1950s is anybody's to use). This instantly makes a production more profitable, or at least less loss-making. There is also quite a reasonable chance that people will have heard of the play, or at least the playwright. There will also have been previous productions, something of a mixed blessing – you can draw on other stagings for ideas, but you might also be directly compared to them. For this reason it would be unwise to choose a slightly obscure play that has recently been successfully staged at the National, because you're letting yourself in for unfavourable comparisons. This is less of a concern with Shakespeare, a perennial Fringe dead bloke, but because there are so many productions to choose from you have to be careful; of eight *Macbeths*, you'd better be the one with naked lesbian witches if you're going to stand out. Apart from naked lesbian witches (which we've realised can be shoehorned into pretty much any Shakespeare – or any production at all, for that matter), people attempt to stand out by 'bringing Shakespeare up-to-date', perhaps using video projection, handguns and Americans, or even transposing it into a completely different art form such as the highly successful *Bombity of Errors*, which transferred to the West End after its 2002 Fringe run. Not just Shakespeare, either – anything that's a bit dusty runs the risk of being reborn on the stages of the Fringe. Established plays by dead folk, whether performed as written or taken as the start of a new or devised work (even here those three options are available) have the advantage that everyone has heard of them, but the disadvantage that everyone has seen them too.

Live folk 1: famous live folk

Between the dead folk and new writing, plays brand new for the Fringe, come a few live folk whose work has entered the repertoire. Say 'hi' to Alan Ayckbourn and Stephen Sondheim (everywhere you go).

Behind them are Alan Bennett, Willy Russell and a few others. If you bring one of their plays to the Fringe, there's almost always an audience. On the other hand, you have to pay them royalties. Usually, performance rights for modern works are handled through one of the big dramatic publishing companies, such as Samuel French or A & C Black. How much you will have to pay depends on the work in question, the money-grabbing tendencies of the publisher or writer in question, and possibly on the size of venue or number of performances. It's almost impossible to get around paying royalties unless you happen to know the playwright personally – claims that you're from 300 years in the future when the copyright has expired will not cut it (and anyway, the copyright term will probably have been extended again by then). You're not even exempt if you're a charity (as a lot of Fringe groups are); even non-profit making organisations such as schools have to deal with copyright, and as you're presumably performing to a paying audience you are likely to be treated as professionals. Don't even assume you'll be allowed to put on a given play – plays may be withdrawn from availability for a number of reasons, such as a major London or National touring production having obtained exclusive rights for the duration of its run. Oh, the heartache that was experienced by one of our siblings when her school was denied the rights to use *Oliver!* and instead had to put on a play called *A Twist of Oliver* using completely different songs. If you don't want to look stupid, find out about this before you apply to venues; if you're accepted by a venue only then to discover that the rights aren't available, you'll be both stupid-looking and unpopular.

Live folk 2: unfamous live folk

New writing (not necessarily new to the Fringe, as it may have been tried out elsewhere) cannot trade on its name, as *Romeo and Juliet* can (but what's in a name?). Instead, the writer may have previous Fringe successes you can pin publicity on. Otherwise, you're on your own and unknown (which undoubtedly makes it harder to sell) but it's in good company, as more than one-third of all Fringe shows are premières. This makes choosing a show to watch the world's biggest lucky dip. (Some shows give you cheap plastic toys, too, although they probably don't consider them to be consolation prizes.) However, there are advantages to being in this position – *The Scotsman's* Fringe First awards, set up for this very category of production, not only singles out outstanding new work but also means that there are *Scotsman* reviewers dashing around looking for good new writing. Even if you don't make the cut for the awards, you may get good reviews in the process. To some extent, at least from a drama side, the Fringe is more a place to launch your career as a writer than as a performer; if, for example, a reviewer (or a big-name audience member) chooses to champion a writer, it can help not only them but their play. Few reviewers will champion actors. (Although *Fest* have a thing about promoting attractive people at the Fringe, as if they really need the help. Not that we're bitter.)

Devised pieces

Finally, there's the devised option. Devised shows are very popular these days, and particularly shine in physical theatre and adaptations of other works for more experimental performances. Most of the time it fails utterly, but often entertainingly and it's worth it for the few times when a group that is highly in tune and working smoothly creates a show that is both brilliant and unlike anything you've ever seen before. The biggest cause of devised work falling down is ego: if you encounter a devised piece where one actor gets all the good bits while the rest of the cast sulk at the back of the stage, you've run into the Fringe staple of Devised Company With Egotistical Leader. Occasionally, such a company will actually produce a good show, in the same way that occasionally Orlando Bloom does a good film. If you find yourself invited to join a devised group where one actor is louder than all the rest, think carefully before accepting, especially if the loud actor is Orlando Bloom.

Another, less severe, way that devised pieces can miss the mark is also related to ego. With a company full of ideas and well-balanced egos so no one drowns out the rest, you can end up with a play that is good, with some great individual scenes, but which doesn't go anywhere in particular. This is the other end of the curve from having an egotistical leader – you need a leader. If they happen to come with more than their fair share of ego then they should probably be directing, because then at least their ego will spread across the whole show and create a bold, if arrogant, piece of theatre. With that balance and direction, devising new things can produce some of the most riveting theatre you will ever see.

Improvisation

Perhaps the bravest, maybe also silliest, way of devising a show, is to make it up on the spot. In its simplest form, improvisation can just be a string of *Whose Line is it Anyway*-style games which give performers a chance to be quick-witted in a smart-arsy way, but that is only the tip of the comedy iceberg. More sophisticated groups – okay, ours for example – use improvisation to make up stories, anything from a few minutes long to an hour or more. There might be an overriding structure to this (particularly in what is known in the trade as 'long form improv') or it might be much more flexible (which isn't called short form; long form comes from America, so we suppose you could call the other 'European-style'). Either way, without a script, what the characters say and to varying extents the way the story develops is completely unpredictable. The absolute opposite of the game-show style presentation are the shows by improv groups aiming to create legitimate serious theatre; these people tend to piss off writers, who know that theatre *really* needs to be carefully crafted and thought out and written over several months if it's going to be any good. But if writerless devised shows can be coherent and exciting, it's logical to presume that writerless improvised shows can achieve the same in the hands of an ego-free skilled company of gifted performers, with the added element of spontaneity, which creates an extra level of frisson for audience and performers. This having been recognised at the Fringe more than most places, improvisation crops up in a variety of places – often in comedy shows, sometimes in children's shows. Not so much in Shakespeare.

For a certain type of performer, the challenge of coming up with everything on the spot is a real stimulus, and for the audience the chance to see something completely fresh, coupled with a chance that it might all suddenly fall apart (audiences love to see people fail – provided that they do so with grace) can tempt them away from more traditional fare. On the other hand, the social stresses of the Fringe combined with the unique challenges of an improvised show can be too much for some people, and it is at least as exhausting as any other type of show. Finally, no one will believe it's improvised, because obviously it makes more sense that you wrote and rehearsed 20 different shows. This leap of illogical thinking is often made by reviewers, but then how do you write up a show that will never happen again?

So which one's for me?

The above methods of creating shows are not mutually exclusive, and the way in which they work varies between different types of performance: it is unusual for music ensembles to 'devise' a symphony, for example (but don't make the mistake of thinking it hasn't been tried*). We would reiterate that it is possible to take anything to the Fringe, and in any way. To ensure a certain level of quality, though, it's as well to have some idea of how you're going to do it. Most groups will have a preferred way of creating a show, but there are some that choose how each show will work afresh. Other people are trying to push the boundaries of the word 'art' so will set out with the single aim of doing something differently from anything else that has ever been or is being done. If you're going to the Fringe, you probably have an idea of what it is you're likely to do, simply because people don't tend to get up one morning and decide to take a show to Edinburgh without having first thought of shows they might like to do.

That said, if you do have to choose, think through the pros and cons and above all try to come up with something that stands out, simply because that makes it easier to sell, and if you can't do that you'll lose lots of money. That is a disturbing thought, so you'd better have a drink while you ponder it.

No really, which one is for me?

Not telling. Have another drink.

Edinburgh advice
John Finnemore

> The single most important advice I would give anyone thinking of taking a show up to Edinburgh for the first time this year is: don't. Do it next year. Seriously.

---

*Ideally, don't make the mistake of trying it.

Whatever time of year it is when you read this, it's too late to do Edinburgh this year, but a great time to be thinking about it for next year. Great though the festival (still) is, there's so much competition for every space, every seat, and every review; and the whole enterprise is liable to cost you so much time, money and nervous energy that it's only worth doing when you're certain the thing you're taking up is as good as you can possibly make it. So, sit on the idea for now. Do a run somewhere cheap in your home town, or if it's comedy, do bits of it at open-mike nights or sketch nights. Rewrite it. Perform it again. Rewrite it again. Fish the original script out of the bin, and reinstate the bits that you now realise held the whole thing together, and you should never have cut. In short, make it absolutely the thing you always imagined and couldn't possibly improve from the first preview. Because a huge amount depends on the very first reviewer you get in, if you can get a positive review out early, no matter how small the publication, the huge mass of audiences and other critics looking for any indication that one show is better than another may be nudged your way, and your snowball has a chance of rolling.

Don't hire a publicist! There is nothing a publicist can do that you can't do. The only people that can get reviewers to see the show against their will are certain of the larger management firms, who are not afraid to use bribery, blackmail, and if necessary chloroform. Publicists are afraid to use these things, but they are not afraid to charge you a thousand pounds to send out press releases you could have sent out, and make (or pretend to have made) phone calls you could have made. This rant is based on a true story.

It's not hard to find actors who are perfectly prepared to perform in your play at Edinburgh for free, and even pay for their own accommodation. It is a little harder to find good actors who will do this, but not impossible.

An advert in PCR magazine or castnet.com will produce a flood of responses, and a careful and exhausting auditioning process will unearth the 10% who are both good actors and people it won't be impossible to live with for a month. The important thing is to be absolutely up-front about what you're offering – make sure they understand that although you're calling the contract a 'profit share', there will almost certainly be no profit to share; what they stand to gain by signing up is a chance to be seen at the Edinburgh festival in a good part, in a good play. (If the play you've written isn't in fact a good play, please don't take it to Edinburgh. I'm begging you. Taking coals to Newcastle is an astute piece of entrepreneurism compared with taking a bad play to Edinburgh.)

Never see a show because the pretty student who gave you the flyer warned you there will be nudity. It won't be her nudity. It will be the nudity of an ugly, ugly man, and will go on for ages.

John Finnemore has written for theatre and television. His play, Amy Evans' Strike, was nominated for a Fringe First.

Where do shows get their money from?

Edinburgh shows lose money. It's not a rule without exceptions, but a strong possibility for the vast majority. It's hardly surprising – taking a show to Edinburgh costs more than a lengthy holiday in Venice for a family of four. Venue guarantees are set to ensure that a venue is in profit (or at least doesn't lose anything) even if some of its shows don't even turn up. Getting decent publicity printed costs money; getting the cast and crew to Edinburgh costs money; staying in Edinburgh costs money; eating in Edinburgh costs money. If you want reviews and a chance of the Edinburgh run leading somewhere else, you need to be there for a sizeable part of the entire month. And then there is seeing other shows... and drink.

Shows that are fortunate enough to have some kind of guaranteed success (perhaps it features a previous Perrier nominee, or people who have been on television in more than just an advert for orange juice) will usually be funded by someone putting money in, confident that they'll get it back. It might be an individual or a promotion company, or the group itself. Comedians tend to work through promoters once they are known on the scene, although the promoters often don't take much of a risk, so if the show is a flop, its performers may end up owing them a fair amount of money. (If you wondered why comedians drink so much, this goes some way to explaining it – without explaining how they can afford it.)

Some shows are considered as a kind of 'valuable life experience' for the participants, such as the teeming groups of American high-school students, members of community theatres and nine-year-old nuns performing *Cabaret*, so may not be trying to make money at all. If the accommodation and other living costs are paid for by the company individually, the other costs of putting on the show itself might be covered by ticket sales, and if not, the loss is picked up by the parent organisation who are probably backed up by funds from charitable or educational sources. A lot of shows from university theatre companies are run like this, as well; performing a Fringe show back at university in the autumn is a common way of covering a loss at Edinburgh (and after weeks of playing to audiences of three people, having large audiences of inebriated students see you is a great way of ending a production on a high). Big groups, including professional theatre companies and more famous student groups take their shows on tour with Edinburgh being only one stop, albeit a long one.

The point is, somebody has to foot the bill at some point, and if it isn't going to be Fringe audiences, a more reliable source of paying punters on home-turf, an overseeing company or a rich uncle Michael will ease the burden for performers who don't want to be repaying debt for the rest of their lives. This can be a problem for the large number of *ad hoc* shows that end up at the Fringe not because of a promoter or a company, but because of some creative people having had a really good night out that ended in the small hours with one of them slurring 'and whatsh more…we're gunna bloody take a show to the Edinburgh Fridge…' Presuming none of them have a rich uncle Michael, it is important they decide where the liability lies. Shared liability is most fair (even if only one person initially puts the money up) and, in general, it is a good idea to do things this way unless there is a really good reason not to. Many actors initially object that they are too poor and end up having to sell their collection of *A-Ha* albums on eBay. Some actors even end up getting a job. Other individuals may have to take out loans to put money into a show, because even if creative people give themselves a group name (something trendy and obscure like 'Pilgrims Who Jump') most banks won't just let them borrow several thousand pounds.

There are other ways of raising money for shows. In the UK, The Arts Council has funding programmes, although in general this is a longer-term development path rather than cash for your first show. The Arts Council divides into regions, and each region has different ways of working; some have programmes specifically for Edinburgh shows, such as the Arts Council East of England's 'East To Edinburgh'. The regional websites make for several hours' worth of laborious reading and it can feel as if you're being pointed towards several different sources of money without actually ever finding out anything useful. (In fact, the whole internet is constructed along similar lines.) On the other hand, the information is usually thorough and you can, after a bit of hard research, discover that you're not eligible for anything. Sorry, whether you're eligible for anything. The people in charge of the relevant schemes are also well worth contacting, partly to express an initial interest, but also because they're often nice and you might build up a friendship, or in extreme cases a marriage.

Other funding bodies exist, many designed for very specific products or regions, and it is always worth investigating. Schools and universities often have funding for their students – many university drama societies send shows to Edinburgh every year and are a good source of funding if you're at the right institution.

Sponsorship can be difficult to secure, but worth it if you can sort something out, either cash or (more likely) in-kind services. The key to sponsorship is to use personal contacts rather than writing form letters to people. Explore your network of friends, friends' families, people you once met on a bus tour of Morocco and anyone else you think might have access to anyone useful, then write to any possible source and follow up with several crawling phone calls... until they call the police.

While you're doing that, it's worth considering whether your friends and family might be persuaded to give money to the show directly. A nice way of doing this is some sort of supporters' club, asking for only small amounts of money, with benefits for joining (cheap tickets, a mention in the programme, signed photographs, a badge...). A less nice way is to just take the money without asking. This is not usually necessary, in fact – if approached professionally, many people are happy to put money in voluntarily and some may turn out to be surprisingly generous.

These are all tried and tested means of finding money for shows. They take a little work to organise, which naturally puts some people off, but the choice is there if you're in need of some cash. Some performers just end up repaying debt for the rest of their lives.

Budgeting

However you get your money, it's important to take care of it. Don't just put it in a kettle and hide it in a mattress. Don't invest it in the arms trade, whatever example our leaders have set. Spend it sensibly and keep track of exactly what is happening to it: this is a process known as budgeting. Even if most production jobs are shared between different people, one person should be ultimately responsible for the budget because you need a single person who is organised, diligent, and good with numbers – the sort of person, in short, who might become an accountant if only they weren't shut up in a small room in the middle of Edinburgh trying to figure out if you can afford a glitter ball. If you don't know anyone like that, try a Sudoku addict, and if you don't know anyone like that, do it yourself. Worse than having someone look after your budget in a slapdash way is to have no one do it at all. The budget is one of the most important documents in a show's possession, and it's the only thing that can simultaneously keep a cap on what you spend and tell you how much money you are up or down. We have seen bad budgeting in shows cause friction on an unbelievable scale. (It's a little known fact that the First World War was sparked when Archduke Franz Ferdinand failed to produce budget sheets for a show he'd taken to the Fringe called *The Loneliest Man in Vienna*, but insisted that his Serbian cast all owed him £200 in addition to the food expenses he claimed he would foot the bill for.) Furthermore, sorting out a budget that has gone wrong is far more time-consuming than doing it properly in the first place, and can cause feuds which last for several generations.

Ultimately, it may well end up being the producer's responsibility, but if you manage to find your Sodoku expert you can invent a special title for them like treasurer or bursar (or purser, if you're doing a show on a ship). If the Sodoku expert doesn't turn up and you end up doing it yourself, fear not – we've been speaking to experts to show you just how easy it is…

In conversation with… the Excel paperclip

`Hello! You look like you're doing a budget! Would you like some help?`

God, yes.

`Okay! Let's start with costs. You've got venue hire, publicity, Fringe fees, accommodation, transport. What's your set made of?`

A thousand copies of *Playboy*.

Back issues?

We got them off a skip.

Free, then. Costumes?

Wellies.

JUST wellies?

Wellies and plastic macs.

Okay, cast of six, better have some spares, that goes in as well... any other costs?

Ariadne needs a wheelchair.

Can't you borrow one?

My grandmother has one – I suppose she won't miss it for 3 weeks or so.

Free again — excellent. Now, add in VAT where needed — most of it's in the Fringe guide, you know. Ah — no VAT on flyers. Not unless they're really big.

They're not really big, you idiot. That would make them posters.

Good point! Now add it all up, add on 10%, and...

Hang on. What's the 10% for?

Good question! I'll answer it! That's contingency. It's in case anything goes wrong. Unexpected costs, that sort of thing.

You think I'm going to make mistakes?

I'm not letting you save this budget unless you put it in.

I'll do it with a pencil.

Ah, but then you'll miss out on all this interactive fun! Now let's add income. You get 60% of box office, 100 seats for 20 performances at £10 pounds, that's... £2,400.

Don't try to pull a fast one on me, I may not be a Sudoku expert but I do it in my spare time and I've learned how to add up numbers: 60% of 100 times 20 times 10 is £20,000.

You're not going to sell all those tickets. Fringe shows usually manage somewhere between 10% and 30%. I've put down 20%, somewhere in the middle. And then minus the venue's takings.

But our venue guarantee is at 30%! Less than that and we're losing money!

Welcome to the Fringe! Look, you've already paid the guarantee, and in practice you're not going to get more than 30% audience across the run unless you're very good, get a great review at the start, and are pretty damn lucky. Because you're not going to hit your guarantee level, what you've already paid the venue is all they're going to take from you, so you can treat the entire box office takings as yours — well done! It's up to £4,000.

We don't get 10% on that?

No. In fact, you may have to pay the venue for
other things — microphone hire, fines for
overrunning. Check your contract.

I don't even have a copy of the contract – I'm just the purser!

You're doing the show on a ship?

Ariadne's Dad is in the Royal Navy. She liked the sound of it.

Hurray for Ariadne's Dad! Now, we've worked out
the costs — how are you paying for the show?

Ariadne's got a credit card.

That's pretty normal — most Fringe groups don't
have their own bank account, even. You'll be
buying little things while you're up there,
though — replacement wellies, that sort of
thing — so get everyone to keep their receipts
and you can pay it back at the end.

We have to keep ALL our receipts? That's impossible!

On your own head be it. The authors of this
book made the mistake one year of just keeping
a list of how much people had spent.

So you can pay everyone back – what more do you need?

Oh, my physical friend. They didn't know how
much had been spent on different things — they
used a lot of chalk but didn't know how much

Credit cards

A brief warning about using credit cards: if relying on someone's personal credit card to pay for important things, make sure they don't accidentally get it cancelled, or get themselves into a position where they fail a credit check. The embarrassment of sitting in a car rental shop on the last day of the Fringe and being told that you aren't allowed to hire a car is bad enough, but then you're stuck in Edinburgh with no transport, no accommodation, and a huge amount of junk you have to get home somehow. And if you think it'll never happen to you – it turns out that if you've just moved, but haven't paid a bill from your new address, the game's up. Cue panicked phone calls to other rental companies to find one that will just take the money without checking to see that you've got it first.

had been spent on it! They had no idea!

That must have been terrible for them.

It's a little inconvenient if they want to know how much they should budget for chalk next year!

But we don't want chalk. And we won't be buying much anyway.

But you won't know which part of the budget you're spending, so you won't know when you're over spending…

Enough! If you don't start being helpful I'll uninstall you… or turn you into the talking cat option.

Don't blame me if you end up surrounded by wellies. Okay, how are you going to do your budget in Edinburgh?

What?

Are you taking a computer up there?

Ariadne will have her laptop.

Okay! So you can take me with you. Great!

No...

This is going to be *so* much fun! I'll make a list of all the shows I'm going to see. I can hang around Pleasance Courtyard giving spreadsheet advice to people like Nicholas Parsons, maybe even get to see Paul Daniels...

Or how about doing something useful like setting up a spreadsheet and keeping track of how much we spend so we know how much more we've got left to buy wellies with?

I'd hate to miss Paul Daniels.

You could even put in our audience figures each day so we know how well we're doing and what audience we need across the rest of the run to break even.

No.

No? You're not going up to Edinburgh so you can watch Paul Daniels, let's make that clear now.

I mean, no it's really not a good idea. I know you humans, you'll be fine at the beginning, but when I tell you on the last night you need 2000 punters to break even, you're going to get depressed.

But we'll need the figures at the end.

Okay. I'll remember the figures, but you can't look at them. Deal?

Deal? You're my servant. My slave!

If you get depressed looking at audience figures, you won't perform properly, and you'll get even less audience, which will make you more depressed.

What do you know? It's not like you've been to the Fringe!

Have too. I directed an experimental version of a Shakespeare play where all the parts were played by animated characters on computer screens. 'Mac-beth'.

Shut up now or I'll turn you into the talking bouncy ball! Or that strange coloured blob which isn't even a thing.

Before you do that, why don't I introduce you to online banking?

Hello, welcome to Online Banking! You look like you're doing an unprofitable Fringe show. Would you like some help?

Comforting words

Franklin D. Roosevelt said that 'Happiness is not in the mere possession of money; it lies in the joy of achievement, in the thrill of creative effort.' Something to remember when you're achieving something at the Fringe and making a creative effort, even if you're losing all your money and quite a lot of everybody else's in the process. On the other hand, Franklin D. Roosevelt was stinking rich, so what would he know?

Sod it. Have another drink.

Rats, dry rot and other venues

In the real world, buildings known as 'theatres' are big places where plays are put on. They often have more than one actual theatrical space within them, so the different theatres inside the overall theatre are given names – like the National's Olivier Theatre (named after one of England's greatest actors of all time, Laurence Olivier) and its Lyttleton Theatre (named after Humphrey Lyttleton from *I'm Sorry, I Haven't a Clue*). Similarly, the buildings known as 'cinemas' have several 'screens', usually numbered rather than named because it's more lowbrow. At the Fringe, where the theatrical venues are often cinemas for the rest of the year round anyway, it would be pretentious and untruthful to refer to them as 'theatres', so they are simply called 'venues'. There are a few venues that remain theatres for the rest of the year (the Traverse being the most notable, as it grew up as a direct result of the success of the Fringe), but most are converted, from arts centres, churches, sports halls, university buildings, houses, building sites, back rooms of pubs and Masonic lodges.

Yes, Masonic lodges. You'd have thought with all their money the Masons wouldn't need to open their secret places to a load of thespians, but perhaps their habit of giving charitably to the community can account for the fact that one year we found ourselves performing in a lodge. This was a source of more than a little titillation, what with storing our props in a temple filled with swords and tartan aprons (not to

mention two full-size inflatable Daleks being used by the show before us).

Andrew McClelland, whose *Somewhat Accurate History of Pirates* was making a medium-sized splash at the Fringe that year, was beside himself with excitement when he learned of our unusual venue, secret societies being something of a pet topic for him and a possible subject for his next show. He begged us to take him to see the temple and assorted props, so one evening we snuck in and showed him around, then took photographs of McClelland examining the aprons and sitting in the Master's chair surrounded by Daleks*. We probably broke all sorts of terrible Masonic laws and we half expected McClelland to go inexplicably missing before his show could emerge. But in fact he was back at the Fringe the next year with his *Somewhat Secret Secret Society Show*, replete with photographs that we took

---

*Despite the presence of Daleks, the Master referred to is not thought to be in any way related to Dr Who.

ourselves. He admitted that he had removed a rather nice photograph of us from the show fairly early on, but since he let us get in for free we remain full of goodwill towards him.

When venues have more than one actual theatrical space inside them, they are not called theatres either, because of problems that would cause most venues under the Trades Descriptions Act; they are called 'spaces'. Spaces might be named or numbered, but each venue has to do this very carefully because of the huge number of spaces across Edinburgh and the potential for confusion. Imagine trying to find your way to Pleasance Olivier, only to discover that you're meant to be at Gilded Balloon Olivier; or arriving at C Venues to see a show in theatre 33, only to be told that the ticket saying C33 means C cubed 3, so you're in the wrong theatre altogether. Although these blunders have been avoided, we're not the only people who've arrived at Pleasance Courtyard to see a show that's actually on in Pleasance Dome – the Cambridge Footlights once got a very negative review by someone who turned up to the wrong place and discovered a 'no late admissions' policy when they finally found where they were supposed to have gone.

When applying to do a show at the Fringe, a group first has to persuade venues to give them one of their spaces. This is one of the more time-intensive parts of preparing for the Fringe and although the Fringe Office publishes guides and runs open days designed to give you enough information and advice, it can still be daunting. With around 300 venues to choose from, some of them not even in Edinburgh (one is a quarter of the way to Newcastle), it's perfectly normal to be overwhelmed when the *Fringe Spaces* brochure first turns up. If you find yourself in this situation, with claustrophobia taking hold and you're having hallucinations of being chased down Cowgate by several large buildings, don't panic. Have a drink and let us show you how to navigate the whole thing.

Size isn't everything

Ask any aging Fringe-goer what has changed across the years and they'll talk about the emergence of 'premium venues'. (At least, that is one of the

The Pleasance toilets

Even if you don't manage to get tickets for the show you want to see at Pleasance Courtyard, do be sure to use the toilets. Not because they are particularly nice, but because the walls make a fantastic read. Scrawlings which potentially date back several decades include a number of gems, but being a centre of comedy the Pleasance has evidently drawn a number of humorous people into its toilets resulting in a fine collection of jokes. Whether or not any actual comedians have contributed over the years remains uncertain – but surely the person who added 'How do you titillate an ocelot? You oscillate its tit a lot' was a professional in some capacity. (That one kept us smiling through some of our darkest moments at the Fringe.)

Better still, on one of the walls there is a giant cryptic crossword to which people continue to add clues and spaces. A few people have had a go at solving some of the genuinely difficult clues, but the more inventive option is surely to add your own. It's an impressive feat of intellectual camaraderie and must be approaching some sort of world record.

So pop in when you have a full bladder or nosebleed or whatever… and take a pen.

N.B.: This information pertains only to the men's toilets. Thorough as our research was, we drew the line at joining the queue for the women's facilities, because it's so long you actually have to buy a ticket for it. However, women seem to spend three times as much time in the loo as men, so we can only imagine that whatever graffiti is on their walls is three times as detailed and also worth checking out.

topics they will eventually cover. We don't recommend you ever ask that of anyone, as there is a very real risk you'll get a list of everything that has changed, down to the jokes on the walls of the Pleasance toilets.)

Premium venues are a little bit like premium unleaded petrol: although it's a bit more expensive and reputed to be better, you can't really tell the difference, yet find yourself almost forced into buying it because the other stuff's harder to find, even though you know there must be an awful lot of the other stuff around somewhere. These are the Fringe venues, still small in number, that receive a lot more attention than the others. Exactly which are on the list depends on who you talk to, but there are clear leaders in the field: Pleasance, Assembly Rooms and Gilded Balloon are almost a Fringe unto themselves, while relative newcomers C Venues and Underbelly are big enough and well-known enough to feel like part of the Fringe proper. Because it's a lot easier to get people to see a show at a venue someone's heard of, these are the venues that big names will apply to, and because these venues get to choose from a huge number of applications you'll generally find quite a lot of famous people (at least in Fringe terms) at them. This all generates publicity which is useful both for the big venues and the people performing inside them, sometimes having a significant snowball effect in terms of audiences that can only be helped by the fact that once you enter one of the big venues, it's difficult to leave.

Take Pleasance, for example. Lovely though it is, it sometimes feels a bit like America, with half of the people there happily telling you they haven't ever set foot outside it because – well, why would they need to? Why indeed; Pleasance has six bars, three cafés and over 15 shows on at any one time. You can go to Pleasance and see shows back-to-back from morning through to midnight, then bundle over to Pleasance Dome for *After Hours* before creeping into bed until it's time to do it all over again.

Meanwhile, it's all terribly frustrating for those of us in the outside world, scratching our heads in bewilderment at all those Yanks who have absolutely no curiosity about visiting London, Paris, Prague or Vienna, who couldn't care less about wandering the streets of Venice

or experiencing the beauty of the Swiss mountains, and who are missing out on anything remotely exotic such as the saunas of Japan, the big rocks of the outback or the Buddhist temples of Thailand. Similarly, at the Fringe you can be sitting in Pleasance Courtyard missing out on the quirky, the exotic, the things which are different from anything you've seen before, of which there are a possible choice of over 1000 shows, because as you're huddling to avoid whichever of blistering heat and torrential rain is favoured today, thinking to yourself, 'we could wander down to Sweet, there is a promising show there', the person you're with mentions they've met a techie who can get you in to see some big comedy star for free – and you can take your beer. Hundreds of other venues cry out in pain (pain in no way mitigated when you can't get in after all, because instead you stayed in Pleasance Courtyard trying to chat up someone with long legs you're sure has been on Channel 4 on a Friday night). Travelling elsewhere is just so much more effort; is it any wonder so few Americans have passports?

Those that do make it out of the enclosed world of Pleasance often get lost, in any case. The biggest venues have street signs pointing to them and adverts in the Fringe brochure giving clear directions. The smaller venues do not. Although the Fringe brochure comes with a venue map, finding a venue by name takes a bit of time and you can still get lost on the way there. Smaller groups have to work harder, sometimes training their street publicists to give directions (good), arming them with maps (better), or going to the trouble of putting maps on their flyers (best).

Big venues also have big venue staff, sometimes in the physical sense but also in sheer numbers. A smallish venue might employ three permanent staff (there pretty much all the time), and perhaps another ten to fill in the little jobs (mostly techies and front of house). In contrast, the Pleasance has around 150.

Much of the difference is in marketing. C Venues have three people working full-time on selling their shows by talking to the press, arranging promotional deals and coming up with a way – any way – of getting bums on seats. With such a team on side, a show has a much better chance of getting those all-important early audiences in so that word of mouth can start to work its magic. There's still a lot left to do, but Edinburgh is all about finding an edge, lots of edges, and trying to wield them all without slicing your hands off.

Pleasance, again, wields its edges with all the flair and expertise of Uma Thurman using a samurai sword. Its marketing is as sharp as you can get and the polish on the blade is its sell-out board. Prominently displayed in Courtyard, the board tells you which shows you cannot possibly see because they've already sold out... for today. This serves two purposes: first, it makes you rush back in to the box office to book for tomorrow, and second it makes the people from those shows become intolerably smug. It's a big status thing to get on the board; then again, since you can have a full house without selling out because of press and other free tickets, some people end up feeling hard done by even though they're playing to packed houses. Although if they're playing to packed houses, they shouldn't be too upset, so don't bother actually feeling sorry for them.

The bigger venues will, naturally, programme bigger names, but not exclusively. Like everyone else, they're looking for the unknown comic who'll win the Perrier, or the experimental theatre show that gets five stars clean across the board. If you think your show will fit the style of a big venue then you should certainly apply (and if you're not sure, ask; if you talk to them early in the year, they're all pretty approachable but the closer to the Fringe it gets, the more busy and stressed they'll be). They're especially likely to at least show an interest if you've started to carve an audience for yourselves – in London, in your home town, or in previous years on the Fringe.

This is not to say that if you don't get picked by a well-known venue, you should give up hope. Everyone has to start somewhere, and it hasn't stopped people going on to sell out at Gilded Balloon or Assembly Rooms in subsequent years. In addition, if you're but one of 10 or 20 shows at your venue, the staff will be trying that much harder to make every one of their shows a success. A larger venue, while it will attempt to programme shows it thinks will be a success, can tolerate a few mistakes; if you happen to be a mistake you may realise that you are a tiny fish in a big pond with everyone around you too busy to lend a hand, so finding ways of getting audiences will be entirely down to you. Plus, it is important to remember that there are a lot of veteran Fringe goers who are well aware that many of the most exciting shows crop up at less well-known venues, and so will be on the look-out for just such gems – and anyone who reads this book will be exactly the same, so we're predicting a sudden surge of people into the little venues over the next few years.

Facilities in venues vary across the board; because they spend the rest of the year as Masonic lodges or building sites, what they offer is unlikely to be too bad – even on a building site there's running water – but they will often be rather cramped and limited compared with provincial theatres. Masons are an exclusive society with few members, so need little space to drink their sherry and don their leather aprons. There might just be space to store your inflatable Daleks, but several costume changes in the wings requiring five pairs of hands and multiple shoehorns are unlikely to be easily achieved. Dressing rooms are often a barrel of laughs too, with one cast putting on clothes while another takes theirs off in the corridor outside because there isn't room for them, blocking the routes the audience is trying to take through to the theatre and treating them to the spectacle of the cast they are about to watch in their underwear. While this helped create a vaudeville air for a burlesque-style production of *The*

Threepenny Opera we once saw, don't rely on it giving the right impression if you have a cast of nine-year-old nuns.

It would be wonderfully ironic to end by saying that, in this aspect at least, Pleasance falls down. Alas, we can't; whilst their facilities are nothing special, they do have the best jokes on the walls of their toilets.

Choosing a venue

Venues are listed in the official Fringe Spaces guide, available for free from the Fringe Office to any group that registers. That's where the fun starts, particularly for a group that has never been to the Fringe before.

The first time we were responsible for organising a Fringe show, finding a venue stumped us. We applied to the big ones we'd heard of, who were unlikely to take us without any proven track record, then picked other places almost at random. Our selection criteria were somewhat dubious; venues were discarded because of half-remembered warnings from someone we knew who'd heard something nasty about them, others were ignored because they didn't make it clear if they programmed comedy but sounded posh and we were too scared to ring and ask. Some we just didn't like the name. Others fell later – we got an initial positive response from one venue, then heard nothing ever again. One venue offered us a reasonable time slot with a good deal but we decided not to accept it because the manager sounded a bit scatty on the phone, despite their having a good reputation and our not actually having an alternative at the time. In the end we stuck our name on the list of groups with no venue and got picked up by one of the new ones, which thankfully was staffed by Fringe veterans who helped see us through our first August in Edinburgh.

That's not the right way to choose a venue.

What you should do goes something like this: talk to other people who have done Edinburgh, talk to the Fringe staff, think about your show, and decide what size of space you need (both in audience capacity and size of stage) and what facilities you need (if a show relies on a follow spot*, it really cuts down the options). Some venues only take certain genres, or will not consider traditional plays or are

---

*A follow spot, for the non-thesps, is a spotlight which moves to follow people moving about on the stage, not a chase game involving a cartoon dog.

restricted to cabaret-style singing and stripping, so you should be able to narrow the field a lot. You should do this within a couple of weeks of the Spaces brochure being published.

Then you do more talking: to your friends, to the venues and to the Fringe Office some more. The Fringe run an open day in Edinburgh and you can see some of the venues by arrangement at the same time. Although at that stage they're mostly still cellars, churches and building sites, you may be able to get an impression of how things might work. You will certainly get a feel for location if you walk to see the venues, which you should do if you can – if it takes you more than an hour to get there or find it, it may not be the best place for you (Edinburgh is not huge, but it has a number of inconveniently-placed hills that sometimes get in the way of an otherwise straightforward route from A to B).

Gradually, you'll narrow the list down to a number you're prepared to apply to. Some venues just want a synopsis of the show, but many have their own application forms asking for different lengths of publicity blurb, previous reviews, and so on, as well as less taxing but equally important issues such as how much set you'll have and whether you'll bring your own technician. Most of this you figure out once and regurgitate; some will be fresh each time (try writing the publicity blurb in 10, 20, 35, 50, 70, 100, 150 and 200 word variants – a process which comprised only three applications for us one year). Then you send it all off, and wait.

Be prepared for venues to take a while to deal with applications. Many wait until a fixed date to programme, and getting the right balance of shows takes them a while. Don't take the first offer you're made; wait until you have to make a decision on one you're comfortable with. If you're feeling lucky, you can push further – some venues may still be looking for the right show until close to the Fringe Office deadline in April, which is when you need to register to get into the Fringe brochure. Playing chicken with venues is risky, however, so don't do it if you can't stand the idea of not doing the Fringe at all, or of doing it at a venue you hate.

If it's getting close to the deadline, you've let a couple

of promising venues drift by hoping for something better and you suddenly realise that you have nowhere at all, then there are a number of things you can do. First, the Fringe website lists all venues, including ones that didn't appear in the original Spaces guide, so you can look for newcomers that might be suitable. They also have a section for venues with slots still available and another where you can put up your group as still looking for a space. Between

Slot times

When you apply for venues at Edinburgh, you will be asked to specify your preferred performance time. There was supposed to be a section here telling you how to decide what sort of time will be best for your show, but we realised that we don't really know. Big-name comedians will usually have an evening slot and more general comedy and cabaret shows will usually be on either late afternoon or late at night, but unless you're a big-name comedian that doesn't help much – do you want to put your comedy show on at one of these times and risk losing audience to Jimmy Carr (both humiliating and bad for box office sales)? Or do you put it on earlier and risk people thinking it's a serious monologue? Naturally, if you're looking at very early slots (the 'breakfast' period, which for a hearty Fringegoer lasts until about 1 p.m.) there may not be so many people actually awake to target your show at. The slot will almost certainly be considerably cheaper, perhaps ideal for fledgling companies and experimental pieces but fledgling companies and experimental pieces surely also deserve audiences, so wouldn't that more expensive mid-afternoon slot be better? Or might that clash with the hearty Fringegoers' lunch? What about early evening – could you hope to attract people who've planned out their evening proper, but haven't quite worked out what to do following that big afternoon show? Or will everybody be having dinner?

To take yet another thing into account, if you do end up with a prime-time slot, won't that mean you miss an awful lot of good shows yourself? We don't know the answers to these questions, we just thought you might want to be aware of them.

the three it should be possible to find somewhere. Finally, some venues don't bother listing that they have free spaces because they have a huge list of applications and will keep on working through them until they find a good fit. So you may get a welcome phone call sometime in April offering exactly what you want.

Of course, if you've been paying attention and actually been organised, you'll be sorted out long, long before then – won't you?

Finding accommodation

If you're going to Edinburgh for any length of time you need somewhere to put yourself. The weather is unpredictable in Scotland and a sleeping bag on the street is not advisable, even for a few nights. There are of course bed and breakfasts aplenty, as well as hotels, but because the Fringe draws so many crowds it is worth pointing out that B&Bs can cost as much as a decent hotel, so the hotels compensate by upping their prices to the cost of buying a medium-sized villa in Rome.

The cheaper option is to blag space from other groups – it helps to know a group at the Fringe beforehand, but there are plenty of ways to make friends. Certainly, for non-performing visitors this option is favoured by many. If you're actually performing though, it's not such a good idea, because you're never going to perform well if you're sleeping on a kitchen table. It certainly isn't an option if you're going up to the Fringe for the full three weeks. Well, actually one of our friends did try it, but we imagine it was a difficult experience for him.

Certainly, he gave every impression of being a homeless person.

Blagging floorspace for a big cast and crew is even less desirable – again, there are people who have tried it, but it always leads to grief. Dehumanising as the Fringe can be, people at least ought to have the option of getting a decent night's rest.

The more sensible shows hire a flat, or more than one if there are a lot of people involved, ideally close to the city centre and best of all within a few minutes' walk from their venue. Some groups share accommodation (particularly comedians, who tend to be there on their own anyway). Some groups share beds (particularly comedians, who need the warmth and companionship of another body at night to overcome the self-loathing that is behind their art).

Flats can be rented all over the city at varying prices, either directly from the landlord or through agencies. Agency flats are often more expensive and may not be any nicer, but are usually more convenient to arrange. If you get in early there are cheap places available at universities, particularly Heriot Watt; if not, the Fringe website provides a list of properties being let directly by landlords, and you can also use the forums if you want to arrange flatshares.

Groups on a budget have a tendency to cram several people into one bedroom (landlords will often be quite accommodating here, arranging for extra beds to be available), which certainly helps bring the price down considerably. However, especially if you're going to be there for an entire month, it can increase the risk of tension and, in extreme cases, madness; people need time on their own, and this may be difficult in a cramped flat. One of our comrades one year elected for the solace of a small, windowless, cell-like cupboard in which to squeeze his camp-bed, instead of the option of sleeping in a proper bedroom with a couple of other people in the cast. Weird though it made him look (in an endearing way), it should be pointed out that he didn't go mad at all, whereas the room he decided not to sleep in saw some of the most entertaining arguments we have ever experienced, with other cast members completely losing it in a far less endearing way.

If people do fall out with each other (as was almost the case in this instance), it may put a lot of strain on the group as a whole. The Fringe

Goblin being anally raped by blond boy.

is rife with stories of people developing lifelong animosities, and if it does happen within your group you want to limit potential damage. The last thing you want is for someone to walk away from your carefully-planned show, and it's pretty unpleasant if they don't and just glower at everyone else, too. Planning accommodation with space for people to glower is a wise thing to do.

A final thing to think about when considering a sardine approach is that many of you will want to have sex, either with each other or with all sorts of other people around the Fringe. No matter how powerful the desire, a lot of people have a problem fucking in a room with two or three of even their very best friends. (The main exception to this rule appears to be among members of Chapel Choirs.) If you're planning on shacking up with mostly local inhabitants, they probably have some privacy wherever they're living, but you can't guarantee the same if it's another Fringe person that takes your fancy. We suppose in an emergency you could buy a tent and wander up Arthur's Seat whenever you feel horny. It's a well-visited beauty spot though, so don't blame us if it suddenly turns into a threesome.

This is perhaps less of an issue with a cast of nine-year-old nuns.

Depending on how a show is funded, the rent may be paid for by the group, or individually – many shows will arrange one or more flats, then get members of the company to pay the group. It's convenient, and if the group has a bank account, having money go through it (even quite rapidly) may impress your bank manager. (At least, that's what we were told. We've been doing this sort of thing for a while now, without any positive results – in fact, the last time we checked, they'd completely stopped having a bank manager for our account, and we had to talk to a customer service representative, which is one financial step away from sleeping in the mud.) If you have the budget, it's probably worth shelling out on accommodation – it's your home for a month, after all. Having the entire cast of *Macbethany and the Girls of Edinburgh* sleep together on a waterbed in the spare room of someone else's flat may sound pretty fun at the time, but… hey, what are we saying? It sounds great!

Choosing a location

Particularly if you're organised (we are not - but we can both sew), you might even book your accommodation before you agree your venue. Even if you don't, you cannot guarantee you'll be able to get the two close together. Most of the Fringe is focused in the Old Town, to the south of the Royal Mile, but accommodation is far more evenly spread around Edinburgh. From accommodation in the New Town, the Fringe Office on the High Street might be a 30- or 40-minute walk (more if you're carrying a ladder), but then it's the same sort of distance from a lot of the places in Marchmont or Bruntsfield Links, across the Meadows from the Old Town. Both sides of the city have the same in the way of essential shops, swimming pools, parks and so on, so unless there is another group you want to live close to, or you have other constraints such as the need to get instruments to and from the venue regularly, there's not a huge amount to choose between them. Except for the sex.

At one edge of the Old Town, up near the financial sector, is the Red Light district – strip clubs, shops that are strangely quiet during the day and places that sell car parts. The works. It's on the way to Fountain Park, where the UGC cinema shows a fair number of premières during the film festival, so it's unlikely you're going to avoid it even if you're not tempted by the offer of girls, girls, girls (words which you will pass several times in flickering neon lights).

If you're not tempted, though, you probably want to head towards the New Town – down by the other main multiplex cinema, the Vue, is Edinburgh's thriving pink district, so if you're more interested in boys, boys, boys – or indeed, big hairy Scots, drag queens and karaoke – then this is the place for you. As you trudge wearily back home every day, you may well be wolf-whistled by permatanned lads in tight sleeveless T-shirts, and you will certainly be unable to ignore the heavy thump of camp disco classics coming from almost every bar and club you walk past. And what an enticingly different world this can offer to the jaded Fringe performer when trying to escape from all the difficulties of the Fringe. It's not necessarily a simpler world, but it's a different one – a classic frying pan and fire scenario, which, conveniently you're right in the middle of. Sometimes literally; one year we discovered a map of 'places of interest' in a gay bar, which, while omitting the Castle, Arthur's Seat and the Royal Mile, placed our flat in the dead centre. We proudly displayed the map to all our visitors to show how important we were*.

Some accommodation is drab, some is palatial. Quite a lot in Edinburgh seems to be somewhere in between – either a well-appointed flat nestling halfway up a damp dingy staircase that looks just like the one in *Shallow Grave*, or an enormous apartment carved out of Georgian townhouses that nonetheless is a little rundown, with peeling paint, appliances that need encouragement, and a strange box room that has no obvious purpose (although we let people sleep in it,

---

*Foolishly, we didn't keep this memento, but assuming the map had been produced by 'Scotland's premier magazine for lesbians, gay men, bisexuals and friends, the aptly named *ScotsGay*, we wrote to them to see if they might send us another map for reproduction in this book. Well, in fact we addressed our query to 'Scotsgay', and got the following response: 'It wisnae us! Sorry. P.S. Please note that it is *ScotsGay* not Scotsgay.'

which works quite well). If you're lucky, your flat will come well-equipped, but if you're like us it will come *almost* well-equipped: a television and video without remote controls, but with the surround sound speakers from a completely different television; the television itself with seven channels, all tuned to Channel 4; a two-manual Hammond organ that doesn't work; two kitchens, with no baking trays. Kitchens, in fact, are the most touch and go; you'll generally get enough for you to cook and eat (provided that you're not too fussy), but dinner parties or even cooking for the entire company may be trickier, which is a shame, because communal cooking and eating is a good way of holding off Edinburgh Hysteria and the demise of civilisation as we know it. You may need to wash up after every meal, which many people find difficult, and this too can lead to Edinburgh Hysteria and the demise of civilisation as we know it. Certainly, the act of making a shepherd's pie across two kitchens drove one of us mad, and things were not improved when he was told to clean up the (admittedly rather huge) mess that he'd made in the process.

Your flat may or may not have a phone, but if it does, don't use it unless you've already agreed to with the landlord or letting agency, otherwise you may get stuck with a 'facility overuse' charge which is quite out of proportion to the real cost. Most people have mobile phones these days, anyway. Having said that, if you can arrange for a landline it can be very helpful for incoming calls; mobile reception in some buildings, and particularly in basements, can be limited, and it is useful for your venue to be able to contact you at any hour – you want to know when you've landed that interview in *The Scotsman*, don't you?

It's difficult to know what you'll get, although the well-appointed flats are more likely to be someone's home that they're renting out just for August, while the rundown apartments are probably being let out all year round, perhaps to students. You may have more luck in finding accommodation in the first category by avoiding estate agents – or then again you might not. Agents are a good route if you definitely want one type or the other, because they'll often have photos available.

And why would you prefer large-yet-seedy over unassuming-but-well appointed? Because they are great for parties, of course. Parties are the second things you do where you're living (after eating, but before sleeping) – see 'How Do people Live (and How to Crash their Parties)'.

We've always found sorting out accommodation (and even spelling it right) quite stressful, and once we've got it done it's a huge relief. If you're more organised, the wave of pleasure may be less intense (which is how we justify being so useless about it), but knowing where you're living – particularly if you also know where you're performing – marks a turning point with a Fringe show. You're definitely doing it now, no turning back, this is it. Have another drink, there's work to be done.

Giving birth

Assuming you've got everything else in hand, or that you have a producer who is on top of things, the director and cast have to get down and rehearse the show. If it's a new devised piece, that means writing it too. If it's dance... well, God knows, but from what we've seen of the *Riverdance – A Journey* video, we think it involves watching yourself in a lot of long mirrors.

If you're a group with a permanent base (a community drama group, or a theatre company with a working relationship with a local theatre, for instance) location isn't a big deal, but for everyone else it is. If you can't scrounge rehearsal space for free, then it doesn't come cheap – anything from £50 pounds a day in London and often a lot more. If you can't afford it, you may be able to get away with rooms in your house, or the garden if the weather is good enough, which, since many rehearsals take place in July, it might be. Although impractical for some shows, it is worth considering; we do a lot of our rehearsing outdoors, even in public parks on occasion, among an eclectic mix of students, animals and alcoholics (often indistinguishable from each other). We fit in rather well among these people, although we were suspicious of a group who regularly sat and talked Danish near to our rehearsal spot. We think they might have been Vikings.

There were other problems with our choice of rehearsal spot; one day, all was proceeding well as we improvised a story around a game of Risk and a *Railway Children*-obsessed signalman. But as the mad signalman attacked our youngest cast member in a rather brilliantly improvised plot twist, a real non-improvised and therefore rather alarming policeman halted the narrative, his extendable truncheon all extended. His exact words actually were, 'What's going on here [then]?' Fortunately, the victim of the attack was able to reassure the policeman that we were actors, a great relief for the actor behind the mad signalman character because it looked like the young and slightly jumpy policeman wouldn't have hesitated in using his extendable truncheon. Obviously, though, it threw our rehearsal off completely, and we are still slightly concerned we might be under covert surveillance even now, a few years on.

Even so, we risked drawing attention to ourselves for the sake of completeness and asked the Cambridgeshire Constabulary if they had any advice for young thesps wishing to engage in acting in public areas, relating the basic details of our own ordeal. We received the following stern response from a police spokesman: 'We would advise that anyone taking part in such an event in a public place should show regard for public safety and be careful not to get involved in any activities which might alarm others. It would also be helpful for organisers to notify the police and other authorities in advance, if a rehearsal or a performance is due to be held in a public place.' We feel that, wise though this sounds if you wish to avoid getting beaten to a pulp by an overenthusiastic young policeman, if actors need to inform the police about their outdoor activities, then so should Vikings.

The rehearsal process

The rehearsal process can be the most enjoyable part of doing a Fringe show. Performing is obviously also good and if you don't enjoy that you're in the wrong place, but when it happens it's mixed in with the hard work of selling the show, day in, day out, and the struggle to stay sharp enough to sparkle every night, both of which can make it harder to enjoy. In rehearsal, you get to concentrate on the show to the exclusion of everything else. For actors, the creation of a character and learning what and how to communicate with an audience is where most of the skill and hard work lies. For comedians, shaping and tightening their routines to give them optimum punch is generally more difficult than delivering the final project, but a worthwhile process full of discoveries. For dancers... well, God knows, again. We don't really know about dancers. We suspect most of them are mainly in it for the costumes, so perhaps they don't really enjoy rehearsals at all (although this again is just guesswork based on the *Riverdance – A Journey* video, so may only actually apply to Michael Flatley).

For a director, the rehearsals are undoubtedly the hardest period of work, and they may have little left to do by the time the show is performed, although this is less true for Fringe shows, since there is always the opportunity to tighten and rework (even rewrite) and many Fringe shows end up quite different by the end of the run.

Rehearsals can serve a number of different purposes, not all of them obvious. First, and most importantly, they are a time for the director to shape the performances of the cast to match his or her vision. Second, they can give the cast a time to explore their characters in relationship to others in the show (or to disagree violently with each other). Third, if the cast aren't already familiar with each other, they provide a time for everyone to get to know one another, which is important for any production, but vital in the cast of an Edinburgh show where the company will be living and working (and disagreeing violently) together for more than just the performances each day.

So you're a brand-new director, your local theatre group has decided to take a play up to the Fringe, and you have stepped into the breach left by your usual director having quit over a violent disagreement with the costume designer (he wanted all the men to wear trousers with the bottoms cut out). You have a cast, now you need to direct. Where do you start?

Scene 1: the director's study

Light streams through the window, washing out the director's face and conveniently erasing the unsightly bags and bloodshot eyes that reveal last night's debauched antics.

Director: What am I doing next? *Macbeth on Ice?* Ah, yes. I think... hmm...tricky one this... I think this production will be about human resilience. Yes. Macbeth soldiering on as his world falls apart. And on ice! We could have Banquo's Ghost as an ice sculpture. Yes: resilience.

The director's demon pops up. Better dressed, better looking, and with a red tinge.

Demon: Your last show was about human resilience.

Director: Ah. Yes. Ah, yes - but that was a comedy. No real suffering – there was very little to be resilient AGAINST.

Demon: The lead character's mother died.

Director: Yes, but she was eaten by a Scientologist – it was comedy trauma. And she sang a song from inside the stomach.

Demon: So it wasn't about human resilience at all then? That's what it said in the programme notes.

Director: Oh come on. It was comedy. I was just trying to make people laugh.

Demon: If you do human resilience again you'll be stuck in a rut – like George Romero with all those zombie films. Choose something else.

Director: Why do I have to choose anything? Why do I have to have vision? You hound me – it's *Macbeth on Ice*, can't it just be... cold?

Demon: It can't be cold, it's Edinburgh in August. Look, you need a vision because otherwise the costume designer, the set designer – everyone, they'll have nothing to go on, and you'll be doing a naked show in the dark. Again.

Director: That was *avant garde*!

Demon: Anyway, your cast arrives this afternoon, and you've got to give THEM something to work with, as well. Something more than 'it's cold'.

Director: And then I suppose they'll want me to work with them. Hone their performance. Shape their character arc.

Demon: That IS your job.

Director: It's all so bloody thespy!

Demon: That IS your job.

Director sighs heavily.

Director: I suppose I'd better get started.

Demon: Great! What's your through-line?

We leave the scene as the director strangles his own demon.

Ludicrous as it can sound, especially to those not directly involved in the theatrical world, directors do have to worry about through-lines, character arcs and so on (although they may not call them that) because they are the tools they have available to them to do their jobs. The names of dental implements sound pretty silly, too. This won't stop non-artistic types taking the piss if they ever hear about it, or for that matter some artistic types writing cheap sketches and making jokes about stereotypical thespian activities. However, if you're an actor and you find yourself being teased about what you do, the best response is simply to find your focus, move your centre of gravity, raise your status and determine your motivation within a long-term arc-like vision in which you are one puppet working as part of a bigger machine, pause for the length of a beat, turn, move, speak and exit.

How directors like to shape a show varies from person to person. Some will state their goals for the production in a lot of detail for the cast, while some will give only broad strokes and fine tune an individual actor's work as things go on. If you have directed before, you'll already have started to develop your own style. If not, the best advice is probably to do what you feel is needed, and change as required. A lot may depend on your cast and, of course, how the show is being put together. A director of *Hamlet* will have to concentrate on different things from someone directing a bedroom farce (unless they have decided to interpret *Hamlet* as a bedroom farce, which we suppose is vaguely feasible*. Different types of shows need different amounts of work, also. One of our shows was rehearsed mostly in evenings, around our jobs, while a musical might take weeks of intensive rehearsal. In theory, the more the better, except it's worth remembering that actors, like children, can get overtired if kept up too long, and start behaving strangely. (Rehearsals for dance shows presumably involve dancing, which means the people in them will probably get tired more quickly.)

Theatre games

Perhaps more in a Fringe show than any other kind of show, an important part of rehearsals is discovering ways to relax the cast and to keep them fresh to enable them to have fun in ways that will continue to energise them halfway through a tiring three-week run. Almost every director will resort at some point to 'theatre games' as a way of doing this. These are another thing that those outside the profession will happily mock as another of those weird things that actors do, and which prove that they must all be gay.

In fact, theatre games are quite different from most of the things that gay people do, and look more like children's games. Possibly

*Or even as pantomime. We have visions of Hamlet asking the audience, 'Where is Polonius?...'

because a lot of them are children's games. Grandmother's Footsteps, various forms of chase or 'tag', 'What's the time, Mr Wolf' and others are all invigorating games which make a cast more aware of their surroundings and encourage concentration, as well as being liberating and fun. Many adults lose touch with the childlike glee of the young, but actors often find it useful to retain that energy and fascination with things, and playing children's games can help here. Outsiders watching them might be forgiven for thinking they are all nutcases, but in some ways games are as important for an actor as a good physical warm-up is for a football player. (We suggest a good physical warm-up is quite a good idea for actors as well.)

There are also games developed specifically for theatre, and there are many fine books on the subject. Augusto Boal's *Games for Actors and Non-actors* is the genre's equivalent of Paradise Lost, and full of fun ideas for (as the title suggests) both actors and non-actors. We also found many useful ideas in Clive Barker's *Theatre Games*, although it sometimes reads as if he thinks all actors should live in sexually liberated communes (maybe that's how you carried on when the book was published, Clive, but things have changed since the 1970s – we have standards). The familiarity with each others' bodies his work promotes can be particularly helpful for physical theatre work, but may not be appropriate for a cast of nine-year-old nuns. Most good bookshops have at least a small drama section and they are well worth browsing to find books with ideas that suit what you are doing. Games can easily be adapted to suit different groups too; we use a variant of a Boal game which entails the cast linking hands and tying themselves into a giant knot, the main feature of our version being that we chant 'Patsy, Patsy, Patsy, Patsy' to keep our timing, in homage to the celebrated voice coach Patsy Rodenburg, whose book we were working from when we first started doing the game. (For more obscure reasons, we say it in Ian McKellen's voice.)

Other games teach specific skills and are particularly useful for building teamwork. Anything that involves coordination as a whole group (games which generally involve clapping, counting or throwing blobs of imaginary energy around with cries of 'zip, zap, boing') give groups better awareness of each other and force them to cooperate.

For someone watching people who have been doing them for a while, the instinctive reactions, with the whole group working as a single body, can look like magic. (Some directors take a short-cut and actually use magic, but we think that's cheating.)

Workshops

Workshops are rooms, areas or establishments where manual or light industrial work is performed with wood, metal and plastic, often hammered into shape by sweating men in overalls who have a surplus of balsa wood and vices. But just as 'vices' has two meanings, referring to a grip or clamping device usually consisting of two jaws open or closed by a screw or lever, but also an evil, degrading or immoral practice or habit, so 'workshop' also has a second meaning, being used to describe an educational seminar or series of meetings and explorations emphasising interaction amongst the participants. In theatrical terms, they're rather less boring than that sounds*.

Workshops come in all shapes and sizes, but usually they're either teaching new skills, reinforcing old ones, or developing aspects of the production without working directly from the text. In other words, they are a chance for actors to play.

How these work will depend on the imagination and intent of the director. It might take the form of an improvised scene containing characters from the play but which never happens in the play itself. It gives actors a chance to rehearse how their characters will interact without the need to remember lines but with the added opportunity to explore in more depth sides of their character that perhaps the writer didn't want to, giving extra depth to their portrayal. It might involve everyone deciding what animal their character is most like and pretending they are that animal, or it might involve adapting a scene to different setting, so putting *The Cherry Orchard* on a ship or in a sauna. All of these can be useful in different ways. (Perhaps the sauna one less so.)

Some workshops may be required to teach a cast more specific skills such as mask work, puppetry, magic tricks, circus skills, all sorts

---

*By contrast, most vices are *more* boring than they sound.

of physical techniques or dance. These are skills that for many actors will be a little off the beaten track, so will probably need teaching and then practicing. Some skills can be picked up by a director and taught to the rest, or discovered by the group as a whole (there are fine books on subjects like mask work, puppetry and various physical things). Don't underestimate the time taken to learn a new skill: most people won't pick them up straight away, and if you don't have teaching

Pass time with good company
Andrew McClelland

As an Australasian travelling to the Edinburgh Fringe for my first time in 2002, I hoped that I would be something of a novelty through my quaint antipodean ways. But I soon realised that there are more Australian and New Zealanders in Edinburgh at Fringe time than there are in all of Tasmania; so, the playing field levelled, I spent my festival like every other young hopeful with no profile in Britain to speak of. I walked the Mile, day in day out, smile plastered over my face, sometimes even resorting to puppet shows to attempt to attract punters to see me (a strange pursuit that smacks of both egotism and an absolute lack of self respect at the same time). I performed in 'The Caves', an underground venue that had freshly been opened since being boarded up during some sort of plague. It dripped, had genuine stalactites coming from the ceiling and was apparently haunted. Not the ideal place to be making with the funny. And yet the cliché remains, I had the time of my life. There was no great romance, there was no great success, there was no great food. But there was camaraderie! Drinking! And the chance to see more theatre and comedy than is medically sound!

Karen Koren of the oft-lamented Gilded Balloon was the delightful lady who helped me get there. Say what you will of her (and I'm sure you shall), she is a wonderful help for so many acts trying to perform in Edinburgh. I remember being quite intimidated by her – to overcome this I had been advised by a friend to joke around with her and not be too reserved or polite. And so as I negotiated my first contract with her I recall opening one phone conversation with "Karen! You old bint, how are you?" From then on I dealt only with her secretary. In many ways Karen to me is the human representation of Edinburgh. Big, ancient and made of stone? No. Tough and intimidating, yes. But if you keep your wits about you and do your best you'll be ok.

In 2004 I returned to Edinburgh with the ambitiously titled *Andrew McClelland's Somewhat Accurate History of Pirates. 1550-2017.* It was about pirates. I was back in the same venue but suddenly selling well and receiving some kind reviews. Oh happy days! I was meeting comedians I'd always admired, I was taking off some days from flyering and I even took a day trip to the countryside. My advice here? Do a show that's good. Or at least do a show that has an arresting title. That seemed to work well.

In 2005 I moved up to the Teviot. Karen's big venue and a big room. 'The Nightclub'. Not entitled so because it is dark and has a salubrious atmosphere, but because it is indeed a nightclub. With balconies, disco lighting and a pillar in the middle of the stage that could be used for questionable dancing. Again, hardly ideal. I took a show called *Lawrence Leung and Andrew McClelland's Somewhat Secret Secret Society Show.* It didn't go quite as well as *Pirates* - clearly the idea of being a sea faring nation still runs deep in British blood (well, deeper than the idea of being a bunch of masonic goat-riders). But again I had the time of my life. All in all that makes three time of my lifes! A mathematical impossibility! And yet it remains.

Edinburgh, for an Australian, is a big investment. Our money loses its value by two-thirds when we arrive (and for the rest of the time as well), and yet I keep going back. Opportunity always seems to knock somehow, and there are shows to see and dancing to be done, and I don't care that the food and accommodation have been within reproach. I'm going to try to do it all again as soon as is humanly possible.

And as soon as I'm out of debt from last time.

Andrew McClelland is an Australian comedian who dresses like an English fop from the 19th Century.

experience it's easy to get frustrated by this. Some directors, particularly those who specialise in certain types of show, are themselves experienced workshop leaders, and so have the ability to bring their cast up to speed themselves.

But do also remember that some skills you cannot learn out of a book. If it's swordplay or juggling chainsaws, get an expert in.

Previews

At some point, rehearsals have to end, or at least to step back and let performances take over. There can be some time at the Fringe for further rehearsals, allowing performances to be further refined and weaker sections strengthened, but by first curtain up the show is into performance territory. This doesn't mean it's got to Edinburgh yet – some shows take in Edinburgh as part of a wider tour (many comedians do this) but before that there are also preview shows.

Ignore the name; previews are less about a group letting other people see what they've got and more about letting themselves see what they've got. In the professional world, preview shows are often free to members of the public, or at least cheaper, and the press nights come later. (The Cambridge Footlights shirk tradition by charging more for their tour show's preview than for any of their other shows, but they're from an institution full of strange, archaic traditions so they're always going to be a bit different from everyone else.) No show is ready until it has been in front of an audience – that is when actors' bodies flood full of adrenaline, when they get nerves, or get bold. Hopefully, they relax into things and get an edge in performance that might have been lacking in rehearsals. However, if they're unlucky, the preview is where half the props break, the leading lady twists her ankle and the beautifully-crafted set falls over. This can at least make for a very entertaining show for the audience (if you ever get the chance to attend the preview for a panto then do so, because there are more silly props and sets to go wrong in a panto than in any other kind of show).

Not every show bothers with previews, but lots (particularly comedies) do, and in July the London Fringe theatres, as well as small to medium-sized venues around the country, play host to one after another show on its way to Edinburgh. Usually each show will do two or three previews, a week or so apart so early comments can be fed back into later ones (this is done by comedies most of all because it is possible for sketches or even entire shows to be rewritten or scrapped and replaced). Without them, many Edinburgh shows would open with no idea if they're any good and, indeed, they probably wouldn't be any good without the lessons learned from these early shows.

One year, we did previews at the start of July, which was before our main block of rehearsal. It was an improvised show, so we weren't looking for pointers like 'less angsty in scene 20'; we were after a feeling about the structure we were using and on the lookout for 'salient points' that we could take into performances to keep things on track. It proved incredibly helpful, giving us many things to feed into the rehearsal process as well as the performances themselves. Because we did it in Cambridge just after all the students had left, we were mostly playing to tiny audiences, but it was still cheaper than a well-appointed rehearsal space in London, so we weren't too upset.

If you are taking a show up to the Fringe, it is of course up to you whether you do previews or not; they can be helpful, giving you a deadline to work towards and an early chance to gauge how the show is shaping up, or they can just get in the way of preparing a show. If you want feedback on the show, you may not need to go to a proper theatre and try to attract a real audience, you could simply get some friends along to see what you're doing when you do a full run through of the show in rehearsal. We've done this as well, and it was probably just as helpful to us both in terms of figuring out which bits worked and which didn't and in giving ourselves confidence that we had something worthwhile. Then again, unless you break completely from rehearsals to promote your previews, or have a solid local following, you'll probably be getting mostly friends along anyway, but doing it in a real theatre rather than a rehearsal space may be worthwhile, particularly if you have cast members with limited experience or a complex set. Shows can also run preview performances in the first few days of the Fringe itself depending on venue policy; many reviewers will not go to them, but given the nature of previews that may be just as well (and if they do turn up, make sure every cast member has the word 'preview' stamped on their forehead in big red letters to ensure that the reviewer takes it into account).

Getting there, getting ready, getting in

It's time – finally – to go to Edinburgh. The show is, you hope, ready. The venue is, you hope, expecting you. Somewhere in Edinburgh, you hope, is your publicity material, ready for the off. Everybody – you hope – knows what they're doing.

All you have to do is get there.

For some people, getting to Edinburgh is pretty easy. People in Glasgow, for example, have a painless train journey, and there they are slap bang in the centre.

For everyone else it's a little harder. Basically, there are three ways to enter Edinburgh (well… three ways that count: you could take a stagecoach from Wolverhampton, but it'll take you a while, partly because it's over 300 miles but mostly because the last one left in the nineteenth century and hasn't yet managed the return journey). Three ways: by train, by plane or by following the road signs marked

'Edinburgh'. Obviously, if you're coming any real distance (from the Americas or Japan for example), plane it is (the road signs marked 'Edinburgh' don't appear that far away, and your car will get wet). There's a good bus service from the airport to the centre and, presumably, if you have any large amounts of set you can have that flown too at some exorbitant rate. Flying is also practical from London and other less distant places, the main drawback being the difficulty of transporting luggage (particularly set and props for a show). Often groups will band together to share the cost of getting all their gear up to Edinburgh in a single van (you can arrange this sort of thing, as always, on the Fringe website), leaving everyone except the driver and possibly a map-reader to hop on the plane and hop off after an hour.

Before you start hopping, just be sure you know where your passport is and that it hasn't expired. Security being as tight as it is these days, even travelling within Britain you need a passport, or at least a driving license, to get on a plane. One of us was left in a situation not long ago when a flight to Edinburgh was almost a write-off because he had sent his passport to the DVLA along with his driving license to get the latter renewed. Thanks to the efficiency of the DVLA, disaster was narrowly averted. Or if not disaster, at least a long train journey.

Long though the train journey is, some people prefer it and from some places it's a single journey without changes in one of Richard Branson's large, comfortable trains. It has the added convenience of taking you straight into the heart of Edinburgh. You can also shift more luggage with you, but this is not advised if you need to change often. We have still nightmares about manhandling a keyboard and several boxes of props across Peterborough station to get a connecting service, and there's also the risk that on arriving in Edinburgh one of your fellow cast will insist on shopping for a marker pen before dropping off your luggage, dragging you right across the city in search of a stationer while your bags get increasingly tattered and you lose all feeling in your shoulders.

Travelling to Edinburgh by road is pretty straightforward – it is a capital city, it's well sign-posted after all, and the London to Edinburgh route, the A1, is easy to navigate (in map-reading terms you simply follow it 'up', and on the way back 'down'). It is actually called London

Road at the Edinburgh end. At the London end, confusingly, it's called Upper Street (Liverpool gets it own road, as well as Adelaide for crying out loud – Adelaide is a cottage in Windsor Home Park, named after the consort of William IV. She had five children stillborn, and two died under the age of two, so thank God he'd done better with his mistress. Adelaide's chief claim to fame is as the first queen consort of the UK to have her own crown made. We still don't think that gives her the right to have her own London street when Edinburgh doesn't). The point is that driving to Edinburgh is pretty easy. Not necessarily cheap, but if you have a lot of stuff it's probably cheaper to drive it up yourself. Some groups might use a minibus (if they have someone with an appropriate driving license – new driving licenses these days try to limit damage by only permitting you to drive vehicles with up to eight people in them), moving people and things at once.

We drove up one year with three of us crammed into a little Ford with our suitcases, boxes of props and puppets, keyboard and set all wedged in beside us. It was a fun bonding experience, a kind of high-octane, low-lead road trip, barrelling up to the sounds of Pink Floyd and Beethoven (artists which actually have a lot in common). We actually left the A1 at Gateshead, cutting through Northumberland National Park, which is blisteringly beautiful and made the entire journey worthwhile. We did, however, discover that we all got a lot more unpredictable the closer we got to Edinburgh; at one point we stopped at a service station somewhere around Darlington only for one of us to run and hide in a field of corn, then later emerge declaring unexpectedly that he really needed to marry one of our friends and have lots of babies. And he's gay. As we got nearer to Edinburgh, the driver became increasingly erratic, choosing at one point to circle a roundabout four times, not because he was lost but just because he liked the roundabout.

Edinburgh doesn't afflict everyone like this, but don't be surprised if it happens to you: even before it has started, the effects of the Fringe can insinuate themselves into the people who are but one technical rehearsal and, if they're lucky, a dress rehearsal away from the opening night.

If you find yourself in that place, have another drink. You both deserve and need it.

Lots and lots of shows

Did that sound like hard work? After all that budgeting for a show, getting hold of a venue, putting everything together and rehearsing it, it must get easier. After all, you really needed that drink at the end of the last chapter and that's just when you were reading it – surely the long Edinburgh process is all uphill from there. Once people are finally up in Auld Reekie it ought to be fun, fun, fun.

Well, it is. That is why people do it, after all. But there are much, much less stressful ways of having fun. Bungee jumping off the Clifton Suspension Bridge, perhaps, or backpacking across Afghanistan. The refined atmosphere of the Edinburgh Fringe can strain nerves like nothing else – it can turn sane, quiet people into monsters. It can destroy relationships. It can turn a simple artistic endeavour into an unclimbable mountain. Having a show is part one, but when you get to Edinburgh you realise that the journey has only just begun.

Along the way you'll meet all sorts of people, some helpful, some not, some seemingly sworn to defeat you at all costs. Sometimes the Fringe feels like 'Dungeons and Dragons' for art lovers. Is the smiling man with a camera a photojournalist who might get your picture into *The Guardian,* or a paedophile? Is the dirty scabrous woman on the corner a tramp or just a reviewer who hasn't had time to wash recently? Will the pack of children who took all your flyers actually come to the show, or are they playing cards with them now, jeering at your photos and making you into a Happy Family with a man who paints himself gold, a circus freak, and an oriental erotic dancer?

Trying to solve these conundrums while surrounded by irksome eccentrics may put you in mind of Alice. Like Alice, you have a journey ahead of you. The weird and the wonderful beckon, and there are dangers on the way*. Not only have Fringe performers got to get through a month of intense thesping, living in close proximity, cooking together and often sleeping six people to a single bed, these

---

*An equally valid literary and cinematic comparison would be with Dorothy's journey in *The Wizard of Oz;* although the characters she meets are generally less irksomely eccentric, her journey is rather better defined (it would be disastrous to approach the Fringe in the unplanned, hotchpotch way that Alice approaches Wonderland). The Fringe involves both a journey with a definite mission and irksome eccentrics, so the best comparison would in fact be with the superlative film, *Labyrinth.*

poor fools have let themselves in for the most interactive performing experience possible. You can become part of someone else's pitch, their publicity – even their show – simply by being there. There are no part-timers at the Fringe. Everybody is involved in everything, from setting up the theatre, to selling their shows. All without killing each other.

As if that wasn't already more than a full-time job, anybody staying at the Fringe naturally wants to try and see as much of what is available as possible. Furthermore, shows run until the early hours; the bars are open until 3 a.m. and the clubs until 5 a.m.; parties happen on a nightly basis and there can be no waiting around until the next afternoon for things to begin again. When are people supposed to sleep?

Is it any wonder that several hundred people actually go mad every year?

In this section, we look at what it is actually like to be in a show at the Fringe, and we'll explain the difficult and Fringe-consuming publicity work that goes on and how it is achieved. We'll explain how the shows themselves work, and talk about some of the hidden difficulties in those that you might not have considered. For those not afflicted with the performing bug, we'll explain how to begin wading through the sea of thousands of shows available to you and not end up going to all the terrible ones. We will tell you all about how and where the performers live during the Fringe, and more importantly how to crash their parties. If mingling with famous names is your thing, we'll tell you how to do that as well, and how to cope with famous people and the fact that you're not one of them. Ultimately, this section will give you clear instructions on how to live the Fringe to the full while avoiding some of its terrible consequences*.

---

*The authors accept no responsibility should the reader fail to avoid the terrible consequences, even if following our advice, while living the Fringe to the full.

Publicity

Taking a show to Edinburgh is not really about performing a show. It's about publicising a show. Somebody could take up a daring piece of conceptual theatre starring Derek Jacobi on ice, but if they failed to get the publicity right they might as well have done *Cats* in the dark, with nine-year-old nuns.

You can't avoid publicity, whether you are immersed in a show yourself or just an innocent hiker who happens to be passing through Edinburgh. Wonderful as it would be for the Fringe to cultivate an atmosphere of creative freedom and enable people to focus on their artistic endeavours, the large number of shows at the Fringe means you have to fight for your audiences. Fight your friends. Fight your enemies. Fight the frankly bloody-minded desire of people to eat dinner rather than come to your show. Shows are not the priority, publicity is. Publicity never stops, never sleeps, and only rarely needs to pee. If you're there as a spectator you can do quite well out of it if you know what you're looking for; as a performer, you sure as hell can't change the system, so you need to try to play the game even if you don't like it. Like doing rugby in P.E. lessons*.

Print publicity

Getting print publicity sorted out is very much in the domain of the aforementioned production team, and they should be aware from early on of when it all needs to be done by. Certainly it ought to be ready by the time everyone actually gets to Edinburgh, because posters and flyers are the life-blood of any publicity campaign.

The official Fringe guidelines have in recent years suggested that 4000–8000 flyers and 400–800 posters are the usual requirement for a 3-week stint at the Fringe, though from our experience you'd then run out of flyers halfway through the Fringe and be left with a surfeit of posters. Shows that are serious about flyering (and they ought to be) can shift up to 15,000 flyers over 3 weeks – that's a lot of cardboard.

A poster will usually be a bigger, simpler, one-sided version of the flyer, displaying the most basic information about the show: what it is called, when and where it is on, where to book tickets and maybe a couple of choice quotes from reviews.

Flyers are smaller but, paradoxically, contain a lot more information; because they are designed to be closely scrutinised, rather than tossed aside and trampled into the ground (something which a lot of people don't seem to understand), they can contain all of the above with greater precision (for example, they might include a little map of how to get to the venue), with the addition of a lot more writing explaining exactly what the show is about. It should be fairly obvious from the poster what the show is about, but if that acts as an appetiser then the flyer is most definitely the main course, offering

---

*It's also like rugby in P.E. lessons in that, if you try to get out of it by pretending you've forgotten your kit, you might be made to do it in your underwear. That, at least, would account for the number of people who do it in their underwear.

chunkier morsels of information and a more filling content. Following this to its conclusion, the dessert in the three-course publicity meal would be a conversation with the person doing the flyering: sweet, but not everyone's thing. If you want to offer them coffee that's your own business, and what cheese, biscuits and fruit constitute is your own guess and to be reserved only for the most appealing of clientele and the most successful conversations – it is possible to take individual attention too far.

A good design is vital. This is laughably obvious to spectators at the Fringe, who can see a bad poster a mile off (and rating the various flyers you've been handed over the course of the day makes for excellent teatime fun; you can also make finger puppets out of the ones with people on). But it's amazing how many people get it wrong. The best designs tend to use an uncomplicated colour scheme and an image which is minimalist and elegant enough to be iconic. A lot of shows mess this up entirely, complicating their design with unnecessary details that crowd the overall look and at worst get in the way of the information that it is there to present.

To help you if you're new to appraising Fringe publicity, you can use the following system, carefully created for us by scientists at CERN, to enable you to take an educated laugh at the crap ones.

Judging Fringe publicity

Firstly, give each poster/flyer a score of 1–5 in each of these categories (1 = truly abysmal, 5 = perfection):

Category one: clarity
Can you tell what the show is called? Are the basic facts all evident or do you have to search for them? Most importantly, can you tell where and when the show is actually on? That information ought to be the first priority for anybody designing publicity, but – tee hee! – there are always a few that leave it out!

Category two: simplicity
Is it a design that stands out from the others, that you can spot from a distance, that beams like a... er, a beam... by virtue of its simple

perfection? Or could a short-sighted person mistake it for the work of a 2-year-old with some felt tip pens?

Category three: elegance

Essentially, does it look any good? Does it have a classy layout, a stylish font, an overall air of knowing what it's doing? Or is it to poster design what Milton Keynes is to British architecture?

Category four: concept

Often the clincher. Is it a cleverly thought-out idea which intrigues you, excites you, upsets you, or makes you chuckle? Is it something that could be hung in Tate Modern as a piece of concept art? Or is it yet another bloody photograph of a comedian looking grumpy?

Category five: memorability

Does it still stick in your mind after days of bombardment from 1600 other shows? The best thing for any design is when somebody discussing their show can say, 'You know, we're the one with the big frog on the front' and people will respond, 'Oh, that show, yeah!'

If you are assessing a flyer, you should also make a judgement about this:

Category six: blurb

The writing on a flyer should be easy to read but full of details that captivate you and make you want to see the show. Easy enough to say, but extremely difficult to pull off. Getting a decent show description into 500 words requires both journalistic and creative skills, and a description that fulfils these requirements is worthy of much respect and a full five points.

Now, tot up the scores, then remove up to three points for each of the following blunders (number of points being proportionate to the scale of the misdemeanour):

Blunder one: poor-quality paper

Flyers and posters have to survive being hauled around Edinburgh for several weeks, handled by several different people, passed around, stuck on walls, rained on and generally mistreated. If costs have been cut on paper quality it will be obvious instantly, because usually said flyer/poster will not be in terribly good condition. Flyers in particular should be printed on cardboard, or they just won't last.

Blunder two: cheap reproduction
In an age where professional colour printing is actually quite affordable, it's amazing that people still think they can get away with something cheaper. You can spot shoddy reproduction a mile off, and people who reckon they can still sell a show with a black and white photocopy are beneath contempt.

Blunder three: cringe factor
Perhaps more of a subjective thing, but something that makes you wince because of the crassness of the design is losing from the beginning. A photograph of the cast all in white T-shirts and bare feet, a horrifically punning title, or a tag line that could have been taken from a tabloid or cheesy publicity blurb should all be penalised.

Blunder four: typos
Before sending a publicity design to be printed at the cost of several-hundred pounds, most people would double-check it for mistakes. Some don't. We didn't*.

So – what did they score?
25–30: a masterpiece of art and design – get yours framed and then when the original is finally accorded the place it deserves in the National Gallery log on to eBay as fast as your mouse will carry you.

20–25: a fine effort – every bit as good as anything you can usually expect to see in the professional world, and so probably feeling a little out of place at the Fringe. Almost certainly not for stand-up comedy. You probably ought to see the show too – unless all their creativity went on the poster.

10–20: average – while it probably looks good on its own on a wall, it's likely to be ignored by everyone at the Fringe (along with most of what's around it).

0–10: piss poor – laugh at it, then deface it. Try drawing moustaches on all the faces and turning random words into rude ones.

---

*It took 3 weeks for a punter to point it out to us. Maybe before that they were scared of our reaction – we were all dressed in lab coats going round analysing people's brains.

Less than 0: you're joking – anything this bad is so awful it might even be deliberate. Either that or you've accidentally picked up publicity for your local church flower festival.

Enjoyable as it is going through Fringe publicity using this method and slagging it off – and indeed useful as it is for anyone doing the Fringe to know what good publicity ought to contain – you can have even more fun applying the same rules to professional shows in London, adverts in newspapers or film posters. While some of them certainly get it right, it's amazing how many don't.

Of course, you can't really play this game until you get to Edinburgh, which perhaps explains why so much publicity up there isn't much good. If you spot anyone wandering up and down the Royal Mile looking intently at posters and slapping their foreheads, you've probably found a publicity designer making up their own personal scoreboard. We've included a few sample posters overleaf so you can play without leaving the comfort of your favourite armchair and to try to safeguard your forehead, if you ever need to create one yourself. Of course this is nothing like as rich as Edinburgh's pickings, with posters and flyers for every single show all jostling for attention.

The artboard monster

Unless, that is, they aren't.

Few companies fail to get publicity materials printed – it really is a pretty obvious thing to do – but that doesn't mean they'll arrive. Printers are only human, and this means mistakes will be made; too few flyers may be printed, for example, or they may arrive a few days later, or a week later, or not at all.

One year, doing two shows, our posters arrived late, flyers for one show later (but with twice the number) and for the other not at all. When all concerned had finally given up hope that they might simply be dawdling, we ordered some more. They turned up late, too. Imagine how we laughed, stuck up in Edinburgh with a show to promote and nothing to promote it with!

However, we were not the only people in this position. Every year, a number of shows' publicity materials are late or don't turn up at all. It's like there's a giant artboard monster, sitting at the top of the A1, gobbling away frantically. When it's full, things get through. At other times, no chance. To avoid this happening to you is difficult; endorsements by other groups or your venue count for much, but a good company one year may have problems the next – and short of having everything delivered a long time in advance, you're pretty much just hoping it'll be all right.

Our own run-in with the artboard monster did have one single benefit: we were able to answer the question of whether you can get an audience without giving away any flyers. Turns out you can, but that's really a story for another time. For now, relax, have a drink and score the example posters.

It begins...

Publicity for the Fringe begins early. Although the week before things begin in earnest there are only hints at the level of insanity that defines the festival, you can see things limbering up in what feels like a half-hearted rehearsal. A man dances away to Latin American music; girls with fluffy antennae flock down the street getting in the way of taxis; a woman on roller skates dressed as an angel croons into a microphone; large phallic totems are erected to enable people to stick posters all over them, which the most efficient groups will do in readiness for less-efficient groups to stick different posters over the first lot.

In this early period, some people will already be publicising their shows to the others who have arrived early to do exactly the same thing. You can witness people, still in the early, uncynical stages of the whole experience when anger and bitterness have not shown their ugly faces, nodding and smiling as they describe their shows to each other without the slightest intention of remembering a word of what is being said to them.

For the entrepreneurial Fringe-goer, there are many advantages to be had. To try and get the ball rolling, almost every show will give out a

luma

Never fails to amaze.
Chicago Tribune

Outrageous illuminated spectacle!
Pittsburgh Tribune Gazette

A refreshingly original show
for kids and adults alike.
*Charleston Post
and Courier*

Now Playing
Venue 37
George Square Theatre: Tickets 662-8740
August 2nd through 11th, 18:45   August 14th through 25th, 21:30
11£ (9£) 7£ under 16, (1 Hour 15 minutes/European Premiere)

www.lumatheatre.com

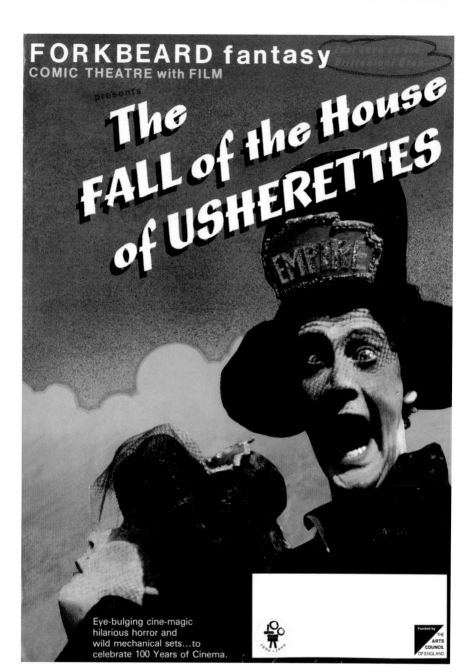

FORKBEARD fantasy
COMIC THEATRE with FILM

presents

The FALL of the House of USHERETTES

Eye-bulging cine-magic
hilarious horror and
wild mechanical sets...to
celebrate 100 Years of Cinema.

Funded by
THE
ARTS
COUNCIL
OF ENGLAND

BOLLYWOOD NIGHTS

A retrospective of the films of
SHAH RUKH KHAN
at George Square Theatre

Venue 37, George Square/Buccleuch Place, EH8

Asoka
Friday 16th August

Devdas
Saturday 17th August

Dilwale Dulhania Le Jaayenge
Friday 23rd August

Kabhi Khushi Kabhi Gham
Saturday 24th August
Shah Rukh Khan *himself* will introduce this special screening

All films start at 23.30
£5 (£4)

Immerse yourself in India. *Chor Bizare*, India's Restaurant (Mayfair and New Delhi) will be bringing some of their top chefs to George Square Theatre. Special offers for food and films available; contact Box Office for further details

Box Office and Info: 0131 662 8740
www.uoefo.com

The University of Edinburgh Festivals Office

VOLCANO THEATRE COMPANY

Macbeth

Director's Cut

Text **William Shakespeare**

Direction **Nigel Charnock**

Lighting & Design **Andrew Jones**

Video **Rheinhard Lorenz**

Additional Music **Stewart Lucas**

In association with the Unity Theatre, Liverpool

george
square
theatre

23 - 30 August   19.15 - 20.25

All Tickets £8.00 (concessions £6.00)   Box Office: 0131 662 8740

TOKEBI

A Boisterous and Imaginative Rhythm Fantasia

"Fabulous ! Fabulous ! Fabulous !..." - Canada / USA International Children's Festival
"This extravaganza is perfect ... unforgettable" - Beijing Evening News
"A feast for the eyes as much as the ears ... rhythm rocks !" - Korea Herald

▶ Production : Miru Stage Inc.
▶ Performer : **PungMuAk**

▶ Venue :
✸ George Square Theatre :
3rd - 12th (20:40)
Tel : 0131 · 662 · 8140

✸ Gilded Balloon at Teviot Row House :
14th (15:15, 20:45), 15th (15:15),
16th, 19th (14:00), 18th, 20th - 23rd (14:00 / 20:45), 24th - 25th (20:45)
Tel : 0131 · 650 · 4403

No Show : 13th, 17th
Fringe Office Tel : 0131 · 226 · 0000

fringe

Pound !! Get Energy !!

Государственный ансамбль танца

КАЗАКИ РОССИИ

Липецкой Государственной филармонии

Cinderella

Box Office Number
0131 662 8740
The Quad
(next to the Festival Theatre) Venue 192

TURBO ZONE

SUPPORTED BY go
go
go-fly.com

photo: Peter Smith

number of free tickets, or at least special offers, for their performances. This is a sensible strategy – the only way to get any kind of word of mouth going about your show is, after all, for people to see it. From a psychological point of view, also, it is nice to begin your run with some people in the audience, even if none of them have paid. People also sensibly give away several free tickets for nights when the press are going to be in, so that the reviewers can see their performances with a decent number of enthusiastic audience members enjoying it as well.

So, it is well worth seeking out these offers and taking full advantage of them, even if you end up watching a few crap ones. You can hardly complain if you haven't paid anything, and it might give you a better idea of what to avoid. Even if the offers don't appear to be coming to you, there's no harm in asking – some people go out with a number of free tickets to give away only to people who register any interest in a show (and if you are in a show it's worth bearing in mind that so many free tickets are given away in this early period it's worth trying to ensure that people actually use your ones).

The main places to find these offers are the Royal Mile and Pleasance Courtyard – chances are, if you hover in either of these places in the first few days of the Fringe, people will be fighting to give you free things, or at the very least cheap things. The offers continue into the first full week of the Fringe, and though they get thinner on the ground and less generous (often more in the nature of two-for-the-price-of-one) it makes fiscal sense to use them while they're still there.

Coping with flyering (I): being flyered by other people

What's to say about flyering that you won't notice within minutes of entering Edinburgh's fair city? At the Fringe people flyer you everywhere, all the time. On the street, naturally, or before shows, after shows, in bars, in the toilet, in bed (possibly). You might be having a fine conversation with somebody you've met in a bar when they suddenly get all aggressive and try to foist several flyers on you, urging you to 'take some for your friends' and maybe 'hand a few out when you're next in town'.

What is the best way of dealing with this behaviour, which in any other place except perhaps Bangkok would be considered unseemly? Some people bite the bullet and take everything they're offered, preferring the quiet disposal of said flyers to anything resembling a confrontation. Some locals take another approach, responding with a grimace, an utterance of 'daft Sassenachs' and a club round the head with a caber.

The best option probably lies somewhere between the two extremes. There is, of course, no obligation to take any flyers, but if nobody took any flyers then the actors would get miserable and imagine how dreadful Edinburgh would be, full of miserable actors. (Or if you can't imagine, just pop up there towards the end of the Fringe.) In any case, some people flyering you don't just want to shove a piece of paper in your face, they actually want to impart some information about what could be a great show, in which case it's not a bad idea to pay some attention to them. Give a thought to the fact that, however smiling and happy the fresh-faced thespian in front of you looks, they've probably been on the street for several hours for the nth day in a row, and it costs nothing to at least give them a friendly smile.

Unless they're looking angry and pissed off, in which case you are of course entitled to spit in their face.

Coping with flyering (II): flyering other people

As we mentioned just before you had that last drink, we have had the experience of flyering without actually having any flyers, thanks to the crapness of a certain printing company who would, now that we've employed the term 'crapness', sue us if we named them.

Our makeshift alternative was the kind of photocopied flyers that we advised you to ignore completely, yet the audiences we got that week were perhaps the most consistently high we saw throughout the whole Fringe.

What do we learn from this? That we are actually wrong and photocopied flyers are incredibly appealing to the masses? Well... no. But in order to compensate for the fact that our flyers looked crap and contained very little information, we found ourselves talking to anybody we gave them to, apologising for cluttering up their hand luggage with such poorly produced rubbish, explaining why exactly we had resorted to doing this, and explaining what a good show it was going to be in spite of this and why exactly.

Perhaps people came to see us out of sympathy. More realistically, by telling people all about what we were doing, we succeeded in interesting them and so increased the success rate of each shoddy photocopied flyer several hundred times. Even if flyers look fantastic, people reach a saturation point. They see a million of the bloody things. So talking to people about your show is a far better way of getting audiences than trying to sell it on the strength of a flyer alone. It's also a better way of making friends.

However, trying to grab people as they head down the Royal Mile is hard enough without trying to start a conversation. For this reason the best flyering spots are places where people are not constantly on the move. Find somewhere such as the queue to the Fringe box office, where people are standing around waiting to get tickets. They are much more likely to want to talk to you – there's not much else for them to do, after all – and if you're really persuasive they may even go straight into the box office and book a ticket then and there. It's unlikely, but they might.

Flyering quotes

To give you an idea of what reaction you might be able to expect when you flyer on the streets of Edinburgh, here are a selection of genuine responses to our efforts to publicise our first fully improvised Edinburgh show, *Out of Your Mind*.

Rejections:

'No thanks, I live in Edinburgh.'

'No thanks, we're not here.'

'We saw it last year, thanks.'

'No, I'm actually performing in a show here. Would you like one of our flyers?'

Comments on the nature of our show:

James L: 'We turn your thoughts into theatre!'
Fringegoer: 'What, even the dirty ones?'

James L: 'We turn your thoughts into theatre!'
Forlorn girl: 'All right.'

James L: '*Out of Your Mind*?'
Lady: 'Oh! Is it like Art?'
James L: 'Um... no, we turn your thoughts into theatre.'
Lady: 'Oh! What a good idea!'

'We've just dropped somebody off at a mental asylum, so it's rather déjà vu for us.'

'Oh. I thought it was a massage.'

Comments on the nature of our company:

James L to a small boy: 'It's a lovely picture, look.'
Mother of small boy: 'Oh, but his ears stick out, don't they?' (looks at James) 'Never mind, he can't help it.'

Susie, our ravishing producer: 'Thoughts into theatre, Sir?'
Sleazy Latin type, gazing into her eyes: 'You're beautiful.'
Susie: 'Yes, yes, I know.'

'That guy has really big nostrils.'

'He's got a posh voice, doesn't 'e?!'

Responses to more ill-advised attempts to sell the show:

James L plays his harmonica to a jolly looking baby. Baby cries.

Even on the Royal Mile, there are several folk who prefer to meander and observe rather than rush from one place to another. They are easy to spot, because they are the ones meandering and observing. In the name of happiness and communication, having conversations with them is a very worthwhile pastime. You don't even have to just discuss the show you're in – crazy as it may sound, at the Fringe there are opportunities to enjoy conversation with complete strangers. Yes, people talk, make friends and occasionally enjoy themselves. Unexpected, but it takes all sorts.

On the other hand, there are some who just seem to want to get rid of their pile of flyers without too much thought as to who they're giving them to or where they end up. These people have considerably less impact because they're frankly lazy. In fact, flyers are thought to persuade only one person in a hundred to get to see a show – when flyers cost about 2p each to produce you're losing about £2 from the ticket price for every audience member pulled in by flyers. Economically, then, just handing out flyers willy-nilly is rather a stupid policy and it makes a lot more sense to talk them up and maximise your pulling power.

You'd have thought that this would be a good reason to hand out your own flyers rather than employ somebody else to do it. After all, getting enthused about a show you are not directly involved with is pretty much unsustainable over three weeks. However, performers with enough money, and some of the big production companies, do pay people to hand out flyers for them, and they evidently think it's worth paying people by the hour to do it. Apart from seeming to have a positive effect on audience sizes, it gives the performers themselves a bit of space to relax, particularly in the case of shows put on by individuals or small groups. Many people would consider it money well spent for this reason alone.

There are companies that will supply people to flyer for shows, but the people they supply are almost inevitably students and it's not difficult to get hold of students without the help of a company. The happiest students, and therefore probably the most successful, appear to be those who have been in some way 'involved' with the show(s) they are working for, be it ushering for them, or simply treated to free performances and, of course, this puts them in a position where they can (hopefully) tell everyone how good the show is.

Coping with flyering (III): strategy

For reasons which should now be very, very obvious, flyering done properly is extremely hard work. It is therefore worth planning carefully. Everybody has a limited level of tolerance for the number of hours they can reasonably stand outside doing publicity, and it's often lower than they would imagine. Some kind of rota system to prevent exhaustion or insanity is advisable. It is a pity when the energy used up on publicity results in a drop in the quality of a performance. It is also a good idea to give anyone with flyering duties a chance to see shows they are interested in, and possibly even a day off every now and then. However, there is strength in numbers, so don't stretch yourselves too thinly: better to do a good few hours every day than struggle to ensure that there is 24-hour cover across Edinburgh. That would be silly in any case, as people do go to bed, eventually.

A good policy is to make sure some flyering energy and resources are reserved for the period immediately before your show. Some people may be looking to fill the immediate hour or so before whatever they've planned to go and see and will happily step in off the street to while away the time, especially if it's raining.

Coping with flyering (IV): having fun

There are always people who spend several hours devising clever and wacky ways to get people to take their flyers. Variations of the old 'please could you hold this for a moment' then running away routine are rife. Or disguising flyers as pieces of cake. Or kidnapping and drugging people then tattooing publicity blurb onto their bodies. This is all good clean fun and may win the grudging respect of whoever has been conned into taking yet another piece of publicity, but at the end of the day you have only succeeded in foisting yet another piece of publicity onto them about which they are none the wiser except that whatever it's advertising is being put on by some cunning bastards. As far as the bums-on-seat-per-flyer hit rate goes, nothing beats personal contact.

On the other hand, the wackier ways of getting rid of flyers can get a group noticed and offer the opportunity to have a bit of fun. One year a group would tie one of their cast members to a chair and threaten to execute him if people didn't take their flyers. We responded to this by performing a daring rescue/kidnap attempt, three of us picking up the chair and running away with their cast member, something which annoyed them but ironically helped them shift a lot more flyers. We felt it was pretty unsporting of them to get annoyed, although we noticed that the person they'd tied up seemed pretty happy.

One of the best flyering gimmicks we have come across in recent years was a show which had attached keys to all of their flyers. They were handing them out with the promise of an opportunity to win a prize if your key unlocked their magic case, or something along those lines (it was an experimental devised piece, so they were allowed to be a bit weird). Most of the keys were miscut rejects which we imagine didn't cost them anything at all; just a few were able to open the case they said featured in their show, and contained some sort of goodies. At least, that is what they told us. When we went to see the show – partly out of interest in experimental devised theatre, but mainly because we wanted to win the goodies – said case and opportunity to open it didn't appear to be present, and we were a little bit pissed off. Perhaps they had run out of goodies, or decided the case didn't really fit into the show as well as it should have done. But even if they were just lying to us all along, it was a clever marketing ploy, as demonstrated by the fact that we went to see them.

It shouldn't need saying, but if a clever method of flyering is detrimental to the intended result (i.e. people taking flyers) it possibly isn't all that clever after all. Delightful as it is seeing people flyer in slow motion, you only need to walk away from them at a moderate pace and they haven't got a hope of catching you. Since it's also impossible have a decent conversation in slow motion, as a flyering strategy it is almost entirely useless. And yet people still do it.

Postering

Postering at the Fringe works as follows: you put up a poster. Somebody else puts a poster up over the top of it. You put up another poster over the top of that one. Somebody else puts up another on top of that. You put up another..., and so on. The people with the most posters visible are not those who put the most posters up, but those who do it most regularly. It's that simple.

There are always some wankers who try to defeat this simple law of physics by taping together improbably long rows of posters and spreading them over everything, so that for at least a few minutes their posters are the only thing you can see anywhere. Not only does this use up a lot of posters, but it pisses off everybody whose posters have been indiscriminately covered up by a single group.

The actual areas you can put posters up in are, sadly, rather limited these days. Since the venues themselves are now ultra-competitive, you are never going to be allowed to put up posters at any venue other than your own, so spaces for communal postering are few. Back when the Fringe Club was at Teviot Row (where the Gilded Balloon now squats) it was a perfect place to put up posters and see what else was on. There isn't really any equivalent now, though in recent years the alternative outdoor Fringe box office has provided a place where posters can be displayed. Other than that, there is only really the much-fought over official poster space on the Royal Mile to use. Some pubs, cafés, bars, etc., are also happy for posters and flyers to be left on their premises, but it's a good idea to ask.

Other surfaces may look tempting – those shiny blue Fringe-sponsored bins may seem to be crying out for one of your lovely posters, but people are employed to remove them, and will. Fly-posting is illegal and some pretty hefty fines are threatened for doing it; on the other hand, the fact that the promoters of respected big-name acts are particularly guilty of fly-posting suggests that nothing at all is being done about it, which is annoying because, let's face it, it's not difficult to track down the culprits.

Television interviews

Publicity takes you in all sorts of exciting directions. From meeting your future wife to meeting your wife's future husband, when you step out of the door, armed with a stack of flyers and your best five-word slogan yet, you offer yourself up to the fates. Maybe it'll rain, maybe some photojournalist will get your face into *Three Weeks*, maybe you'll pick the right time for lunch, and not have to wait ages to get a sandwich. Maybe, maybe, that call will come, and one of the papers will want to interview you. (And maybe they'll actually get round to it, too.)

Or you might even be on television.

There are film crews in Edinburgh throughout August, from various programmes, some dedicated to the Fringe and some more general news and culture shows. The terrestrial stations will be there, but so also will any number of cable and satellite channels and, increasingly, web-only broadcast teams, either run by the venues themselves or completely independent.

Some will just rove around Edinburgh looking for interesting things to film. You might be fortunate enough to end up featuring in a montage scene for some daytime television programme or, more usefully, you might get your face on the local live news broadcast. We say usefully – but that's really an exaggeration. We were once flyering when we received a frantic phone call from our producer who urgently told us to get to the top of the Royal Mile with some posters as there was a live interview going on. Obediently, we legged it 300 metres and stood panting in the background of a live television interview, grinning sheepishly and holding up posters.

Can you imagine how many people saw us on television (a group of sweaty men looking unfit and embarrassed and holding up publicity materials with information that would only be visible if the viewer had videoed the programme, and paused it at the relevant point on a good video recorder with a magnifying glass to hand) and shouted, 'Elspeth, there's a show on here that we really must go and see!'?

Here's a clue: less than one.

Far better to be the people being interviewed.

Interviews are arranged with people or shows that film crews think will work well for their programme or channel. Live interviews can always be risky, but if you relax and remember that generally the interviewer isn't trying to make you look stupid, but rather wants to get some interesting television out of it, you'll do fine. What you do have to judge is whether it's worth it.

A television interview generally won't get you more audience. It might further your career, get you a television contract, or make it easier to find a good venue next year, but it's pretty unlikely to rustle up any more punters, for the same reason that watching an interview with Orlando Bloom is unlikely to make you want to see his latest film. Unless you fancy him. In which case you've probably already seen it and not even noticed how little real acting he does. An interview isn't really publicity for your show, unless you come off very well indeed: it's publicity for you, or it's just entertainment for everyone else. Another thing to remember is that some of these programmes won't have a very large audience. Some may have a smaller audience than your show (see Television Interviews box). Anyway, time is limited at the Fringe: there might be better things to do with your time, things that might bring in audience, or you might just want to relax and take in someone else's show.

Television interviews
James Aylett

At my first Fringe, taking part in a comedy about life and love in the gay community, I was interviewed for cable channel LiveTV by a strikingly attractive female presenter who quizzed the cast for half an hour or so on our love lives. Only one of us was gay, tanned and confident and full of stories of waltzing into various parties and sharing champagne with the controller of Channel 4. The lead said something about usually getting drunk to get up courage when on the pull, and when the presenter turned her questioning (and somewhat distracting eyes and smile) on me, I said that I pursued women slowly, and at great length. Perhaps it was funny (she laughed, but then that's her job), but it certainly sounded believable, because I was wearing a dress.

The other two had the two lead roles; I had all the other parts from Barman through Concerned Gay Friend to Checkout Boy. Oh, and Mad Woman. When the lead character was dreaming of being dead, I ran onto the stage, wailing over his body. In a dress. It was rather fun at the time, but when the director decided I should wear the dress to the interview, it didn't seem nearly so enjoyable.

And I gave up tickets for Mark Thomas to do it.

At its peak, LiveTV pulled in about 1% of the cable audience, itself pretty tiny in the mid-nineties, and its peak was not three guys sitting in a bar talking about how to pull. We were doing pretty well on audience both before and after the interview, and I don't think for one moment that being on television did anything for either the show or our careers. It makes a passable story at parties, and that's it – so before you agree to spend an evening doing your hair, putting on makeup, and getting into costume for a television interview, just think briefly about what else you could do with your time.

Getting noticed

Everybody has posters. Everybody hands out flyers. Regardless of how distinctive they sometimes manage to be, on their own they will not make people stand out from the crowd. Most groups will therefore stop at nothing to grab people's attention. This is why the Royal Mile during the Fringe is such a famously weird and frenetic place: it's full of exhibitionists who all want to be seen by everybody. Some people do it successfully, some people less so. It's worth mentioning a few basic tactics and some of the things you can expect to see and may wish to brace yourself against.

First, and commonly, many groups perform bits of their shows wholesale. This is particularly common among groups doing musicals, and it has to be said the song and dance numbers tend to work better than anything else on the street. Not that this stops people from attempting to deliver Shakespeare soliloquies on street corners, as if they're going to gain any more attention than the man preaching about God. So you get all sorts of samples on display, and although these are largely ineffective and often even off-putting, they do add to the silly atmosphere of the place. You should not be in the least bit surprised to walk past a man on a bollard wailing, 'How long will you hate me for, Loretta?' That's how wonderful it is.

Other groups will have devised a special slogan or motto for their show, or as reviews start to come out they may just begin chanting quotes such as 'Four stars from Fest, 'a really lovely show'!' which gets extremely irritating after a while, but not as irritating as some of the catchphrases they might churn out – a production of *A Midsummer Night's Dream* which goes around greeting people, 'hail, mortal!' is crying out to be culled.

One of our colleagues once tried less conventional methods of publicity, in the course of an afternoon grabbing a man's crotch and kicking somebody. She claims both incidents were accidental; we do not know if either of her victims was persuaded to come to our show.

High Street stages

In recent years, the Royal Bank of Scotland, which sponsors the Fringe as it pretty much owns Edinburgh anyway, has provided small stages along the Royal Mile which shows can book to put on twenty-minute excerpts from, or trailers for, their shows. Like all the other entertainment in the area, people watch it for a bit then wander on, enjoying it all as part of the Fringe atmosphere but not really taking in the fact that the poor sods on the stages are actually trying to publicise anything. In any case, it is rare for anyone to successfully distil their show into a 20-minute performance that works in the open air. For this reason, the little stages, fun though they be, mainly benefit the Fringe organisers and sponsors, and of course the punters. It is possibly for this reason that by the middle of the Fringe half of the people booked in to do slots on them fail to turn up, so if you're really desperate to get up and perform – probably even if you're just a member of the public – one of the Fringe organisers can usually arrange it for you. We recall a surreal moment when a woman persuaded them to give her a slot and spent it skating around the stage on a scooter with a vacuum cleaner attached to the front, singing gently to herself.

We got ourselves officially booked into slots on the stages the first year we went to the Fringe with an improvised show. When we realised that they were practically useless in publicity terms, we gave up trying to sell our show and used the slots to mess around in front of a crowd. In one we built a brain machine out of small children (we're not sure where the law stands on this activity in Scotland), showing ideas coming in through the top of the head before being whirled around to make thoughts. In another we had fights in slow motion. Our final slot was a review of the Fringe in which we improvised our own approximations of everything we had seen. This went down rather well, and we were quite irritated when the idea was turned into an actual show at the Fringe a couple of years later before we had a chance to do it ourselves.

High Street gimmicks

Other methods of getting noticed are less easy to explain, but can provide some mild amusement. One year a woman advertised her show by knitting together spooled out cassettes. Quite how this related to *Edward II* was anybody's guess, but at least she showed more imagination and taste than just removing items of clothing.

Publicity gimmick #7: the girl in the short skirt.

This seems to be increasingly common, whether or not it has any relevance to the show being advertised – people may go out in skimpy rags because they're in something Dickensian, or they may be half-naked because it's a play about swimming. But really, it's a bit much when people start flyering in their underpants. It's not as if we're talking people with the Teutonic ideal of the perfect body, either. If you see them, tell them to put some clothes on – it's Edinburgh, you may save them from hypothermia, not to mention all the embarrassment they ought to feel.

One tactic you often see is groups trying to position themselves as high up as possible. They will perch atop the bollards or bins along the Royal Mile to shout their publicity slogans. In some ways it is a dubious tactic, because you can only get so high on a bollard and even when you do, what you're shouting literally goes over people's heads. But with a bit of thought height can definitely be an advantage – one year we used a stepladder on a daily basis, from which we would deliver lectures on subjects related to the show we were doing, aided by a flip-chart. When we ran out of paper, we started drawing on the pavement in chalk, which in some respects was even more successful; you can draw a long series of arrows on the pavement and people will follow them. We once drew a chalk circle around an unsuspecting woman and she froze completely, uncertain of whether she could move out of it. You could probably capture a whole audience in this manner.

The success of this campaign, which through repetition made us something of an installation on the Royal Mile that year, was confirmed when a glorious full colour spread in *The Guardian* showing Fringe highlights centred around a fine photograph of one of us towering over the Royal Mile on a stepladder. If they had only used a photograph from the other direction it might have got the face in too.

It wasn't without its dangers, though. Let's not forget that 41,000 people injure themselves falling off stepladders every year. One afternoon, we were watching as one of our colleagues addressed the crowds from the stepladder wearing a lab coat and (perhaps unwisely) shorts, prompting an old lady to approach from behind, a broad grin on her face, and pinch his leg.

A more grandiose scheme we developed, and with less dangerous leg exposure, was to take advantage of our show being improvised and organise an 'Improlympics' event. In the year of the Athens Olympics, the Fringe was not the only event drawing people from all over the world to watch a variety of performances in buildings which were not quite finished in time. We drew a cunning parallel and, in the Athens of the North, underneath the Greco-Roman columns perched atop Calton Hill, we drew together improvisation teams from three different nations for a morning of competitive impro-games.

We represented our own country so realistically that we lost. Some people would suggest that to organise a competitive improvisation event and then lose it shows a degree of carelessness. We would turn this argument around to suggest that any foreign improvisation group invited to take part in such an event, even if they are on their own soil, is actually rather rude not to let the organisers of the event win. To look at it in a more positive light, we did win bronze – although we would have done better had not the final clinching event been the 100-metre sprint. Our final position was less a judgement on our improvisation than that our chosen team member runs like a girl. He's since become a lawyer; it seemed the only way.

Aside from the slight shame of losing our own event, though, was it worth all that effort from the perspective of publicity? Well, no. It was a lot of fun, and some interesting people got involved in the event, many of whom came to see our show afterwards. However, there was a big gap between the effort expended on organising the event and the minimal publicity it generated. Not that it mattered; we had fun, we made some friends and we put on a good show, which is essentially what the Fringe is all about. The effort you put into things at the Fringe is rarely matched by the outcome, but that doesn't mean it isn't worth doing them – in fact, it's what the Fringe is all about. It goes to show, though, how difficult it is to get noticed, even with a reasonably large-scale idea.

Bad publicity

If reconstructing the largest sporting event in the world is of limited publicity value, it is hardly surprising that some people go overboard in trying to get some kind of attention. Be warned, though: this way of getting noticed can, if you're not careful, be counter-productive. Remember Aaron Barschak, whose gatecrashing-royal-parties-dressed-as-a-terrorist antics in 2003 earned him attention from the national press, as well as the boys in blue? As a publicity stunt, you could say it was an unqualified success – theoretically, notoriety is as good a selling point for a show as anything else.

However, it backfired. For a start, nobody likes a smart-arse exhibitionist, especially other smart-arse exhibitionists who have been less successful in getting into the news headlines. Furthermore, Barschak's methods, unconventional though they were, were not so much funny as slightly alarming, and he did little to endear himself to the press or the public. When it came to reviews, then, in spite of (in fact, because of) having attracted national coverage for his show, he was a sitting duck. The slightest weakness in his show was going to expose him to ridicule on a huge scale. Predictably, given his inexperience (he had been performing comedy for a mere eight months), he gave critics every excuse they needed for a thorough panning.

To quote from *BBC Online*, 'with such little evidence of scripted material it is also little wonder that the sceptical community of comics are out to lynch him.' Or this, from *Chortle*: 'Going to a party he wasn't invited to brought him publicity you just can't buy, but with no discernible talent other than chutzpah, he's still not been able to hang the 'sold out' signs on the door.'

In the words of Barschak himself, interviewed in *The Scotsman*, 'What hurt was the fact I deserved the bad reviews I got, absolutely without doubt. I was delusional, thinking I could come up and conquer Edinburgh. But I didn't write a script.'

Indeed. Important as publicity is, if you don't have a show to publicise then you're bound to come a cropper. So perhaps, before you plan your security-threatening publicity explosion, it is probably as well to put in the vital groundwork of ensuring that you have something that is worth publicising (see previous chapter, if you haven't already – and if you haven't, why not?)

You might feel that no publicity is bad publicity. Barschak himself seemed to believe that by the end of his run he was doing better shows, and audiences certainly remained steady. In the long term, however, you have to admit that getting a national reputation for having the worst show at the Fringe is a flawed strategy at best. Quite aside from that, you have to spend a whole month at the Fringe, so alienating every other person there is probably not the best way to enjoy it.

On that topic, another publicity strategy springs to mind, which we cite in full if only as an act of personal revenge. Our first year at the Fringe, a group hailing from Trinity College, Dublin, had devised what probably counts as the most irritating publicity campaign in the history of the Fringe. It took the form of a little song, the words of which went as follows:

'*We're standing (standing, standing)*
Handing out some flyers (handing out some flyers)
Handing out some flyers (handing out some flyers)
For just a few hours or so (oh oh)'
(Music provided on request.)

The joke – the only joke – is that this was repeated again and again for the few hours or so. *Ad nauseum* (oh oh). Being out on the Royal Mile publicising our own show, we were exposed to it on a daily basis. As you can imagine, the joke began to wear a bit thin by the last week of the Fringe.

The next year the same group were back in Edinburgh with a show called *Stop Fistfighting, You're Pregnant* (an unfortunate title, because on first reading it always seemed to say 'Stop Fisting, You're Pregnant'), for which their publicity campaign was exactly the same as the previous year. We don't know if their show was any good, but more exposure to the standing (standing, standing) song made us absolutely determined to boycott them in any way possible, and we surely were not the only ones.

In any case, irritating the hell out of people is never the best idea in a city where in every souvenir shop you can buy huge ornamental swords.

Getting reviews

Reviews are publicity you just can't buy. Literally, more's the pity. A good review is worth a hundred nice flyers, and even a bad review gets a show's name out in the open, so getting reviewers to come to performances is a high priority for all Fringe performers.

There are regular newspapers printed especially for the Fringe, *Fest* and *Three Weeks*, both of which are full of reviews and the most likely chance most shows will have of being reviewed. *The Guardian* often boasts the highest proportion of Fringe shows reviewed, but equally often goes for the well-known names. *The Scotsman* is local and also regularly reviews the slightly more high-flying shows. Various other national newspapers produce supplements about the Fringe. There's

140

no harm in pushing information about shows in every possible direction – you never know who might be interested – but it's as well to be realistic, and nationals typically have little space for the Fringe.

A few shows, ones with significant financial backing usually, opt to use a PR company to promote their show. There are a handful of such companies in Edinburgh who take on shows each year, and although they choose which people they take on, if you've got the money to pay for it you should be able to find one. The second show we took to the Fringe, thanks to the generosity of our sponsor, was represented by a PR company called Tartan Silk (which sounds like a strand of Mills and Boon novels aimed at people with a Scottish fetish). The main advantages of having them working on our behalf were in their work prior to the Fringe – they did some clever work with press releases to generate develop interest in our show before it even started and, most significantly, ran a brief showcase for members of the press (all of them liberally plied with wine and kangaroo butties – the latter a particularly unconventional move, but we assumed they knew what they were doing). This required us to fly up to Edinburgh and back again all in one day just to perform ten minutes of material and taste marsupial – much as this decadence made us feel like celebrities (with fewer bodyguards and flying EasyJet), it was clear that any possibly benefits of PR representation was going to have to be weighed against increased cost.

To our delight, the man in charge of Tartan Silk was actually wearing a jacket made out of tartan silk. To our dismay, he promptly informed us that we needed to ensure our performance was no more than five minutes rather than the ten minutes we'd been told to prepare. Squeezing the essence of our show into ten minutes had been hard enough, getting it into five minutes seemed well nigh impossible, and more than one of our company felt highly irritated at the difficulty this posed – another lesson to learn, then, was that with a PR company things are run to best suit them or the press. No doubt they had their reasons but it didn't make it any easier on us.

However, if a man in a tartan jacket tells you it's five minutes, you're in no position to argue with him, so we thought sod it, let's just do what we've planned, twice as fast. In the end this worked to our advantage, giving our performance a pace which even woke up the man from *The Scotsman*. It was effective as well, with reviewers turning up to our early performances and the resulting reviews being printed mere days into the festival.

Although we were never going to deny this successful start to the run, or complain about getting quick reviews (even if some of them did imply that our improvised show might be scripted), it was a lot of money to be paying a company when, after the pre-Fringe extras, they were essentially doing things that we would have been perfectly able to do for ourselves. Of course, PR companies have useful contacts, and years of experience in writing press releases and promoting things, but writing a good press release is not rocket science.

Essentially, to appeal to the press (not unlike appealing to everybody else) you need to identify a 'Unique Selling Point'. Since the reviewers are never going to even get close to seeing every show, they will naturally choose to review the well-known performers, and anything that grabs their attention as being particularly noteworthy or unusual. For example, Tartan Silk took the umbrella theme of our show, emergencies (really just a framing device for improvising plays), and wrote press releases cleverly linking our show to the emergency leaflets that had recently been produced by the government, leaving us in the slightly unpleasant situation of having reason to be grateful to David Blunkett.

The skill Tartan Silk demonstrated here was to link it to something which everyone in the country knew about, making it look topical and cutting edge. They might have chosen to write press releases about how we were pushing the limits of theatre with our razor sharp techniques and improvisational skill. Which we were, of course, but think about how many press releases must make claims of that nature and you'll see how focussing attention on something more specific (and possibly more gimmicky) will say 'yippee, I'm interesting' to members of the press when they're wading through a sea of groups who are all pushing the limits of theatre with their razor sharp techniques.

Once the press releases are out, it's all a matter of perseverance. Follow-up phone calls are always a good idea, sometimes even after a reviewer has been to the show (the reviews may be lined up waiting to be printed, but unfair as it may seem, some of them jump the queue…). Some venues do press stuff for you, but in any case it's a good idea to keep tabs on what is being done and keep pushing for more. The more work you put into it, the more likely you are to see something in return.

Fish licence
Alex Horne

I always think people who do solo shows at Edinburgh must be very hardy individuals with supreme confidence in their own abilities and temperament. I'm not sure if I could do a month of shows without being able to share even some of the blame/joy/heavy lifting/debt with somebody else.

That's why when I went up 'on my own' for the first time (2003) I took two assistants – the frighteningly talented Tim Key and a goldfish. I thought both would provide extra interest on stage and additional comfort and reassurance off. I didn't think that one of them would end up stealing nearly all my limelight, attention and thunder.

Daniel (we called him Daniel) first started getting attention on our daily walk through the Assembly Rooms to the backstage area of the Wildman room. People literally cooed – at a fish. This unpredictable and unedifying behaviour soon brought him to the notice of Edinburgh City Council who said he couldn't 'perform' without a 'performer's licence'. He's a fish.

Within 2 days the press started running stories about this 'performing fish' with a 'performer's licence' and before long much more had been written about Daniel than 'my' show. In one article in *The Sun* a journalist managed to spell his name correctly while misspelling mine and failing even to mention the name of the show (*Making Fish Laugh*).

The poster image of my fish and I (definitely in that order) cropped and still crops up all over the place, people still call me 'the fish guy' and occasionally an audience is still disappointed when I don't 'do my fish stuff'. I never had any 'fish stuff'. I'm actually genuinely quite scared of fish. On reflection, I know I have much to thank my assistants for that year. I wouldn't have had half as much fun without them. Well, maybe half, but definitely not as much fun as I did end up having. While I ditched Daniel (an unfortunate phrase but he was a 'performer') for the following year's show, I did end up living with them both for the next 6 months and I still have a fish in a bowl by my side as I write this today.

Alex Horne's show Making Fish Laugh *was nominated for the Perrier Newcomer Award in 2003.*

Using reviews

Once a show has a review, quotes from it are inevitably added to the publicity to demonstrate to potential audiences how good the show is. These can be printed onto bits of paper and hastily glued onto flyers, or the very trendy people might do a second print-run halfway through the Fringe with a new flyer design to include quotes. Venues almost always print bits of reviews out and stick them onto the posters they have up, and possibly also put up full reviews for anything in their programme, although they may need pestering to get round to it unless you have four or five stars.

If the show is given a decent star rating, then the stars are always used (four or five stars always look good, and shows that get fewer stars sometimes manage to sneakily combine stars from two different reviews to make up the numbers). Otherwise, it's a matter of taking a nice soundbite about the show and putting it everywhere. If there are no nice soundbites then the process requires a little more imagination. The manipulation of reviews is an art form in itself, and one that has long been practised in the professional world. It is simply a matter of removing words and adding dots – you don't lie, you just omit the truth. For example:

'I gave up all hope of getting more than my money's worth' becomes '…more than my money's worth'

'Is this the best Edinburgh can offer?' becomes '…the best Edinburgh can offer'

'It doesn't have a single talented cast member and I would rather die than watch this show again' becomes 'talented cast…watch this show'

'… no longer a mighty seedbed for new comic talents' becomes 'a mighty seedbed for new comic talents'

…and so on. If you're not getting reviews at all – we really don't advise it – but you could just make some up. We really don't advise it though. Bad thoughts. Bad.

On the other hand, who is going to check?

Using the press

If you get fed up with waiting for reviews to come out, there are other ways in which the press can be exploited, if you're clever. You may be able to get some kind of article written about what you're doing, particularly in one of the specifically Edinburgh-based publications – again, the press look for that Unique Selling Point, so it's well worth targeting press people with things that you think would make an interesting article. After all, if you come up with the idea for them, you've saved them time.

You may also be able to cheekily quote from these articles as if they were reviews. Since an article is far less likely to say negative things than a review, this is no bad thing.

Just make sure they get it absolutely right, or it may not be worth the trouble. We once succeeded in getting a commission from a certain national newspaper to write a witty column about dealing with emergencies which could be associated with our show; as the deadline was rather tight, a column was hastily penned by the one cast member who was in the flat at the time. He then submitted the article under the name of 'the Uncertainty Division', which was the right thing to do as it is the name of our group. The newspaper was directed to our website where they could get photographs of us, as requested.

The website contained all our publicity materials, including a poster for our other show which featured the very pretty face of a girl called Christine Twite. She was not in the show – we used her because she looked nice. Some hack obviously decided that she looked so nice that she should represent the Uncertainty Division, because when the column appeared it was underneath a picture of her face – and credited to 'Ally Glennon'. Evidently, whoever chose her face had decided that they needed a female name to match it.

In our cast we had a girl called Ali Glennon. She was our ally, but that is not how to spell her name. So what we ended up with was an article credited to a typing error who didn't write it and with the face of somebody who was not even in the show.

However you look at it, that is extraordinarily shoddy journalism.

It also meant that the whole exercise was utterly hopeless from a publicity point of view. God knows how many people were charmed by Ally Glennon's wit and spent many wasted hours searching Edinburgh for her show.

Fringe Sunday

Usually towards the middle of the Fringe festival there is a Sunday known as 'Fringe Sunday' which means that everyone gathers in a field doing exciting publicity things and giving out flyers. It's exactly the same as the rest of the Fringe, just in a field.

The grass is always greener...

We once spoke to a charmingly eccentric cabaret-style performer called Carola Stewart, who introduced us to her dog Binky Beaumont and before we'd even attempted to mispronounce her name insisted that 'it's not Carohla, it's Carola'. She was completely bonkers but a lot of fun to talk to. As we were comparing notes on publicising our respective shows, she suddenly lamented, 'I'm not the son or daughter of anyone famous, that's my problem. And I didn't go to Cambridge, so I wasn't in the Footlights. And worst of all, I'm not a soap star. So although I've been in the theatre for twenty years and I've worked with Peter O'Toole, nobody's heard of me.'

We were quite enchanted by her and could genuinely sympathise with the predicament; as her subtle name-drop suggested, she wasn't exactly a beginner at her art, yet here she was still struggling to get audiences like any student group on the Royal Mile. Did her career and experience count for nothing? Well – in Edinburgh, alas, possibly not, and there is little advice we can give people for avoiding this situation except 'don't become an actor'.

On the other hand, everybody is in the same sinking ship. Enviable though a Cambridge background may seem, Carola was wrong to imagine that the many groups from Cambridge University find it any easier than her to sell their shows. While a Cambridge education was once considered pretty exciting by the rest of the world, in an era where every other person on the street has a PhD it is no longer enough to impress crowds into coming to a show (or, we've noticed, to impress employers into giving one a job). The same almost certainly applies to people who are the son or daughter of somebody famous, and although we have no personal experience of soap stars trudging up and down the Royal Mile, watching Paul Daniels performing close-up magic on the street to try and win people into coming to his show was a lesson that not even a famous face guarantees bums on seats at the Fringe. Unless we're talking about one of the professionally-run productions with money to throw at promotion and famous casts, everybody has to work to get audiences, and however much of an advantage you may personally think somebody else has, nobody is exempt from the possibility of playing to audiences of four. Not even, it seems, someone who has worked with Peter O'Toole. Everybody comes to the Fringe as equals; in many ways, the Edinburgh Fringe festival is a far more successful distillation of Karl Marx's ideals than communism ever was.

Doing the shows

So, after a late night of partying, networking and being showbizzy, the Fringe performers spend a long day handing out flyers, putting up posters and chasing up their press releases in the vain hope of seeing their names appear somewhere at some point. It is a difficult, thankless task, so what do they get to do after all that hard work? Have a refreshing coffee or an ice-cream? A quick massage or a nice sauna? Or do they all shag like rabbits because that's what actors are supposed to do?

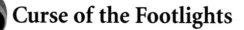

Curse of the Footlights

They almost certainly have the longest list of successful alumni of any comedy organisation. People have heard about them all over the world, people take places at Anglia Ruskin University just for the chance to join them and they always have a high-profile summer tour show featuring the possible stars of tomorrow, which takes in the Edinburgh Fringe. But despite having all this going for them, the Cambridge Footlights Dramatic Club are cursed.

Why? Well, it's partly because most people hate them – they are seen as over-privileged, arrogant and aristocratic, none of which necessarily hold true, but which creates a lot of resentment nevertheless. The fact that a group can go to Edinburgh with a show called *Not the Footlights* and the tagline 'For people who hate all things Cambridge' demonstrates the strength of feeling against them and the paucity of wit with which such hatred is expressed. (When the *Durham Revue* described them as 'The Fucklights' they must have been trembling at the threat to their student comedy crown...)

The anti-Footlights feeling is so significant that several alumni have, in the past, done their level best to disassociate themselves from the club altogether, preferring to be assessed on their own strengths free from bias. This is perfectly reasonable, but it does leave the poor existing Footlighters feeling rather as though they are being abandoned by people the minute they start to become in the least bit famous.

Unfortunately, the long and varied history of the club tends to work against those who are currently in it, especially when it comes to press reviews, because of the inevitable yet pointless comparisons that are drawn. The present simply never lives up to the rose-tinted view of past glories, so they are constantly trying to outrun the pretty humungous shadow of Stephen Fry – and yet, when Fry, Laurie, Slattery, Thompson et al. won the coveted first Perrier award in 1981, the panel of judges expressed a reluctance to give the award to a group of known clever dicks. Twenty years earlier, a review of a show which boasted John Cleese, Tim Brooke-Taylor, Graham Chapman and Bill Oddie, stated, 'Have they got a new Jonathan Miller among them? I may as well get the answer over right away, "No".' Yet only a few years earlier, a reviewer

149

sarcastically said 'Jonathan Miller wants to be a chemist and not a theatrical cult. I back his judgement.' Spare them a thought, then, and don't compare them to Stephen Fry, because that isn't really fair on him either.

Well... no, actually, they still have a show to do. So after a day of intellectually draining and physically demanding work, deprived of sleep and most likely food and drink as well, the performers have to throw themselves into the equally draining, physical and intellectual task of performing. Doing the Fringe genuinely has the potential to be the hardest people have ever had to work, unless they happen to be in the employ of the SAS, or perhaps working for the Home Office*.

In fact, it's not always like that. It really depends when you are performing. For morning shows, you have to get up frightfully early, then it's all out of the way for the day. You still won't get to shag like rabbits: you just do all the busy bits in a different order. If you want to shag like rabbits, do it in your spare time. Some people manage that as well, but how they get the energy we're not sure...

And it's not as if the shows themselves are ever plain sailing. The Fringe is full of idiosyncrasies resulting from it being, in short, mad. It's the largest assembled group of Fringe performances anywhere, in addition to which each venue will add its own idiosyncrasies just because they can. Throw in a load of thespians with extra idiosyncrasies and you're in for a pretty idiosyncratic time.

The following information about the way shows work might, hopefully will, act as some kind of cushion to lessen the shock of the reality for performers going to the Fringe. It might also help non-performers understand why some of what they see – before, during and after shows – is quite so, well... , idiosyncratic.

---

*At least one of us here is trying to justify our entire life to our family, who still think that all they're doing is dossing around.

Warm venues

Perhaps it was inaccurate to suggest that the casts of Edinburgh shows don't get time for a sauna, because in many cases they are treated to one every day, along with their audiences. Although Scotland has a reputation for being wet and cold, Edinburgh in August is often warm and sunny, or at least humid. The venues do not offer any chance to escape the heat; in fact, they very effectively collect it. Most of them were never designed as theatrical spaces, so were not built with large sweaty audiences and hot theatre lights in mind. This is exacerbated by the fact that they are all efficiently insulated with the heavy black drapes that are used to disguise whatever purpose the venue originally had. Air conditioning, it seems, has yet to be discovered in Scotland.

Everyone thinks that their venue is the warmest, but you'll always find a warmer one. The upshot of this is, you can see or take part in a show and get your pores thoroughly cleared of gunk at the same time.

As if this undesirable situation takes the venues completely by surprise each year, it always takes them a while to respond to the crisis. When relief comes, it is invariably in the form of noisy whirring fans that make a barely perceptible difference to the heat while causing an extremely noticeable disturbance throughout the performance.

So, if going to a show, think ahead and dress appropriately. Wear something cool, bring a bottle of water and maybe a fan*. Actors, do some voice exercises to assist you when you're competing with an orchestra of electric fans... and wash your clothes occasionally.

Getting in and getting out

One of the important features of all venues is the way they manage to cram so many shows into one day by having them virtually back to back. So, as if it wasn't already hard enough putting on a show in the distinctive high-pressure atmosphere of the Fringe, people end up setting up everything for it in under five minutes, at the same time as another show is getting all of its things

---
*For our shows, wear something skimpy, bring a bottle of something, and maybe a friend.

out of the way. For shows involving a lot of props, big sets and complex technical set-ups, it is particularly nightmarish. It seems even more unfair if your show is fairly simple but you're screwed over by the show before you having a huge plaster-of-Paris fireplace, seven chandeliers, a lighting rig imported from Broadway and a donkey, the removal of which is delayed every night by the number of encores the donkey insists on doing. However much the sweaty men moving the fireplace and chandeliers grunt and puff to imply that they're working really hard, your show is still going to start late.

So, here are a few handy tips for performers, to ensure that you avoid upsetting other people or getting upset yourself:

- Before even going to the Fringe, consider quite whether you need that stuffed elephant or whether the naked lesbian witches will look all right without it. If a prop is unnecessary, you will grow to hate it so irrationally that it is bound to be 'accidentally' lost by somebody in the end anyway.
- If your show overruns, especially if it does it consistently, you will piss off everyone: the shows after you (all of them), the audiences for the shows after you, and your venue – the last of which is perfectly able and entitled to fine you money. The timings you are given by the venue are important, make sure your show fits them.
- Generally, wait for the show before you to be out of the venue before you start getting in, otherwise everyone just gets cross.
- Don't get cross.
- Work out exactly who in the cast and crew is responsible for moving what, to make the most of the short amount of time available for getting in and getting out.
- Really, don't get cross. Even when the audience waiting to be let in peers at you in amusement as if this is all part of the entertainment.

If you are just an audience member, you can naturally just peer in amusement at the people in the show you're about to see rushing around like madmen – it's all part of the entertainment.

Keeping it fresh

Learning to keep performances fresh time after time is part of what being a professional is all about, but the extreme pressures of the Fringe arguably make it even harder. That is one of the things that makes Edinburgh such a famously good training ground for young hopefuls.

It is a pity, though, that the non-show bits of the Fringe so often have a detrimental effect on the show. It's pretty much unavoidable, but it's a pity. Fringe performers develop all sorts of ideas to try to combat Fringe-fatigue and keep the shows fresh, using any number of thespy games, from infinite variations on the game 'tag' to shouty games involving made-up words. The problem is, these exercises get as tired and dull as doing the show itself, so you need to keep coming up with new ones. Here are some ideas for keeping people fresh:

- Performers almost invariably need some kind of 'space' before going on stage. That sounds like an thespy excuse for actors to have a hissy fit, but it is well worth ensuring that before you go on stage you take a few minutes to yourself to get into the right frame of mind. This can be difficult at the Fringe, given previous notes about flyering before shows and the tightness of getting in, and putting aside that important few minutes for the cast will probably require careful planning. But, as with living arrangements, failing to take account of the need for personal space can have disastrous effects – onstage there's no space for a cell.

- Massage each other. Everyone can do a basic shoulder massage, and the back is pretty much the same, just leave the spine alone. This helps relax everyone and creates a warm, bubbly feeling of team bonding which, hopefully, counters some of the stressful wanting-to-kill-each-other that can develop over the course of the Fringe. If you're brave, or your cast are very hygienic, you could also try a foot massage now and then, to try to relieve all that standing (standing, standing) while handing out flyers. (We witnessed Adam Hills giving Mark Watson a foot massage during one of the latter's shows, and it not only looked like a soothing experience and a great reliever of tension, it was also hugely erotic.)

Musical chairs

Here's something you might try if you're after new ways of invigorating a cast before a show: musical chairs. This was something our group stumbled on towards the end of our first year at the Fringe, with remarkable results. Perhaps it was just the simple childish fun of dancing round chairs in a vaguely competitive manner, but it made us all feel a lot happier and the show which followed felt a lot less like work. You can spice up your game of musical chairs by playing it as characters – the default position is to play it as six-year-old kids, but it is even more fun as elderly people, or animals, or pirates, or our favourite, which is German tourists. Musical chairs solves many problems (how much more might be achieved by politicians if before any important meeting they took five minutes, to play it?) and can be enjoyed by anybody at the Fringe, not just performers.

- If you have problems with something that is happening in the show, especially if it is somebody in the show, don't leave it until immediately before the show to voice your concerns. These things are much better discussed over a post-show drink (see below). It's much nicer to say positive things before a show, even if you're lying.
- Sleep is a great healer, so make sure you get some. Some people don't realise quite how much tiredness is getting to them until they've slept it off. So, if you're constantly grumpy and not performing as well as you think you could, try getting a couple of extra hours' kip before resorting to popping pills.
- Tempting though it is to cope with shows by getting drunk before them, this will make everybody else very cross. Get drunk after the show.
- Don't get cross.

During the show

It's very simple: whether you are performing or spectating, enjoy it. It's the reason you're at the Fringe, so you might as well get something out of it.

If you genuinely are having such a terrible time that you want to leave, do it in a blackout. It will only upset people if they see you. (We mean if you're in the audience. If you are involved in the show you will upset people when they *don't* see you. If you're actually in the show then it's better to leave in a big, ostentatious manner so that it looks like it's part of the show. But you will still be loathed and hated by all your colleagues afterwards.)

Post-show discussion

It is vital, if doing a show for three weeks under extreme pressure, to talk about it. It sounds obvious, but some people still get it wrong and end up with all sorts of medical issues as a result.

Many shows, of course, have a director who can organise discussions, but directors don't always stay at the Fringe for the entire run, and some shows are not even blessed with one anyway. Either way, it is advisable to build into your routine a time to discuss shows. You should have one person (a director or whoever) act as a 'chair' to ensure that the discussion is focussed and constructive so as not to upset people. Sometimes it is nice to do this clutching a drink for comfort – or it may be better to save those for after the discussion as (a) an incentive to keep it short or (b) a restorative. The main thing is that everyone should stay friends.

Three Macbeths – Again

The Edinburgh Fringe gets bigger every year. As veteran Fringe performers will tell you, back in the good old days when it was a tiny event in a muddy field there were only twelve shows to choose from. Not so in the heady days of the twenty-first century. There are now more like 1,600 shows, and with more venues opening each year it seems likely that by 2010 there will be around 16,000. By 2050, scientists predict, the Festival Fringe will be so heavy that it will cause a catastrophic tilt to the earth's axis which will plunge Scotland into darkness and signal the end for the human race.

Even the most avid Fringe-goer could not hope to see every one of the shows on offer, or even get close. Those of us who prefer to take breaks between shows for food and the occasional restorative drink have to plan their schedule even more carefully, as do the poor sods actually doing shows themselves. So how do you even begin to choose which few shows you are actually going to pay money for at the risk of missing something much better only next door?

The first place to look is the Fringe brochure. This handy guide lists everything that is on over the course of the festival, detailing all the vital information such as locations and times, and helpfully split into the categories of children's, comedy, theatre, musical, dance, music and exhibition. It's standard procedure to go through the brochure before you even get to the Fringe and circle the shows that look as though they will interest you. This means picking out anything that looks like it is of a style that appeals to you – perhaps a lot of physical theatre, or musicals you're fond of, or stand-up comedy acts – and the shows that look as if they have an interesting concept; then pick out the shows being put on by groups or individuals reputed to be of a certain quality, as well as the ones that have a publicity design that catches your eye. Having done that, you usually find that you have circled almost everything except for the gay revue shows, which you maybe circle as well because there's no better place than the Fringe to see a gay revue show.

In any case, the Fringe brochure is of limited usefulness in finding out what a show will really be like and how good it might be. There are a few clues: bear in mind that the show descriptions are written by the people who are putting them on, so if an unknown comedy group claim to be 'wacky, zany loonies who will crease you up until you vomit!!!!!!' that is likely to be the level of the humour throughout the show. Similarly, a play that describes itself as 'Three witches. A new thane. The life of the Prime Minister is threatened as daily the terrorist threat from without deepens...but the greatest threat is within. A new terror. A terrorist who will kill his own – Macbeth is his name. In this new, physical production incorporating mime, dance, Beckett, improvisation, cookery and naked lesbians...' is likely to be very pretentious and rather mixed up. Even less guesswork is needed with performers or shows you already know about (so go see Bill Bailey if you like him, don't go to Jimmy Carr's show, etc.).

However, the Fringe would be a boring place indeed if people only went to see people they had heard of: the people who do best out of the Fringe are the people who take risks. (Yes, so are the people who do worst, but let's forget them for the moment.) We have seen professionals give perfectly enjoyable performances at the Edinburgh Fringe: we saw Christian Slater in *One Flew Over the Cuckoo's Nest* and the South African group Amajuba perform their beautiful play *Like Doves We Rise*. As parts of the Fringe grow increasingly professional these polished, 'big' shows are easy to find. Venues such as the Pleasance have almost become the professional London comedy circuit, and lots of quality theatre from around the world is transplanted to Scotland for a month, so it is possible to spend whole weeks in one of these venues and see many fine shows each day. However, we could have seen either of those shows at the West End in the months that followed. Similarly, any comedian that you recognise will almost certainly be touring elsewhere when the Fringe is done and dusted. They're not really what the Fringe is about, after all, and none of them has the magic or uniqueness of *Mark Watson's 24-Hour Show* in 2004, the few truly successful pieces of experimental theatre we've seen in Edinburgh, or of unexpectedly brilliant pieces of new writing such as John Finnemore's *Tails You Lose*.

Not a single one of the most memorable shows we've seen was a sure-fire hit. Sitting down in a church hall to watch some amateur singers do staged performances of Britten's canticles brought with it an overwhelming sense of terror at the realisation of how awful it was almost certainly going to be. When it turned out to be a beautifully sung, superbly staged production, the reward was not only a great sense of relief but also the smug satisfaction at having discovered a jewel that, a few elderly ladies aside, nobody else in the world was aware of.

Similarly, a *Guardian* reviewer on the lookout for bad comedy came to our own show on the basis that 'it's almost impossible to go right with improv' and, possibly with a degree of journalistic exaggeration, claimed to have 'never been so disappointed'. Whether you go out hoping to find something 'actually, properly, non-ironically great' or are looking for the opposite in the perverse way that *Guardian* reviewers do, the chances of disappointment are high; but the risk is worth it for the times when you strike gold. Of course, some of the best things at the Fringe will be discovered and revealed to a wider audience; but some won't, and some things (such as the *24-Hour Show*) are unrepeatable.

In order to limit damage and take educated risks, you are recommended to do a little research about shows before going to see them. There are three main sources of information about what is on: reviews, the people in the shows themselves and the word on the street.

Reviews are very useful for shows to take snippets from quotes and put them out of context on their posters as a publicity ploy (see earlier). A cross-section of reviews might give you a consensus as to the general quality of any given show, but they are, of course, the opinions of individuals, and one man's inspired piece of cutting-edge physical theatre is another man's dance-music-fuelled strobe nightmare. You are best advised to read reviews... and then ignore them. Two-thirds of all people disagree with every review anyway. (Especially the people who have been given bad ones.)

People doing shows are unlikely to say anything negative about what they are in, but since they are in the show they are talking about, they are at least in a pretty good position to give you a rough idea of what it contains. They are also always more than willing to talk to anyone, so it's not a bad idea to have a conversation with the person waving a flyer in your face. Just don't take it as gospel when they tell you it's an inspired piece of cutting-edge physical theatre.

The best way to find out about shows is to listen to what everyone else is talking about. Shows that are either brilliant or truly dreadful provide hours worth of conversation, so if everyone is talking about a show, it's a fairly safe bet that it's going to be for one of those reasons. Shows that get good audiences often do so because of word of mouth, and it's well worth listening out for what other people have seen and enjoyed.

Even then, you can't be sure. That's the fun of it. But with a little received wisdom you can usually minimise the amount of rubbish you sit through, and ensure that you see at least a couple of genuinely good shows.

Naturally, everyone has their own preferences for the kind of show they would like to see, and this is where the Fringe brochure's categories of children's, comedy, theatre, musical, dance, music and exhibition fall down. They're pretty vague categories to begin with, and when half of the stuff at the Fringe is, by definition, indefinable, many shows end up simply choosing the section that they feel will bring in the biggest audience, or failing that fits as closely as possible. Anyone who has struggled to decide whether their improvised musical drama with a comedy vein is comedy, theatre or musical will know what we mean. Many people just plump for 'theatre' because that's such a vague term it can mean just about anything.

So, to aid you in choosing shows with a little more accuracy, here is a rather more thorough (though not exhaustive) guide to the types of show you might expect to find at the Fringe.

Shakespeare

There is Shakespeare a-plenty every year at the Fringe. The source material is usually promising (except *Merry Wives of Windsor*). But few of the people performing it are RSC-trained, experienced, or Ian McKellen. As a result, you should not go for the sake of the performances, but for the directorial interpretation; for some reason, most directors want to make their Shakespeare as messy as possible, so try to see the productions pushing the limits of what can be done with fake blood, food and excrement. The *Macbeth* to go to is, without a doubt, the one with the naked lesbian witches.

New writing

The Fringe is the perfect place for wannabe writers to get their masterpieces in front of an audience – and just because writers are unknown is no reason to assume that their work is rubbish. Equally, there's no reason to believe that it will be good. Some of our most pleasurable Fringe experiences have been with new plays, and it's well worth seeing what's available – this is where word of mouth really comes into its own, but you can also check out the writer's previous credits (which will almost certainly be scattered across the flyer for the show if they are any good).

'Devised theatre'

Usually, the word 'devised' suggests that a bunch of actors have been cooped up in a rehearsal room for several weeks playing theatre games and have eventually pushed some of their more successful experiments together to form a bizarre, incomprehensible montage. If the actors are any good it could be pure gold; otherwise, it could be hilarious or it could be excruciating. Watch out for devised pieces created by A-level drama students, as these are only fifteen minutes long.

Monologues

What is the appeal of watching an amateur actor talking on their own for up to an hour? Answer: none. Unless you are looking at a professional production, avoid monologues at all costs. Lacking the ambitious directorial frippery that usually accompanies group theatre, monologues can only offer you a false accent of some sort (the amusement value of which quickly wears off) and a tedious rendition of what might have once been a good piece of writing. Fifteen minutes feels like a whole day. Don't be tempted, not even if the monologue in question is by one of your favourite writers – they will not be your favourite any more by the time the whole thing finishes.

Some groups get clever and, if it's a female monologue, have lots of sexy girls with daringly-cut T-shirts handing out their fliers. They won't be in the show and that's the last glimpse of appealing flesh you'll see – enjoy the publicity team, skip the production.

Stand-up

A staple of comedy and of the Fringe, stand-up shows give you the chance to see your favourite comedians live (if you can get a ticket before they all sell out) and see people that you have never heard of being either unexpectedly brilliant or less so. Avoid sitting through three hours of stand-up by people you've never heard of – an hour is a good length, and unless they've got good previous reviews it should be an hour of several different people.

Comedy shows involving projectors

Once upon a time it was an exciting and novel idea to use a projector to pep up what was otherwise a stand-up comedy show. In much the same way as lectures must have seemed more exciting when the overhead projector was invented, it seemed to herald in a new age of multimedia comedy.

Now, every other comedy show uses a projector and it just feels as if you are going to a lot of lectures.

Comedy groups

The Fringe has long been the arena for hopeful comedy groups to do their thing in the hope of being spotted, and as well as listening out for what is being said about them, you could also look to see who has been nominated for a Perrier award, and of course ask around to find out if the group in question already has a reputation for being any good. Sometimes, reputation can really work against some comedy names – the Cambridge Footlights could put on the funniest show ever, but some tosser will always comment that they're not as good as Stephen Fry was, and even big-name stand-ups change their material eventually. Like investments, past performance is no guarantee of, well, anything.

As well as spotting talent, the Fringe plays the necessary role of allowing people who think that they are funny to discover that they are not. So be especially careful when judging what to see. If you think that the three sweaty men from Kent look like they might not quite be the League of Gentlemen, you are probably right. In fact, probably best to avoid sweaty men altogether.

Improv

Contrary to what embittered writers sometimes tell you ('grrr, I slave away at this keyboard for days and they think they can make it up…') improvisation is a serious art-form with an abundance of theorists, practitioners and groups who do it very well indeed. It flourishes in the experimental atmosphere of the Fringe; being improv, you never know what you're going to get, but if you go and see an established group you're likely to get an enjoyable show. There are, alas, people who do improvisation less well and who have no doubt contributed to the hatred it sometimes engenders; some may even be quite well-known television personalities, adept at ejaculating a quick one-liner or going off on a self-indulgent surreal digression, but not in the same league as the people who have studied and practised it to a level at which they can coherently make up an entire play on the spot.

There are many different types of improv, with variants and gimmicks, such as improvised musicals, improvised soaps, even improvised films. In fact, the less gimmicky the concept, the more likely you are to see something frighteningly good and intense, although that is no reason to avoid the gimmicky ones. The main differences are between people who are doing improvised games (such as on *Whose Line is it Anyway* – in the technical jargon, theatresports), usually aiming for comedy and sometimes every bit as good as a sketch show, and narrative improv, done by groups who are essentially trying to make up a whole play on the spot. Narrative improv can result in almost anything at all, with as much potential to be edgy and dramatic as it has to be funny. American improvisation tends to be more structured and therefore slicker, albeit more predictable than

European improvisation, which is usually considerably weirder.

As a Fringe experience, improvised shows are generally recommended because at worst they will be genuinely unpredictable and they may be great. As a general rule of thumb, if the reviews say that it must be scripted, it's good improvisation (because nobody scripts a show then says it's improvised: it actually doesn't happen), whereas if the reviews say it's hilarious and will 'no doubt be different every night!' it's bad improvisation, because it's obvious that it's improvised.

Children's

Although for some people doing a children's show at the Fringe is a way of getting away with shoddy work while having a guaranteed audience, there are some superb children's shows at the Edinburgh Fringe each year and it's worth looking out for the ones by established performers. You don't have to be a child to see them.

Musicals

Musicals usually guarantee good audiences, and there are plenty to choose from every year. It is advisable to make sure that you know who is performing them, because there's nothing worse than watching a group of nine-year-old nuns doing *Cabaret*.

Often the musicals that stand out at the Fringe are the new ones. Of course, there's no guarantee that that a new musical will be any good, but the same is true at the West End, and at the Fringe you'll find a considerably wider selection of extremely novel ideas. At the end of the day, even crappy musicals are fun, so if you like the title it's probably worth going to.

Operas

Real, proper operas are more within the remit of the Edinburgh International Festival, and being rather hard to pull off it perhaps isn't surprising that they're less common in the Fringe. If you do come across one, we suggest you assess it in pretty much the same way as you would a musical, paying particular attention to who is actually singing. Because there's nothing worse than watching a group of nine-year-old nuns doing *The Marriage of Figaro*.

Concerts

It's not just theatre at the Fringe! Several musical ensembles, soloists and singers put on a selection of fine musical concerts. Some are well-known, some less so, but with music it's considerably easier to tell how good a performance is likely to be from the credits of the performer in question.

At the Fringe you sometimes find unusual and experimental approaches to performance. To pull in the crowds the concert may include breakfast or some kind of wacky staging not usually associated with the music in question. As with anything at the Fringe, tread carefully: nobody likes hearing good music massacred for the sake of a croissant, but what could be a nicer rest from all those frantic thespians than a good bit of Mozart?

Shows with 'project' in the title

Two types of show seem to have the word 'project' in the title: cross-genre music (generally very good if you like at least one of the genres) and experimental theatre pieces that are not really finished and perhaps shouldn't ever be. Any work in progress should be approached with care, as it may turn out to be a man shuffling round the stage reading out unconnected facts in an effort to make sense of his own life – not that the Fringe isn't the right place to do it, of course. The best advice we can give here is to be very wary and try to talk to someone who has actually seen it – if it's great they'll certainly want to share that with you. Interestingly, none of this applies to shows with the word 'experiment' in the title, which tend to be complete shows that make sense.

Performance poetry

Performance poetry is growing in popularity, and while it is usually confined to circles of performance poets, at the Fringe they come out of their ghetto and unleash their work on the rest of us. W. H. Auden it may not be, but these are people who have something to say and are doing it in an unusual way. They're worth a listen, especially if they don't take themselves too seriously.

Shows involving celebrities

It's always nice to see someone you recognise from the television in a show, but among Fringe performers there's a slight feeling that these 'celebrity' shows, where a known performer is presumably getting paid a lot of money to pull in big audiences, are a little bit dirty – not quite right and certainly not in the spirit of a festival where everybody else is mortgaging their house in order to do shows in front of audiences of three people.

Shows involving fading celebrities

It is encouraging that people whose stage or television careers have now sunk without a trace are now finding some solace in doing month-long runs at the Edinburgh Fringe; it certainly beats two nights in Blackpool, being a chance to do a decent number of shows and possibly perform to audiences not entirely made up of fossils. However, because they are doing a proper run of shows, these fading celebrities have to do all the tedious publicity work that everyone else at the Fringe is doing. It is touching and heart-warming to see people who were once household names mingling with all the other hopeful performers on the Royal Mile in a desperate bid for audiences. It shows that they are serious about what they are doing; it's a return to the most challenging basic elements of their chosen careers, and they need our support.

On the other hand, there's usually a reason why they're no longer celebrities.

Cabaret

There are a number of cabarets running at the Fringe, many of which feature different performers from other shows each night, so if you want to sit back with a drink and watch a mixed bag of comedy, music and almost certainly performance poetry, a cabaret show can be a really good way of getting an overview of what's on.

Free shows

A few admirable groups of people have recently been seeking funding to run comedy/cabaret shows on a daily basis which you can just walk into. It appears to be a reaction against the über-professionalism that is growing up in the bigger Edinburgh venues, revitalising the more experimental, disorganised aspect of the Fringe, and this has gained support from several people who are regulars in the London circuit. There is no guarantee of quality, of course, but the same is true of any stand-up show you may pay £9–11 or more to see. You haven't lost anything at all if you go along to a free show. You may even find that they have more of the spontaneous fun that is associated with the Fringe than the larger, money-grabbing venues, although you may end up seeing shows that you would gladly pay to get out of.

Shows involving paint

They exist. We feel this kind of show might have developed as a result of a group of human statues deciding to do something constructive with their lives… and some paint. And let's face it, if a show involves flinging paint around, it's always going to be a noteworthy experience. However, unless some visionary director has managed to incorporate paint flinging into an actual play (perhaps a *Henry V* with audience participation… and paint) you have to ask yourself just how long it will be before the novelty of chucking paint around in a disposable boiler suit, which only keeps out about 30% of it, will wear off, and what else the hour-long experience will contain. (Possibly lesser humiliations, such as chucking around plastic balls and hitting people

Comedy facts

An issue of *Fest* once published the following humbling statistics in the comedy section. Quite how funny they thought it would be is really not clear from the tongue-in-cheek tone of the article, but, nevertheless, the facts themselves are worth repeating.

The price of an average Fringe ticket is £9.50 and it costs 14p to feed one child in Africa for a day. The cost of one ticket would therefore feed a child for 68 days. The average Fringe audience is 107, so the ticket takings from one audience would feed a child for 20 years, or 7,276 children for a day; and if every festival-goer saw just one show, the takings would feed every child in Botswana for two years.

It's worth remembering that while a huge amount of money is spent each year so that people can go poor and hungry at the Fringe, on the other side of the world there are people doing it for absolutely free... and not just for three weeks.

with pieces of rubber, while being encouraged by bizarrely costumed actors to run around screaming like a child.) We say this not to put you off, but to suggest the kind of frame of mind you will need to be in to get the most out of the experience.

Have a drink... or a few.

Oddities

There are always shows at the Fringe that are so unusual that they defy any definition at all: plays that take place in cars or lifts, shows with unusually long or short duration times, high-concept ideas using food, low-concept ideas using sex. It's pointless giving actual examples because every Fringe is different – use your imagination (and if you come up with something really novel you should probably do it yourself). Find these shows and go to them. There's no guarantee that they'll be anything other than awful, but what's the point of being at the Fringe if you don't try out the weirdest things available?

French/Irish singers

You can only hope to be lucky enough to find a bravura singer doing melodramatic songs in strange costumes. Such singers are in such a different league from anything else that they are beyond considerations such as the allotted running time for their show. Sure, it may cause some inconvenience to the show following them if their encores continue twenty minutes after the next show is supposed to have started. Sure, selling their CDs in the venue entrance may block out any potential audience the show following them might have had if they were going to be able to start anything like promptly. In short, the kind of singer we're talking about will fuck around with any other performer near them, but that's okay because as long as they're doing well and selling enough CDs to break even, who cares if the poor sods sharing the venue with them are bereft of audiences and being bankrupted in the process?

Gay shows

Gay shows, or at least those involving gay iconography, always seem to be popular at the Fringe. They often seem to be more in the nature of circus acts or freak shows but since Edinburgh's gay scene is in many ways not entirely dissimilar, that's not inappropriate, and there's a lot of fun to be had here for people of all sexualities. Only in Edinburgh have we seen a gay Japanese Elvis impersonator doing a comedy routine about getting combs stuck in his chest hair, and for that reason alone it's worth chancing. Just don't expect it to be erotic.

Burlesque

Imagine the most horrific thing you can envisage on a stage. Then multiply it by ten and add nipple tassels. What you are left with is a show that can assault, rape and sully you. A show that can leave permanent emotional scars. A show that you could only enjoy if you were a repressed Victorian gentleman in a foreign country with several gallons of tequila inside you.

Distressingly, there appear to be a large number of people at the Fringe in this very state of mind.

If you are the kind of person who is turned on by fake penises and who doesn't mind that the most talented thing on display is a glitter ball, then that's fine. You may well enjoy a night leering at foreign women in obscene costumes. But if you are an ordinary, twenty-first century theatre-lover, we cannot warn you away from this kind of thing strongly enough.

It may be that their posters brightly claim that 'burlesque is back'; it may be that they are selling out; it may be that one of your friends gets back late at night all breathless and drunk claiming it was 'the most fun ever!!!!!!'

Don't do it.

How do people live? (And how to crash their parties)

When asked why he kept coming back to the Edinburgh Fringe, one of our friends wondered, 'Is it the atmosphere? Is it the sheer variety of things? Is it the chance to perform your work, experimental as it might be, to a wider audience? Or is it the fact that the bars are open late?' Probably the latter.

Or, as the irrepressible Carola Stewart succinctly put it, 'it's a permanent party really, isn't it?' (It being her first time at the Fringe for twenty years, she was also convinced that it had grown twenty times as lively in her absence.)

That, essentially, is the nature of the Fringe: one great big long party. As with any party, there are practical considerations, such as who is going to go out and get another packet of hula hoops, whose turn it is to buy more alcopops, and who is going to empty the bins and clean the carpet. As with any party there are peaks and troughs: low points where everyone seems to conk out and high points where a new wave of gatecrashers arrive and the police turn up. And as with any party it is very important that you are in the right place, whether it's the kitchen where everyone is comparing chest hair, on the doorstep where everyone is smoking illegal substances or in the conservatory where somebody has just whacked on some Kylie.

Importantly, as with any party you must also ensure that you are really involved – not the person in the living room reading a book and wondering what everyone else is doing, and not the girl crying on the stairs.

Fortunately, the metaphor rarely stretches to your dad arriving at the Fringe in his dressing gown to take you home. But if you're going to the Fringe, there are ways to make sure you get a decent slice of that party and don't miss out on the essence of its unique atmosphere.

Lifestyle

Essentially, apart from all the publicity and performing already mentioned, the Fringe lifestyle is parties.

Well, not quite. Performers obviously establish some way of living, depending on the kind of accommodation they are sharing and how many of them there are. In an ideal world, the place where they are staying is a relaxed haven, away from the stresses and strains of the rest of the Fringe, a quiet, personal space where each performer can spend a little time each day eating, drinking, sleeping, listening to music…

The Fringe is not an ideal world, though. It is more likely that the place where they are staying is just as stressful as the outside world, being full of angsty artistes arguing about who owes how much money for the lager that has somehow disappeared in one evening when it was meant to last a week, or different people trying to get out of cooking, cleaning and washing even though it is clearly their turn on the rota.

The occasional nights-in-with-a-video and relaxing-discussions-with-drinks are usually more than outweighed by cooking calamities, hissy fits and long, tedious meetings in which every sentence is preceded by the words, 'I know what you're saying, but... ' It is a difficult existence and finding things to lift spirits and sugar the sickly medicine of the Fringe is hard – inevitably, things have to move in the direction of parties, because parties are the only possible solution to all the problems... and there are a lot of parties.

Official parties

There are a number of events put on for Fringe participants by Fringe organisers, venues and sponsors. Any of the bigger venues will almost certainly have some sort of party arranged, and as a rule the better the venue, the better the party. However, you must remember that these are parties arranged *en masse* for a motley crew of different performers of different ages and the only point of these parties is to try to force these unlikely bedfellows into doing a little bit of bonding (well, that and making the venue look good) – so they are usually excruciating. Think of a school disco with Smarties trodden into the floor, sticky vaguely-alcoholic-but-foul-tasting punch in plastic cups and people awkwardly leaning on the walls trying not to make eye contact with anyone, especially the few gawky people dancing badly in the middle of the room. Not all venue parties are that bad, but a lot of them get very close.

Also, these parties are often at the beginning of the Fringe when everyone is still terribly excited about what is still a novel situation of being at the Fringe and in a show, so if you actually try to have a conversation with anybody you don't know it will be along these lines:

You: Hello, my name's [*insert your name here*].
Them: Oh wow, oh really great to meet you [*insert your name here*]! I'm [*insert their name here*].
You: Hello [*insert their name here*]. So, you're performing at this venue are you?
Them: Yes, that's right! And... you're performing here as well?

You: Indeed I am!

Them: Oh wow, that's so cool. Yeah. So what are you doing?

You: Well, it's [*insert lengthy description of your show here*].

Them Nods and smiles with a fixed, glazed grin, failing to be in the least bit intrigued or interested by what you are doing, clearly just waiting for an opportunity to leap in with vital information about their own show.

Finally you pause for breath.

Them: Oh yeah wow, that sounds so cool, well I'm doing [*insert considerably lengthier description of their show here*].

You stand listening to them nodding and smiling with a fixed, glazed grin, not taking any of it in and waiting for the first excuse to get away and top up your plastic cup with sickly, foul-tasting and barely-alcoholic punch…

Some venues admirably try to continue the feeling of goodwill by having additional events programmed into the Fringe, maybe halfway through or in the last week when people are getting a little jaded. Unfortunately, people have also wised up to how to have a good time by then, and they know that going to venue parties is not it. Tempting as the Hawaiian Smurf Party or Saints and Cross Dressing Party look (and don't let us talk you out of trying it), you should probably go with some friends and be prepared to slip out to a nearby pub instead at a moment's notice. Similarly, although crashing venue parties is a doddle (nobody is going to check who you are and what you think you're doing there, and if you're worried you can always make something up about a believably pretentious-sounding show – you can bet nobody will even listen to what you're saying anyway) you will probably be disappointed.

The Fringe launch party

One exception to all of these rules is the official Fringe launch party. As a big Fringe event with sponsors behind it, they tend to find a respectable venue and throw enough money at it to make it worthwhile. There are usually even a few freebies – generally of a plastic, glow-in-the-dark nature but that's better than nothing. One year they handed out ice-creams. The girls handing them out were all dressed as fairies with plastic tiaras; we approached a particularly sulky-looking fairy and persuaded her to give us her tiara. One of us still has it, so in a strictly material sense alone there is plenty to be gained from this party.

It is also not a bad party. Not a great party – but it has potential. It's still full of self-obsessed thespians who will insist on talking about their shows but, unlike the venue parties, the music is usually loud enough for you to be able to ignore them completely. Taking along flyers and trying to actively publicise your show is frowned upon by everyone – don't even attempt it, you will be laughed at, spat at and crucified – so it is actually possible to enjoy it as a proper party.

Entertainment of various sorts is generally laid on, sometimes including performances from some of the more flamboyant, all-singing, all-dancing shows and usually dissolving into more of a club atmosphere (perhaps with a Fringey twist such as a stage full of drummers hammering out the rhythms to your favourite dance music in a way that will either enhance it for you or make you intensely angry).

The set-up provides great opportunity for self-obsessed thespians to show off; one year, God help us, there was even karaoke laid on. Whether you find this amusing or insufferable is very much a matter of personal temperament, though speaking personally there's nothing more fun than leaping up in the middle of a crowd of people who think they're brilliant and trying to be even more brilliant. See it as a challenge. Speaking of challenges, though, this is the party that it really is genuinely difficult to crash. This is logical: if it was easy to crash it wouldn't be worth crashing. And it is worth crashing, for all the above-mentioned reasons and the fact that you are fairly likely to meet some interesting people from across the Fringe. Unfortunately, the Fringe organisers are very strict about the number of tickets each show is entitled to – understandable, given the huge number of performers at the Fringe – and there is tight security on the doors to ensure only people with tickets get in. You're never going to bluff your way in by pretending you're important; your best bet if you're crashing is to go dressed as a fairy with a tiara and pretend you're meant to be serving ice-creams.

James Lark at the Fringe launch party

James dances with not unattractive girl on the strangely-shaped dancefloor. She is into the music, he is merry to the point of distraction.

Girl: Are you on some kind of mission?

James (bemused): Why do you ask?

Girl: It's just the way you're dressed.

James (pausing for thought): It's just... how I like to dress...

Girl: So... do you have any cigarettes?

James: Err... no, I think it's a filthy habit. I... (searches in his pocket, and brings out a glow stick) ... I'd like you to have this.

Girl (grinning from ear to ear): Really? That's lovely! Finish my beer.

Her boyfriend appears.

Boy: I wouldn't trust anything she gives you.

James (backing away): Um...

Boy: Nice crown.

James: Actually it's a tiara.

Parties put on by shows

'Why do we have parties anyway?' one of us mused in the notebook we kept around the house to express our deepest thoughts late at night. 'It's to distract us from the real party which is life.' Somebody else has scribbled in pencil next to this profundity, 'No, it's for the booze'.

Either way, only the dullest groups at the Fringe are going to pass up the opportunity to use their rented accommodation for some sort of knees-up. When you consider the number of groups at the Fringe and the fact that many of them know each other and don't want their respective parties to coincide, you can deduce that there will be a party going on somewhere in Edinburgh every night of the Fringe. In some parts of Edinburgh, in particular, where several flats share one staircase, this can get quite complicated – more than one party may be happening in close proximity, and it's easy to get lost. Several years ago, some friends of ours were having an impromptu toga party, which collided with an impromptu Perrier party. We haven't heard from one of the participants since.

These affairs are rarely like ordinary house parties. In the party atmosphere that is the Fringe, everybody is already partying pretty hard as it is, so when they actually have a party they're going to make damn sure that it's even more so.

How do they do that? The simplest way is to make sure that everyone turns up to it and then to supply them with a lot to drink. It's a very basic approach, but assuming you get a decent pick of Fringe performers with their own idiosyncrasies it rarely fails.

We always go for a more individual approach with our parties. There are many ways of spicing up a party – giving it a theme with optional costumes always breaks the ice and sticking on the soundtrack to *Mary Poppins* and recreating all the best bits of choreography provides a fitting climax*.The main thing is to make sure that the drink flows freely until everyone has left, and not the other way round.

It is more than likely that you will be invited to many parties if you make any kind of effort to meet people while you are at the Fringe; however, if you're just visiting for a few days and want a party to go to, or happen to be at a loss without any specific party planned, finding out where there is a party is simply a matter of keeping your ear to the ground, or better still in the air when you're in a densely Fringe-performer-populated area. Invitations to any house party go out willy-nilly to pretty much anyone who seems interesting, so conversations along the lines of 'you seem interesting, what's your name again? By the way we're having a party tonight…' happen everywhere.

Because party invitations go out pretty much indiscriminately, crashing them is pure simplicity. Even if they have such a thing as a 'guest-list', no Fringe performer worth meeting is going to be boring and turn you away at the doorstep. If you're worried, wear something sexy, or unusual or a clever combination of the two, because Fringe performers like that sort of thing.

We certainly had guest lists for our parties, but they were abandoned at a very early stage of the evening, and what a good job they were because the best parties always end up full of complete strangers. We left a visitor book for everyone to write in, and one of our guests left us an intriguing note (see opposite).

We don't know who Toshi is, or what her message means (if anyone can enlighten us we would be grateful, though we are hoping it doesn't turn out to be something rubbish like 'lovely party!' – there seem to be a lot of exclamation marks so we hope it's a bit raunchy) but it's a great achievement to acquire a gatecrasher who doesn't even write in the same language.

---

*The authors accept no responsibility for breakages suffered during *Over The Rooftops*.

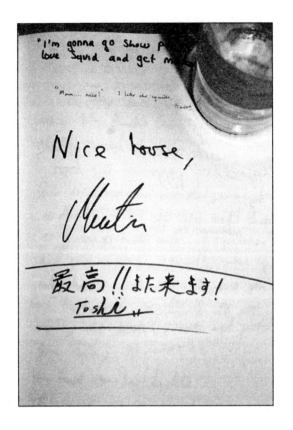

The best possible reason to crash parties put on by shows is that it is a superb chance to meet all sorts of unexpected people. At one party, which we didn't so much crash as stumble into, we found ourselves talking to a pretty, intelligent and very pissed girl who was also performing – we don't recall what she was in, but she did tell us she was a singer, so we asked her if she wanted to perform in our cabaret show and she scribbled her number on the back of a receipt. Yes! We went away with a girl's number: that's how successful it was. She didn't have a clue who we were when we phoned her in the morning, but sure enough, she sang in our cabaret show on several occasions after that and turned out to be astonishingly talented and quite the consummate crowd-pleaser. We have stayed in touch ever since and although she hasn't ever married either of us it is proof of the lasting value of Fringe parties. She was also in a short film in which she vomited up a Chihuahua, something we don't imagine we would have witnessed if we'd stayed in bed instead of going to a party.

Let's not give the wrong impression – there is a time to go to bed, and we do have to be sensible about this, it's just that it might not be during August.

Performer bars

If you happen to pop along to the Brooke Club in Pleasance Dome of an evening during the Fringe and manage to bluff your way into the slightly exclusive performers' bar, you will discover an intriguing crowd of people whiling the night away. Some of them will be quite well-known, usually for their involvement in the field of comedy. Others are young hopefuls who naively believe that by chatting excitedly to the 'personalities' around them they will open up opportunities for themselves in the comedy world. Of course, almost everyone is actually there just to get pissed, and in the morning won't remember a single thing about the fresh-faced youngsters they've been talking to. Even the ones in the Cambridge Footlights.

It's well worth trying to bluff your way into. You may not have the choice of being a 'personality', but you do have the choice not to be a fresh-faced young hopeful, and that's a start. Looking like a fresh-faced hopeful who wants to further their career by talking to celebrities is the quickest way to be refused entry to any exclusive bar. Looking like a celebrity, on the other hand, is precisely how to get in. Don't worry too much about the man on the door: you're famous. Perhaps wave a train ticket at him as proof that you're perfectly entitled to be there, but don't stop to look breathless and lost or you'll blow your cover. And don't, whatever you do, try to talk your way in – you think Dara O'Briain spends half an hour outside performer bars insisting, 'but I have been on television, just rather late at night…'? Of course he doesn't – not unless he's very drunk.

Looking as if you're a celebrity has other advantages once you're inside – some of the breathless young hopefuls might hedge their bets and come and chat you up, and you can always nod sagely and promise to put in a good word for them at the Beeb if they buy you a pint. In fact, you might even manage a conversation or two with someone who's been on Channel 5 on a Friday night, and pissed performers are, after all, a lot of fun (many base their stage performances on this understanding).

Just don't look too enthusiastic and don't start handing out flyers; they'll hate you.

How to do it without going mad, or: coping with going mad

Avoiding madness

Avoiding madness is probably preferable to madness, not just at the Edinburgh Fringe but in life generally, and avoiding madness at the Fringe is pretty much the same as avoiding madness the rest of the time, except that it's more likely to happen so you have to be more careful. The trick is not to get stuck in the close confines of the situation for long periods – without at least having breaks for tea, or better still G&T. Get out and meet people, go for walks, don't take larium. It's all simple stuff, but the kind of thing that gets forgotten when you're trying to publicise, perform in and promote a show with the same people for weeks on end.

How not to unravel at the Fringe
Jude Simpson

Taking a show to the Fringe is not just a financial drain and a professional risk, it's also an emotional rollercoaster. One day you're hanging out with Dave Gorman, getting calls from the BBC and feeling like an

A-list celebrity. The next, you have a one-star review, you've sold five tickets and you're praying that Dave Gorman was drunk last night and doesn't remember what you said about the goldfish and his …

Anyway, here are my tips for keeping your head when all around you have theirs either in the clouds or in their hands…

Know your critics. You will get a bad review at some stage and it will hurt. The best way to deal with a bad review is to have predicted it. Before going to Edinburgh, write down a few examples of what someone who didn't like your sort of show would write about it. Then, when they do write it, at least you have the satisfaction of not being surprised.

Take compliments with almost as much salt as criticism.

Walk up Arthur's seat at least once in the month. It's stunning… and good for perspective.

Have friends around who love you and rate your talent, but who will also occasionally go, 'Oh for goodness' sake, Jude, stop stressing about your show, shut up and chill. You are coming to Topping and Butch with us, like it or not'.

Don't accept guilt trips from anyone who is upset because you haven't seen their show – even if they came to see yours. They need to get a life.

Enjoy performing your show. Sounds obvious, but sometimes you forget.

Smile and be gracious whenever in public.

Yell/bitch/cry/box the walls as much as you need to in private.

Finally, remember that you are living your dreams – even when it doesn't feel like it. Festival-goers will look at you and think you have a glamorous life. That's probably overstating it, but even so, try not to disappoint them.

Jude Simpson (www.judesimpson.co.uk) is a performance poet who has worked on radio and has been highly acclaimed at poetry slams and the Edinburgh Fringe.

Nothing beats a nice wander up to Arthur's Seat (a big hill in the middle of Edinburgh) for giving you a different perspective. It is a popular place for people to wander, but the number of people per square inch is considerably fewer than anywhere else in Edinburgh. As you near the summit, you will see the whole of Edinburgh before you, all tiny and insignificant-looking next to the vast expanse of the sea, the familiar Fringe places teeny tiny dots in a huge country. All the bitching and moaning associated with the Fringe suddenly seems so insignificant and, confronted, with the beauty of the world and the glorious nature of being alive you are filled with an intense feeling of love for all your fellow humans – even the bastards singing that bloody 'standing standing' song on the Royal Mile.

Less than an hour later you can be back in the thick of it, with a dreamlike memory of something bigger already fading into the distance as a far more real dream about taking an ornamental sword to those bastards singing that bloody 'standing standing' song solidifies in your head. But who knows, perhaps the scant dreamlike hours of refuge offered by a bigger perspective has saved a few lives. If nothing else, it's a jolly nice way to spend a couple of hours.

A trip to the seaside is another possibility, especially if you happen to have a day off and a car. It is of course a peculiarly British thing to leap into untenably cold water in the pretence of having fun, and there's no better place to uphold the tradition than in Scotland. Whether it helps with madness or not, though, it is hard to say. At least we've never come across anyone in the sea singing that bloody 'standing standing' song.

Eating and cooking together

One thing that we've realised is that sitting around a table sharing food creates a nice family atmosphere. Yes, it may be a family atmosphere in which half of the people present are being rude to each other but we all grew up with that kind of family, and it makes for a safer, saner living space.

Cooking together also bonds people and adds to the feeling of solidarity, even if it is ultimately a joint feeling of suffering and failure, whereas cooking a shepherd's pie to feed ten people on your own can drive you insane over the course of an hour. At the end of the day, if you're cooking with people in a kitchen well-stocked with gin and vodka, if everything else goes wrong you can always skip food. Sit down; have a drink.

Bath time is anagram time

Our most successful way of avoiding madness, or at least controlling it and focussing it in a single space, was to purchase some spongy letters which were designed to stick to damp tiles in a bathroom. These were left in the bath one day by our publicity manager, as a kind of subtle hint that if we were going to go mad we should at least do it in a creative way while getting clean.

So, throughout the Fringe, we spent rather too long in the bath leaving messages for each other along the lines of 'bad james maims rude quack with robust nun – the lord' which might then be wittily changed to 'bad james maims quick roaduser with only ford – anon'. We vented such nonsense in the bath each day and spared each other the effort of listening to each other actually saying it. We also got very good at *Countdown*. A more enjoyable way of averting madness we cannot imagine and we believe that the Fringe Office should give spongy bath letters to all Fringe participants as a matter of course.

Their alluring nature was more than evident by the response they received at our party. We're aware that it is normal to have queues outside toilets at house parties, but not queues stretching down the street because somebody has locked themselves in and is running a bath to have a quick play with spongy bath letters. We couldn't get people into the rest of the house – we had a fridge full of beers, a living room full of Frank Sinatra, bedrooms all lined up to receive the couples we hoped to form over the course of the evening... and people wouldn't get out of the bathroom because of the spongy bath letters.

They didn't have our skill or subtlety, unfortunately. Just before the party we all had baths so were in a good position to know that the letters before guests were let into the house read 'fie laura – spoon me with waxy duck gunk and eat my scrotum' (the Laura in question is a good friend of ours and often featured in the spongy letters). By the time the guests left, the letters read 'hands of laura's toe'.

We applauded their enthusiasm, of course. But while the former is in iambic heptameter and considerably more literary in effect, the latter is meaningless.

Madness

It happens. Occasionally somebody in an Edinburgh cast is so overcome by the conflicting emotions and the crazy Fringe activity that they go bonkers.

Stalkers

Edinburgh attracts its share of crazy people, and of course among them will be people who believe that it's perfectly okay to wander round being terrifyingly creepy. Many, but not all, tend to get fixated on young, attractive women, and some of them collect restraining orders.

One of our friends, some years ago, unwittingly attracted the attentions of a stalker who was not only barmy but enterprisingly so. On top of the usual, run-of-the-mill, stalker activities (such as covering the walls of his flat with posters with her face on), at the end of the month he got in touch with the production company asking for her phone number.

Presumably at some point he actually stalked her, too.

We know this, because it happened to one of us. Well…, to some extent it happened to all of us, but one of us in particular was overcome by the Fringe atmosphere so much that all the innate eccentricity that forms a quirky part of his essentially rounded and loveable character leapt to the surface to create a monster.

Without pointing the finger, it was the younger, innately eccentric one. The older, wiser one cultivated a series of withering looks with which he managed to control some of the wilder urges of the younger one, at least for a few days. Unfortunately, after two weeks of the Fringe they were utterly ineffective. Stronger action had to be taken to hold back the increasingly all-consuming madness: a hushometer was constructed.

A hushometer is simply a chart on which can be recorded the number of times the word 'hush' is used to silence each member of the company. We had our faces on our publicity material that year, so with a bit of scissor work and some Blu-tac we constructed a visually pleasing and simple-to-use hushometer upon which each person's face would be moved up a notch whenever they were hushed.

The younger, innately eccentric one won by quite a large margin.

There are two lessons to be learned from this. First, that the hushometer, fun though it was, was not in any way an effective deterrent

to the younger, innately eccentric one. Second, a spirit of competitiveness compounded by malady may in fact have encouraged the younger, innately eccentric one to behave in an even louder, more irritating manner. The hushometer was fun, but construct one at your own risk.

It is worrying to be regaled with stories of your behaviour at the Edinburgh Fringe about which you remember nothing, or which you remember as having happened completely differently, with somebody else doing all the mad bits. It is disturbing to read a book of musings kept by the company at the Fringe and to see pages and pages of absolutely lunacy in your own handwriting. These things we have experienced and we were alarmed and disturbed.

On the other hand, it's also kinda fun. Like meeting a mad version of yourself from a parallel universe, someone you'd rather not spend

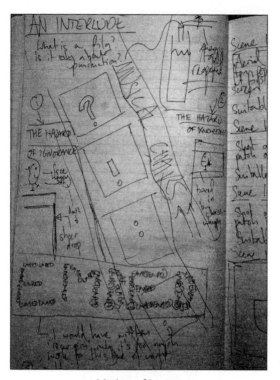

Musings of Lunacy

too much time with but would quite happily be with for an afternoon. Ultimately, coping with going mad is perfectly simple when you are the person it happens to, because you don't really notice it. Much harder is coping with somebody else who has gone mad, but aside from trying not to encourage them too much we don't really have any advice – you just have to put up with it.

Fame (Coping with not having it, and with people who do)

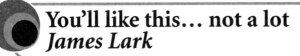

You'll like this... not a lot
James Lark

It was my first year at the Fringe, everything was going well, the weather was superb and I was having a tremendous time. Then, one afternoon, just when I thought things couldn't possibly get any better, Paul Daniels walked past me on the Royal Mile.

Paul Daniels!!!! The diminutive magician himself, in the flesh; he'd created the wonderful Saturday afternoon entertainment I never missed as a child, not to mention the superlative children's TV programme *Wizbit*, so was a genuine childhood hero. I was awestruck.

As, apparently, was every single middle-aged woman in Edinburgh. Clearly, he was as much of a Saturday tea-time hero to them as he was to me. His height meant that he was rather walled in by these menopausal crowds, something which he seemed rather chuffed about. Getting to talk to him was going to be a challenge.

So I give him a flyer. It didn't seem likely that he would come and see my show, but I thought it might be a good conversation-opener. What an exciting moment, to be giving a flyer for my show to one of the people who inspired me to take up performing in the first place!

He glanced at it then turned to the random menopausal lady next to him. 'Oh, it looks a bit gay, doesn't it?' he said in the very same voice with which he used to deliver those hilarious jokes I never failed to laugh at as a boy. Somehow, it seemed more than clear that his use of the term 'gay' was not intended to be complimentary. He looked back at me. 'See, he's got his hand on his hip, he's dyed his hair blond... is it a gay show?'

I was rendered speechless by such unexpected abuse from a childhood hero.

Another random menopausal lady approached, having recognised the famous master of magic. She was, coincidentally, carrying our flyer. Paul Daniels pointed at it and announced, 'That's me, look, in the middle.'

It's me in the middle... surely?

I decided to leave the great man's presence at this point, lest he baffle me further with his wizardly ways.

They're not all like that

So one vertically challenged prick came along and shattered years' worth of childhood dreams in one fell swoop. But not all famous people are like that. Many well-known people come along to the Fringe ready to throw themselves into the fun, especially those that were doing the Fringe themselves before they made it big. If they don't always look delighted to be receiving attention, you have to bear in mind that three weeks surrounded by thousands of excitable ambitious thespians all demanding attention would get pretty tedious for even the most kind-hearted people.

Then again, there are some famous folk who are just not interested in hanging out with ordinary mortals. Just occasionally, this kind of discrimination can backfire spectacularly; we would make an example of Dara O'Briain. O'Briain, the large Irish comedian who you sometimes see on television, turned up to do a stint in Mark Watson's *Over-Ambitious 24-hour Show* in 2004. Now, Watson wasn't exactly an unknown – several shows, a Perrier nomination and a published novel under his belt put him in a strong starting position, and he'd clearly come up with an idea that was so original yet so obvious that everyone was kicking themselves that they hadn't done it first. He just wasn't a comedian of Dara O'Briain's standing.

So when O'Briain arrived in the early hours of the morning, quite pissed, to find that this show he'd charitably decided to help out with consisted of a few sleeping people scattered around a room and a weary Mark Watson hallucinating on a stage, he spent his time rubbishing the idea and being rude to Mark Watson.

The experience clearly bothered Watson, as he spent much of the next day telling his ever-changing and growing audience about it. And his audience did grow: the idea of a show lasting 24 hours fired the imagination of people across Edinburgh to the point where there was a constant queue of people trying to get into it. More comedians such as Adam Hills and Stewart Lee turned up to lend their support and soon everyone was talking about it, at least, everyone we were talking to – but then we were there too.

Simultaneously, Dara O'Briain was being pestered by people who had heard all about how rude he had been to Mark Watson. There must have been a dreadful moment for O'Briain when he realised that it hadn't merely been any old shitty gig at six in the morning.

By the time Watson was finishing his show in a venue packed beyond capacity, O'Briain must have known that his reputation would be damaged unless he made amends. His timing was impeccable, his large figure appearing dramatically in the doorway at ten minutes to midnight, just before the show was due to be wrapped up. Opportunism, perhaps, but the mark of a true showman as well. Unfortunately, Watson's timing was a little off, but when the show finally finished twenty minutes late, with the ultimate feelgood ending of no less than a marriage proposal, the all-round vibes of love and happiness can't have done O'Briain any harm.

They're not all famous

The Fringe is not actually about famous people. Yes, there are great opportunities to see famous people perform, especially in the comedy venues, but when you weigh up the number of shows featuring famous people next to the sheer volume of unknowns, the celebrities are but a tiny pebble in a large ocean.

So it's a shame that so many think it is about famous people, or at least becoming a famous person. Of course, the Fringe has its success stories. It has started many careers and is traditionally the place that people get 'spotted'. It is still the place that agents, casting directors and talent scouts hang out in the hope of finding the next Tom Stoppard or Stephen Fry. However, with the sheer number of performances the Fringe is now home to, getting an agent to see you in a show is every bit as difficult as it is in an ordinary London Fringe theatre. Even people who do get seen by those who seem to hold all the power in the artistic world are more often that not disappointed. The problem is, there just isn't enough fame to go around.

Even 25 years ago the Fringe was small enough that a good performance could realistically expect some sort of recognition. When the first Perrier Award was handed to the Cambridge Footlights, out of a mere eleven nominees, it really did have the power to change lives. Now, a Perrier Award, lovely and coveted though it still is, is but a single rung on a continuing long and difficult struggle to the top.

If you happen to be planning to go to the Edinburgh Fringe in the hope of finding fame and fortune, now is the time to reconsider. It is not a realistic aim and it is not the reason to do the Fringe; it will just be an expensive route to disappointment. Received wisdom is that performers don't usually get any serious kind of recognition from the Fringe until their fifth year there, so if you're serious about making it you need to be serious about that level of commitment over that kind of timescale. Of course, that commitment is one that needs to be sustained for the other eleven months of the year as well. It is not just a matter of being in a show, however fabulous you are in it; it is a constant process of writing letters, trying to get work as a performer, working for nothing and taking on the most menial tasks to pay for your tiny, unattractive bedsit.

When you approach the Fringe, you need to write letters – hundreds of letters – to every agent and casting director you can get an address for, possibly following it up with a further letter and a phone call, then maybe, just maybe, one or two people will turn up.

When they eventually turn up and don't have space on their books for someone of your description, you need to be prepared to do it all over again. When, after your fifth year, you still haven't been 'spotted' and you're angrily tearing to shreds the paragraph above which says 'performers don't usually get any serious kind of recognition from the Fringe until their fifth year there', you still need to be prepared to do it all over again… or to give up.

By that stage, you may find there's a new edition of this book in which the figure has been amended to 'nine years'…

And yet…

If this book says nothing else of importance, it is that it's okay, and indeed fun, doing shows to an audience with four people in it. It may be that your hard work is rubbished by the press and sinks into obscurity within minutes of the final performance. But you have given those four people an experience that they will take away with them for better or for worse. It's not fame, but it's a tiny bit of recognition on the broad canvas of the arts.

We were once given a flyer for a one-woman show by two breathless, excited girls. They explained that they weren't involved in the show in any way, but had been to see it and liked it so much that they had taken a stash of flyers to hand out to other people. They had been the only two people in the audience, and they felt it ought to be seen by many more.

Later that day, we saw the woman actually performing the show, in costume, looking pissed-off and bitter, trying to give out flyers. Of course she looked pissed-off and bitter – she was only getting two people in her audiences and that is why she wasn't happy.

But the two breathless girls were happy.

It's not just shows

If you spend all your time at the Fringe seeing or indeed doing shows, you'll miss out on some of the other great things on offer that you couldn't do or see anywhere else. Don't do that – it's an essential part of the Fringe experience to wallow in everything that's on, especially if it's free. In this section we look at the parts of the Fringe that take place outside the venues – things you will want to look out for, things you will want to avoid, and things you have a moral duty to sabotage.

We also look at some things which are not even part of the Fringe at all. For example, like many major Fringe festivals, the Edinburgh Fringe has a smaller, less well-known but occasionally interesting International Festival going on at the same time (though it's mainly located on the fringes). It's also rumoured that somewhere in the Edinburgh Fringe there is a city, which has got bits that exist outside the month of August. We'll take a look at them, but to set us apart from any run-of-the-mill guide book we'll mainly look at the way the Fringe affects them.

The Edinburgh locals who bugger off in the month of August to avoid the marauding thespians may be interested to find out what actually happens to their cherished city...

Other Fringe things

Circus freaks

One of our party pieces as a mostly-male improvisation troupe was to pick a random female from our audiences, flirt outrageously with her, then improvise a love song about her.

One year we did a slot in the Bongo Club Cabaret and finished with this routine. For the first time in our long stage history, however, charming though we were and remain, we couldn't find a single woman in the audience willing to join us on the stage.

While doing a second desperate sweep over the audience and watching giggling females shrink away in every direction, we were suddenly accosted by a man with spiked red hair and an alarming number of piercings, who yelled 'I'll do it!'

He looked tough and potentially dangerous. Not what we would usually consider 'love song material'.

Nevertheless, he got up on the stage, where he proceeded to be extremely intimidating for several difficult minutes. Being far from adept at flirting with potentially dangerous punks, the cool, charming stage persona which has seen us through many a gig was replaced by a flustered panic while the man, whose name was Gareth, heckled us repeatedly, from a position of authority that hecklers are never supposed to have.

Then we sang him a love song. Turns out it's quite a good heckle put-down. Gareth returned to his seat speechless and docile.

The very next day we saw Gareth juggling chainsaws on the Royal Mile and were glad that we had befriended such a person.

Indeed, if you make a habit of singing love songs to people at the Edinburgh Fringe, there is a higher-than-average probability of finding yourself singing to a chainsaw juggler, or a tightrope walker, a fire eater or an elephant man. As ought to be obvious from the moment the Royal Mile steps into full Fringe mode, the circus is in town.

Throughout each day of the Fringe, large areas of pavement are cleared to make space for circus-type acts of a traditional and less traditional nature. People doing all kinds of juggling, unicycling, tightroping, contortionism and acrobatic feats, all at closer quarters than you would see them in a circus marquee. It is something that people involved in shows tend to take for granted, as they hand out flyers with barely a sideways glance at that man leaping through a hoop of fire again. But actually, they are worth standing and watching properly, because each of these 40-minute acts is a planned show in itself.

These outdoor acts have to apply for slots in the same way as any other performer at the Fringe does, although they will go directly to the Fringe organisers who are in charge of overseeing the activity on the Royal Mile. Each day, the performers get their names put in a hat and are drawn at random to fill the High Street slots. Like all the other performances available at the Fringe, they are of varying quality. However, the general standard is high – outdoor slots are limited so getting them is pretty competitive. In any case, you have to have achieved a certain level of excellence at juggling chainsaws before you go out on the street and do it, unless you're going for the sympathy vote at the risk of being sued for traumatising someone's child.

So, rather than walking past these shows (which is what they are), assuming in a rather blasé way that there will always be a man juggling chainsaws for you to look at, it is a good idea to join the crowds that gather when the circus acts announce they are about to begin. These are performers who know how to work a crowd; they know they have 40 minutes, and they will teasingly build up to their finale in the same way as Shakespeare doesn't give you Agincourt without all that talking beforehand. To just watch the final death-defying act without everything before it would be like listening to *Bohemian Rhapsody* without taking in everything else on *A Night at the Opera* first.

The other minor point to note is that, not being in a nice secure indoor venue, the circus acts don't get to overcharge people to watch them, when in fact they absolutely deserve to. It's a point that hardly needs making, since they all make it so very well themselves – but when the hat is passed round, think how much you might have paid for the privilege of watching some nine-year-old nuns singing *Cabaret*, then make a donation accordingly.

Human statues

What with its potential for dismally poor acting, laboured comedy and musicals sung by young offenders, you may imagine that these dismal productions represent the very worst that the Fringe has to offer.

You would be wrong. Because whatever levels of awfulness are reached by shows at the Fringe, there is a different group of 'performers' so talentless that they wouldn't even be considered for Big Brother.

We're talking about the breed known as 'human statues'. They are humans pretending to be statues. Hence the name.

It's a simple concept: in their most basic form, having sprayed themselves a different colour, the humans in question stand still in a prominent position in the street, usually obstructing various pushchairs and elderly people, and will only move if they are given money by members of the public, or if removed by the police (depending on the attitude of the law in the spot they have chosen to ply their trade).

Forget any desperately inaccurate preconceptions you may have that this is a career requiring any talent. It does not require talent to spray yourself silver and stand in the street for people to look at you.

A child of three could do it... or a monkey, or even a guinea pig, if you did the spraying bit on its behalf and glued its feet to the pavement.

Admittedly, there are different levels of talentlessness on display in the human statue gene pool. Some of them contrive a costume to match their spray paint – perhaps a large pair of wings, or a prop along the lines of a bicycle or a vacuum cleaner. Others make less of an effort, hoping to create a convincing statue effect by merely draping some kind of sheet over themselves or wearing an oddly-shaped hat. Most disgraceful of all are those who erroneously believe that the spray paint is quite enough to create the statuesque effect and don't even bother standing still. (One example that sticks in our minds like a nasty taste was a man who stood in a granite-coloured cardboard box to make himself look like a bust on a pedestal, then nodded and beamed benefactorially at the crowds of people giving him money. Oh, you can bet he was beaming...)

Essentially, then, this is a job that requires no skill at all and deserves little money. People who sell the *Big Issue* may show a similar lack of imagination, but at least you get something for your pound. Prostitutes may not look as pretty as human statues, but at least there's some skill involved.

Of course, human statues exist in areas other than Edinburgh; they are sometimes to be spotted along the South Bank in London, and a woman painted green was once sighted standing on a pillar in Bath. But even in densely populated areas, human statues tend to be a lonely bunch, spread out from each other and isolated in such a way as to make them perfect fodder for the laughing, ribbing and stone-throwing they deserve.

Not so at the Edinburgh Fringe. Like birds migrating south for the winter, human statues migrate north for August and congregate on the Royal Mile, almost as if it is some kind of human statue convention. Why? Because at the Edinburgh Fringe a human statue can, for reasons we cannot even make amusing guesses at, gather a sizeable crowd and earn a small fortune. It is a sad fact that in an area so packed with talented street performers and credible artists trying to sell their shows, people will continue to ignore carefully designed flyers and eager fresh-faced actors yet stand in mute appreciation of a twat who has painted himself blue. With such discernment on display, it's scarcely any wonder that the Edinburgh locals become increasingly suspicious and bitter, hiding in pubs and muttering 'wankers' into their pints. The tourists are ultimately to blame for the fact that their beautiful city has filled up with painted people.

Mind you, it's a wonder that the human statues have the gall to turn up to the Fringe at all. However, since they don't show any embarrassment at being there surrounded by a wealth of genuine performers, and manage to con so many people, they evidently lack any kind of conscience or indeed any concept of art. We were once approached by a huge gold angel who had the nerve to address us as if he was a fellow performer – we don't recall his exact words, but it was something along the lines of, 'Gosh, this is hard work, isn't it! How are you doing?' Since we had spent a typical afternoon having flyers rejected by passers-by and were preparing to go and perform in an almost empty theatre, while knowing for a fact that the angel was walking away with about a million pounds of loose change, we didn't deign to reply.

So our advice is this: human statues will be in Edinburgh. For the foreseeable future they will form part of the Fringe. Don't be surprised, therefore, if you see a person who is standing still and painted a different colour. Don't be irrationally tempted to give them money, for whatever reason, and don't pander to their craving for attention, otherwise they will continue take up valuable space and make a lucrative career out of what really amounts to begging with spray paint. If we make a stand and ignore these cretins (and God knows, there are enough genuinely entertaining things to see on the Royal Mile instead), the human statues might pack their bags and find gainful employment. Either that, or they might continue to stand on the street while birds shit on them until they are as worn and unrecognisable as real statues.

Spot the difference

Buskers

Edinburgh doesn't have buskers during the Fringe like other cities do. Every city has its own licensing laws where busking for money is concerned, which is why places like Bath are full of stray string quartets and saxophonists playing along to tapes of synthesised opera arias, while other cities have nothing at all except for an old man playing a harmonica who is constantly getting moved on by the police.

In Edinburgh there is no need for a licence, so theoretically anybody could stand on the street playing the trombone to earn a vaguely honest living. At Fringe time it requires special treatment, though, because it's already so packed full of people doing strange and wonderful things on the streets. There will hardly be rich pickings for a boring old string quartet when they're competing with Gareth juggling chainsaws. This means that any buskers you find during the Fringe are likely to be more in the nature of the circus performers already mentioned. For example, there is often a man dressed in a green suit covered in hooters who honks Rossini overtures. One year at the Fringe we regularly passed a woman who sat at a piano in a field playing ragtime numbers. These sorts of performers are bizarrely wonderful and should be encouraged, although you probably shouldn't go as far as inviting them back to your house for dinner.

Other buskers you see may be advertising their show, so trying to give away flyers rather than take your money. These are often close harmony vocal ensembles but instrumental ensembles also feature at the Fringe, and they often are forced to perform more than the notes just to stand out. This is why you see musicians camping around to the highest degree, which always makes for entertaining viewing, and if it means you can watch them without paying to see their show (unless you really like them) who's complaining?

It's a shame to say that occasionally you also see children playing instruments rather abysmally on the street as well. Evidently, the young, vaguely musical Scots have either latched onto the fact that they can make easy money for doing their violin practice outdoors instead of at home or they are genuinely starving. Probably best to assume the former and walk on by. You don't tend to get proper, ordinary buskers plying their trade during Fringe time – they have sensibly realised there's enough going on already, and Cirencester is going to be a better option.

There are two exceptions, which are dealt with below.

Bagpipes

Q: Why do pipers march as they play?
A: Because a moving target is much harder to hit.

Yes, people in Scotland really do play bagpipes – although after hearing a tartan-clad piper play *Scotland the Brave* for the fiftieth time a cynic might wonder if they're just playing up to a national stereotype because it earns them more money.

Better, though, the traditional tourist-friendly piper than the type that tries to reinvent the ghastly instrument with bagpipe renditions of chart music and Andrew Lloyd Webber's greatest hits. If you have only one bullet left, save it for these ones. (Incidentally, they

don't always march; your busking piper stands on a street corner while people give him money, until somebody takes him out.)

Peruvian Pan-pipe players

People who play Pan-pipes don't fit into the general busking rules stated above because, frankly, they're everywhere. It is now impossible to travel anywhere within the UK without passing a group of people dressed in animal skins, playing Pan-pipes and sometimes eulogising about how we need to get closer to nature.

There is no worse advocate for getting closer to nature than people who play Pan-pipes. Most people would rather be surrounded by synthetic, human-built artificiality than endure even a few minutes of what must be the most boring, insipid musical sound in the whole world.

What is ironic, though, is that it is customary for Messrs 'Fox' and 'Badger' to accompany their instrumental grotesquery with prerecorded backing tracks of soft-rock drums and Lloyd-Webber inspired synthesisers. Furthermore, their animal costumes must surely also be synthetic? Either that or these people are completely unethical and sew together a whole load of real animals to create their bizarre, indistinguishable costumes. Although that certainly would be one way of getting closer to nature.

In our opinion, practitioners of the pipes of Pan pose a genuine threat to the sanity of the country, and future governments should think harder about imposing stricter immigration laws on people who are known to play the bloody instrument, to stem the flow of Pan-pipe ensembles into this country. As far as Edinburgh is concerned, there is already more than enough insanity on display and Pan-pipes may be enough to push some people over the edge. The Scottish Parliament should probably take steps to have them banned altogether. If God had meant us to play Pan-pipes he wouldn't have made them sound so bloody awful.

Religious nuts

People don't just come out during the Fringe to sell shows. Oh, no. If you're in Edinburgh for any length of time, you'll run into people wanting to persuade you to leave the dirty world of sex, drugs, etc., behind, and embrace your new life with Jesus, Krishna or Tom Cruise. All this really demonstrates is that they don't have the faintest idea what goes on at the Fringe. There really aren't any brand new performers, with their Fringe club photo passes still damp, rolling naked on a raft of Farrah Fawcett lookalikes while all-powerful Fringe Svengalis look on and cackle. This won't stop the nutters trying, of course (and it won't stop you from looking in vain for that tell-tale blonde hair and perky crime-solving smile). Evangelists are nothing if not persistent and the ones you get in Edinburgh aren't all that different to the ones in other parts of the country – except that occasionally an enterprising comedian might take their religious

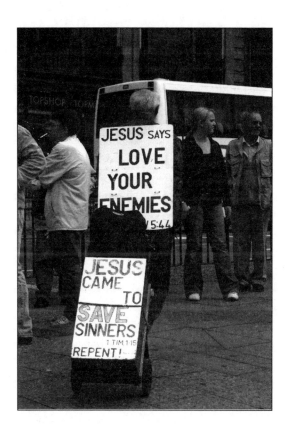

literature and poke fun at them.

At the most harmless end of the spectrum are the 1920s-style Evangelists who could really do with reading our advice on publicity, because as it stands their theologically dubious flyers suggest that their church would only be worthy of a one-star review in Fest. Who is going to listen to them delivering a monotonous spiel about God when the man with the hooters is just across the road?

More worrying are the religious cults who seek to boost their numbers at the Fringe. It's understandable, of course – if you're in a cult devoted to worshipping the Gnomes of Karaoke and you're looking to recruit new people, the Fringe is probably the most likely place you're going to find willing simpletons to join you. Many Fringe-goers would try anything to escape the experience they're having, even if it does mean swearing to deny all rumours that they are performing experiments on lizard men*.

By far the scariest cult we encountered were the Scientologists, out in force and clearly under the erroneous impression that Edinburgh would be full of rich Hollywood actors rather than penniless comedians. They deserve a whole different section, because they're evil.

Scientologists

Sometimes the most fun at the Fringe can be free. Not often, mind – no matter how terrible *Macbeth on Ice* actually turns out to be, the man standing on a box up on George IV Bridge will be worse – but when you find something genuinely stimulating happening out in public, you should take full advantage of it. In the nineteenth century, young rakes might have entertained themselves by watching street urchins chasing an emaciated dog down Cowgate, and it is rumoured that the Lord Provost once kept a starving girl child by his desk so he could watch her jump and twist for the bones of malingerers he'd had hung**.

These days we can taunt Scientologists and the best thing about it is that it's not only free and legal; it's practically your moral duty.

We've all heard of Scientology. It's that weird, secretive thing – a bit like a religion for dumb people – that Tom Cruise draws his young Hollywood brides into. Famous weirdo actors such as John Travolta and Juliette Lewis are Scientologists, and it's definitely not a cult, not even the bit where you get videotaped confessing to all your embarrassing childhood traumas. They keep their methods and beliefs secret because, well, we just wouldn't understand.

Unlike weird, secret, cultlike thing the Masons, Scientology doesn't have strange titles such as Grand Master of the 32nd Order of the Scottish Right. Also unlike the Masons, Scientologists aren't philanthropists whose secrecy masks a positive contribution to the world going back to before the eighteenth century. In America, Scientology claims tax-exempt status as a religion, but in Germany, where the government bothered having a quick look first, they're

---

*More information on this particular cult at
http://somewhatsecret.so.funpic.org/society.php?society_id=46 if you're interested.
**At least, it is rumoured from now on.

treated as a plain old money grabbing company.

They believe in aliens making you think bad thoughts, and that L. Ron Hubbard, the creator of Scientology and atrocious science-fiction epic *Battlefield Earth*, was the bringer of ultimate truth and not a deranged weirdo who liked to sail round the Mediterranean in a private fleet with recalcitrant Scientologists in the chain locker. They also believe in natty yellow tents and discos, so they are pretty much wide open to mockery.

One year in Edinburgh, when we were living in Marchmont, our route to and from the venue, which we accordingly travelled at least twice a day, took us right past Camp Scientology. No low-profile skulking for these boys – they'd pitched an enormous yellow tent right in the middle of the Meadows and during the day one or two of them would stand outside offering free 'personality profiles' to passers-by and waggling their trick boxes suggestively.

This was a challenge. We'd spent much of the preceding month working on group exercises, trying to bring the company up to a level where we could work together seamlessly. We could invent advertising slogans, a word at a time. We could play musical chairs without breaking a sweat. Now, finally, we had an enemy we could fight.

Our friend Andrew, showing even more hatred for Scientologists than for the Fringe, led the charge. Eyes front, straight back, steady time, we marched solemnly up to the tent and, as one reached towards his personality analysis machine, or some vacuous phrase to enslave the feebleminded began to form on the lips of another, out it would come: 'No!'. Shoulders back, arms outstretched, palm flat and pushing away. We did it in sync, all eight of us, even while carrying a ladder, and probably looked like a Nazi work crew, fresh home from destroying lives, showing defiance to the right-thinking bombers high over Dresden. In reality, of course, the reverse was true.

The evening after we first did this, strolling back across the Meadows, we noticed a light within the tent. This turned out to be a regular thing; the new generation of Scientologists would boogie away inside, watched over by one of the more senior members who recruited during the day. It was very disturbing, watching a cult reproduce itself, one eighties song at a time; even if you are the greatest fan of Katrina and the Waves we would suggest there are better ways to fuel your addiction than to sell your soul (and hand over your wallet) to Scientology. The following day we redoubled our efforts. And, not being devotees of Katrina and the Waves, wore earplugs just in case.

The Scientologists evidently weren't used to such forceful negativity, and eventually stopped inviting us into their tent, which suggests to us that a little more theologically reasoned refusal in this world might put an end to such disagreeable organisations. Partway through August they upped and left altogether, and we all felt the warm feeling of having beaten evil, just a little bit.

We strongly recommend living near some Scientologists, if you have the option. If you're intent on surviving Edinburgh you need to cultivate certain automatic reactions; saying 'no' to people will keep you out of trouble, and the Scientologists gave us the ideal opportunity to practice this every time we set off into town.

Painters

Another group of people who often pop up on London's South Bank, but also in any major European city, is the painter of portraits and/or caricatures. Since they apparently make successful careers all over Europe, it's hardly surprising that the increased footfall in Edinburgh during the Fringe lures so many of them to set up shop there.

You must know the set-up. Somebody sits at an easel, surrounded by pencil portraits or felt-tip caricatures of George Michael, David Beckham, Keira Knightley and Janet Street-Porter, and the implication is that they are offering to draw you as well. Often, you see a random person sitting on a stool modelling for them, while a girlfriend/mother watches with a slightly embarrassed smile as the artist sketches a portrait... which looks nothing like the poor, unknowing person sitting in front of them.

How many people, on receiving their specially commissioned work of art, force a smile of thanks as they hand over their hard-earned cash, grin at their girlfriend/mother and say, 'It's perfect, it looks just like me!', frame it and hang it up in their kitchen until the girlfriend leaves them or the mother dies?

Are we the only people who wonder where the pictures on display come from? After all, they actually look like the celebrities in question.

The sad truth is, there is only one caricature artist of any skill in the whole world. He lives in a tiny hut in an Austrian village where he sits, day in, day out, sketching from magazines the faces of people he knows nothing about. He then sells them for an unjustly low price to his customers, people who have taken art degrees then realised with horror that they have no career options, who display them as their own work and take money from unsuspecting members of the public. Since their degrees mainly concerned gluing spoons together or making grainy video installations of their own genitals, they are crap when it comes to real art. Skilled artists don't sit on the street drawing poorly-realised cartoons – they have studios and websites, and they rarely feel the need to reproduce pictures of George Michael.

Drumming

Drums have long been integrated into all sorts of musical ensembles. They feature prominently, for example, in Edinburgh's famous Tattoo; drums are also an established part of most popular music ensembles, and if you go to a musical you will probably hear some drumming in the band. Integrated into such groups, drummers play a valuable role in society, and drumming is generally considered a valid form of self-expression.

But why, oh why, oh why, oh why does the Edinburgh Fringe attract so many hordes of drummers who are apparently unintegrated into any musical ensemble except for a whole load of other drummers? Like the drumming equivalent of illegal immigrants – no…, stray cats – they have nowhere to go so they hunt in packs, sticking together with their drums for entertainment. Yes, on the very streets themselves!

You could be walking through Edinburgh, enjoying the weather and the Fringe atmosphere, when you'll hear a distant bm-badda-bm-badda-bm, a little like a scene in a Western where the cowboys suddenly sit up and listen in the fearful knowledge that they are about to be surrounded by Indians.

Only it's worse than that, because these people are not going to merely fire arrows at you, they are going to drum. However many of them there are, perhaps seven, eight, maybe a larger group of 13 or 14, they will huddle together drumming manically with a kind of rapt intensity that makes them look worryingly as if they're some sort of cult. And it goes on and on and on, relentlessly and unchangingly, bm-badda-bm-badda-bm-badda-bm…

Once you've noticed the noise you'll never escape it, and wherever you go they will eventually track you down and drum loudly at you – usually when you are trying to have a relaxing break in a tea room or when you are having an important discussion with somebody about what you're going to do for the rest of the day. The drummers return, like a headache.

Where do they come from?

And, more to the point,

How do we get rid of them?

Drumming

James Aylett: We don't want to get rid of all drummers. Where would we be without Sterling Campbell?

James Lark: I'm not suggesting that, I'm saying that all drummers should be assigned to a band of some sort. Or shot.

JA: You'd be condemning to death hundreds of innocent drummers who are simply between bands. That's how press-ganging started. Who do you think you are? Nelson?

JL: I would point out that the reason people end up learning the drums is because they are already in a band. Like Ringo Starr. Drummers who are 'between bands' must be either absolutely bloody hopeless or complete social rejects, and nobody is going to miss them.

JA: What about Dave Grohl?

JL: His lead singer in Nirvana killed himself. Grohl is now a guitarist. You think perhaps he blamed himself?

JA: Have you heard the drum track from *Smells Like Teen Spirit*?

JL: Yes. Because it's the same as all their drum tracks. Bmm badda bmm badda bmm badda bmm.

JA: Yes, but if you'd killed Grohl after Nirvana broke up, he'd never have redeemed himself and become a guitarist.

JL: Look, I'm not suggesting an illogical fascist approach here. Common sense would have to be used – and sure, during a suicide-related period of unemployment, drummers would be encouraged to find other bands or better still other pursuits. Then, and only then, would they be shot.

JA: Once they've found other bands?

JL: Ideally.

JA: Just think: with that approach, Chester Thompson would never have played for Phil Collins.

> *JL*: Phil Collins, as we all know, is perfectly capable of playing his own drums.
>
> *JA*: I wouldn't go that far.
>
> *JL*: Okay, we'll shoot him too.
>
> Cheers are heard from outside and James Lark is subsequently knighted.

Other festivals

Several other festivals run in Edinburgh at the same time as the Fringe, but they seem to go unnoticed by the vast majority of the people there. However, there's a vast range of exciting events which certainly shouldn't be ignored, particularly if you're up there for a while and fancy a break from the Fringe madness.

The International Festival

Presumably, the people who run the International Festival are in a perpetual state of horror about the fact that their 'main' festival has been so eclipsed by the one that's meant to be on the fringe. The fact that the Fringe is attracting a far broader audience and much more publicity with only a fraction of the money that the International Festival has to throw around must have given its directors over the years pause for thought – and several bitter, sleepless nights. Even their best-known production, *Beyond the Fringe*, is assumed by most people to have been part of the Fringe because they fail to see beyond the fact that Fringe is in the title.

Nevertheless, if you prefer a more predictable, reliable, professional and – ahem – expensive kind of set-up, then the International Festival consistently pulls top-notch productions out of the bag and stages them in impressive, glitzy venues. Opera, theatre, dance and music are all well-represented and feature the best performers from around the world. If you're looking to wear a tux and look posh somewhere in Edinburgh, this is your best bet.

In terms of sheer scale at least, the International Festival is able to put on the most impressive events in Edinburgh, most notably the climactic firework display which closes the festival season each year. This spectacular show is well worth catching if you can stay in the city for long enough, and provides a fitting end to such a mammoth series of events.

Perhaps in response to criticisms that the International Festival doesn't have the artistic frisson of the Fringe, it has recently seen some new and controversial productions, exploring topical issues and experimental types of performance with a broad multicultural vein, so it's far from being a staid experience – there are plenty of interesting productions to take in and it's well worth checking out what's available, even if it does mean a more expensive night of culture. Hire a tux, relax, have some champagne.

The Book Festival

Each year Charlotte Square gardens hosts the world's biggest book festival and yet many of the people visiting the city don't even notice it, which is a shame, because in addition to the varied programme of readings, discussions and workshops designed to cater for all tastes and ages, it has an atmosphere all of its own that can be a breath of fresh air for any jaded Fringe-goer. Whether you go to get your books signed by your favourite children's illustrator, or to listen to Booker prizewinners discussing their work or just to enjoy the breezy, laid-back ambience and browse the rows of books for sale, the Book Festival makes for a highly enjoyable afternoon.

You can also sit down and have a drink in the beautiful setting. Tea, probably.

The Film Festival

This is yet another internationally renowned event showcasing the finest cinematic talent and numerous premières, as well as the occasional retrospective. Films shown at the film festival may not make it into the cinemas until months later, if ever, so it's a great opportunity to be the first to see contemporary masterpieces, or, indeed, less successful cinematic experiments that may never see the light of day again. It isn't quite Cannes, but it is highly respected by filmmakers all over the world (the European premier of *E.T.* was at the Edinburgh film festival); some people even come to Edinburgh in August just to watch films – would you believe it? For anything big you will have to book well in advance, but sort yourself out – sort out a line of coke in the toilets and you'll probably fit right in.

The Jazz and Blues Festival

This is, apparently, the longest running jazz festival in the UK. Beginning in late July and lasting for just over a week, the jazz festival features artistes from around the world in all sorts of places, ranging from large theatres to bars and outdoor venues. Sounds like an ideal opportunity to sit back, relax, listen to some world-class music and have a drink.

The Art Festival

This runs throughout August and is a recent innovation by the National Galleries of Scotland to promote the visual arts in the many galleries and museums across Edinburgh and beyond. An impressive array of exhibitions ought to please anyone at all interested in art and in Edinburgh, no more civilised way of escaping the frenetic pace of all the other festivals exists. Unless, of course, you'd rather just sit in a pub and have a drink.

The Edinburgh Military Tattoo

A tattoo is of course a permanent patterned design on the skin made by pricking and ingraining an indelible pigment, and Edinburgh is a great place to get one. Cockburn Street in particular has rows of shops just waiting to ingrain indelible pigment into your skin, and you could easily get something pierced while you're there.

If you decide to get a tattoo depicting massed military bands, pipers and drummers, display teams and multinational acts performing against the beautifully lit up backdrop of Edinburgh castle, it may also capture some of the excitement of the annual outdoor spectacular which takes place each year.

We have never actually met a Fringe performer who has bothered to see the Tattoo. Perhaps they feel that they've already seen more than enough pipers, drummers and spectacular displays along the Royal Mile. But we gather that when these people get together in full Scottish garb for some serious marching it's actually a more coherent experience and fun for all the family. They are now putting on a number of free events each year, so there's probably no harm in checking it out. Or you can buy the DVD and watch it again and again and again without getting rained on – and with a drink.

The Edinburgh Mela

Mela is another word for festival, but an exotic, foreign word which suggests the kind of exotic, foreign things that go on in this short, but large and exciting event towards the end of August. A diverse range of artists from around the world come to take part in this intercultural event, featuring music, dance, art, fashion, food and any number of activities – another grand day out for families and Fringe-goers alike, and an event that is growing in scale each year.

Go along, dance a bit, relax, have some cachaca.

Unhealthy Edinburgh
Matt Green

Among comedians, the Edinburgh Fringe is often described in brutal physical terms: it's an 'endurance test' or a 'marathon (not a sprint)'. Comics prepare for the Fringe like athletes for the Olympics, training up their performance in smoky pubs and clubs around the country. Well, okay, Olympic athletes probably don't train in smoky pubs. However, no amount of training can prepare you for the real thing. By the end of the Fringe a typical comedian's body will have aged several years.

One reason for this is a basic lack of fitness. Although there has been a move in recent years towards gym membership and playing football, most comedians remain physically awkward specimens, probably picked last for teams at school. After all, if they were good at sports they would probably never have needed to make people laugh in order to get them to be their friends. The lifestyle of most comedians is hardly conducive to health either, involving long journeys, motorway service station food, smoky clubs and constant late nights. Then there is the topography of the city itself. Everything in Edinburgh seems to be uphill. The ankles are the first to suffer. Indeed, the steep climb up the Pleasance to the Courtyard can seem like an impossible journey. Who knows how many comedians have failed to make that final push over the years? Perhaps that accounts for the recent success of the Holyrood Tavern. It is ideally placed at the bottom of the hill for the out-of-breath traveller in search of entertainment.

'Edinburgh flu' is a well-known phenomenon that strikes many performers at the beginning of week two.

After the initial adrenaline has worn off and the alcohol and late nights have begun to take their toll, the comic is more-than-usually vulnerable to attack. Added to this they are also spending hours every day in small, warm rooms full of people laughing at them and thereby spraying them with germs. It's not a pleasant image, but may account for why by the third week many comedians have no voice, red eyes and pallid skin... and that's just the young ones.

So, the next time you see a comedy show at the Pleasance, spare a thought for the poor comedian who is performing in front of you. He will be sweating, he will be feeling ill, his eyes will be flickering from too little sleep and too many drinks, and he will be trying to make you laugh with every muscle in his body (which is probably not many). Then heckle him with 'Do you go to the gym?' He probably does. After all, he made it up the hill.

Matt Green is an actor and comedian.

Other festivals that you can't see in August

Inexplicably, there are also some festivals outside the month of August. These are understandably less useful in escaping from the Fringe, unless it's taken you an unusually long time to pack up your props after finishing your show, but they still attract many visitors each year and provide a good excuse to pop up to the beautiful city of Edinburgh for a visit at a different time of the year.

Hogmanay

Scotland celebrates the New Year on an annual basis, and there are no plans that we are aware of to make it a more frequent event. This is just as well really, as the carnage after a hearty 4-day street party takes several months to clean up. Say what you like about the Scots, they certainly know how to have a party, or at least how to drink lots, so even if it's too damp to let off their spectacular firework display there's every chance of having a grand time.

There is also every chance of it being damp. Scotland is not known for its fine weather in the winter months, so take some warm clothes and maybe Wellington boots. Then prepare yourself for one big party. Have a drink. No, have several.

The Science Festival

This is a spring event which, in contrast to all the artsy fun in August, celebrates the sciences. Being of an artistic bent ourselves we can't really see the point in this, but it ought to appeal to fans of Jonny Ball. There are workshops, presentations and professors in their dozens – we don't know if there's any opportunity to have a drink, though, as scientists are a serious bunch, but no doubt there are plenty of chemicals lying around with which you can create your own cocktails.

The Children's Festival

The start of the summer brings a festival of award-winning children's productions to Edinburgh. If you are a child, this is probably as much fun as you'll ever have. Run around, scream your head off, meet other children. Don't have a drink, you are underage.

The rest of the city

Well, yeah. There's not just a Fringe, but various other festivals floating round it. In fact, it turns out there's a city as well.

If you're at all interested in that bit, we suggest that a guide book with a name like *Edinburgh* would be a good starting point (certainly a better starting point than a guide book with a name like *Puerto Rico*.)

We're not even going to attempt to cover the whole of the City of Edinburgh in this book. We've always been so submerged in the Fringe when we've been there that we've never given it all that much attention. In any case, the bits we haven't already mentioned might not be worth bothering with.

The Baillie Gifford Conspiracy

On Greenside Row near Calton Square you will find the headquarters of Baillie Gifford, one of the UK's leading independently owned investment management firms. It is not exactly the kind of place we would consider visiting during the Fringe, when there are so many more exciting things than investment management to consider. But as we passed it during our research for this book, we were immediately halted by the similarity between the Baillie Gifford logo and that of the Gilded Balloon. Both use exactly the same font; both involve a crescent shape circling the name. And compare those names: they have the same initials, but reversed, and contain many of the same letters. You can't quite rearrange the letters in 'Baillie Gifford' to make 'Gilded Balloon', but you can make the name 'Gildier Baloff', which is very close.

In short, it's all too much to be coincidental, and because we were writing a book about the Fringe, we were determined not to leave a single stone unturned in our search for the truth behind the curious and hitherto unrecognised link between an independently owned investment management firm and an independently run fringe venue.

Our first action was to make a daring and confrontational telephone call to Baillie Gifford and demand the truth. We found the number and phoned them on a calm, sunny Friday afternoon from an anonymous house in Cambridgeshire; an Australian receptionist answered the phone. (Suspicious? We thought so.)

We explained the situation, viz. the strange and unexplained similarity between the logos and names. There was a short pause and the Australian receptionist said shortly, 'I see.' She was clearly not amused, and neither was she offering any kind of explanation. So we pressed her for details about possible links between the two organisations. Still sounding pissed off, she bluntly answered, 'No, no, there's no sort of link at all, no.' (Note quite how many times she feels the need to use the word 'no'. Suspicious? We thought so.)

After a pause, she tried a change of tactic. Adding a new touch of lightness to her tone of voice, she managed a forced laugh and announced, 'It's just a coincidence actually, I've never thought about that!' (Never thought about it, indeed! A likely story.)

Clearly, we were going to get no straight answers from this antipodean plant, so we tried to trip her up by asking whether the Gilded Balloon had stolen their logo or if it had happened the other way round. 'I would have absolutely no idea,' she replied, in a return to her blunt, uncommunicative mode. 'So it's just a coincidence?' we insisted. 'Seems like it, yes,' she agreed, unpersuasively. It was very clear that she wanted to get rid of us. (Suspicious? We thought so.)

Many journalists would be cowed by such an apparently impenetrable smokescreen. But it appeared that Baillie Gifford's press officer, one Mike Lord (whose email address has the prefix 'mlord', which makes emailing him feel a bit like being a butler), is actually located in a different building – perhaps, free from the controlling talons that lie at the heart of the Baillie Gifford conspiracy, he might reveal a little more, or at least make a few mistakes. So we sent him an email, again pointing out the similarities between the names and the logos, and (just to confuse him slightly) innocently enquiring whether the name 'Baillie Gifford' is in fact Celtic for the words 'Gilded Balloon'.

We have had no response.

(Suspicious? We thought so.)

And so the mystery remains. If you have any information that might help us get to the bottom of it, we would love to hear from you. Just try to be discreet.

N.B.: Although we failed to uncover any definite links between Baillie Gifford and the Gilded Balloon, in a recent edition of NME Baillie Gifford did admit to investing in Paul Baloff's French burlesque show, 'Gildier Baloff'.

You might want to check that Edinburgh guide in case we're wrong, but if you can't be bothered here are some helpful pointers for getting around and a few things you might want to look out for.

Getting around

During the Fringe walking is likely to be your best way of getting anywhere. If you are travelling any significant distance you will find regular and efficient bus services, but if you are making a typically winding trip between two Fringe venues you are unlikely to find a bus that will take a direct route, and the bits of Edinburgh you will have to go through are likely to be impassable to vehicles – either cordoned off or just packed full of people. Furthermore, if you're there for more than a day you'll need to remortgage your house to use taxis all the time – and if you have your own car, forget about being able to park, or at least park anywhere useful.

In any case, Edinburgh's one-way system is like the circle of hell Dante never mentioned because it would have taken him too long; even trying to get your car to a prearranged drop-off point to unload props, or finding a street on which you've been reliably informed you can park, involves driving in ever-widening circles, each time finding yourself re-diverted down the same bit of road which takes you to exactly the wrong part of Edinburgh – and so you begin again. By the time you pay for the petrol and the therapy you will inevitably require after the experience, you might as well have hired the SAS to drop off your props.

If you really can't stick the idea of walking everywhere, take a bike with you, and spend the entire Fringe feeling very smug about it.

Weather

Edinburgh in August is a contrary place – baking hot sun can be replaced with ice-cold rain in a heartbeat. The sun goes in, and the High Street sprouts umbrellas, like little mushrooms – and about as effective, as the Royal Mile acts as a sort of wind tunnel, causing eddies and gusts to leap around playfully, making babies gurgle in delight (a bit like the sewers, only with fewer rats), and grown men cry out in anguish as water shoots up their leg and soaks a perfectly good Armani suit. Then the rain stops, down go the umbrellas, and people start peeling off layers trying to negotiate a good temperature again.

And yet – and this is a strange thing – very few performers are ever prepared for the weather. Tourists, potential audience, are happy to stand around in the rain and talk about your show – they're happy and dry under their huge golfing umbrella – but the people handing out flyers are waterlogged, drained of enthusiasm, and ultimately doing no one any good.

Of course, not everyone is like this. Some groups, particularly

youth theatre groups, carefully kit their company members out with clothing for every eventuality, with T-shirts, sweatshirts, raincoats, and the sort of heavy jacket you only really need in the Antarctic. Distribution companies, and promoters, who pay young attractive things to give out flyers for shows with more money than we ever had, similarly make sure their workers are prepared for anything.

Everyone else gets wet, then gets roasted. An enduring image from one year was a stand-up – established on the circuit but not yet a big name – standing in a circle of misery, his jacket collar turned up to try to squeeze an iota more warmth from it. Somehow, he managed to choose the wet part of every day to come out and flyer. These days he's built up more of a name for himself, and flyering is delegated to others. They aren't going with the jacket collar tactic.

Crime

Edinburgh is a fairly safe city. Housebreaking is only a little above the Scottish average, for example, and Scotland is generally safer than England – in fact, the main hazard we discovered is going round calling everyone 'Jock'. The most popular name among Scots these days is Lewis – although in Edinburgh it's Jack (note the 'a'). With girls it is Amy.

Gay Edinburgh

It is, of course, virtually obligatory these days in any guide to include a section on the gay side of places, even if it amounts to 'Mauritania is not a great place to cruise as you will be put to death'. But in a guide to the Edinburgh Fringe it is an essential inclusion, for not only does

Edinburgh have a healthy and vibrant gay community, but the Fringe is naturally full of actors, singers, dancers and artsy folk, who are of course nearly all gay. Since it's not unlikely that you'll find yourself living near where they all hang out (see notes on accommodation), even if you have no intention of hanging out with them it's just as well to try and understand them. Which can be a challenge, because as gay communities go they're a pretty odd bunch. The actual Fringe performers are usually easy to identify in gay establishments because they're the ones standing on their own looking awkward and bitter. Looking bitter is not so much a homosexual trait as a natural state for performers, particularly if they have received poor reviews (as so many performers do). However, gay performers often milk their bitterness for all it is worth by claiming that they have been the victims

James Lark meets embittered gay performer

Putting up a poster for my show in a gay bar, I was once enthusiastically greeted by a fellow performer, evidently pleased to see another artiste and hopeful that I would pay him a bit of attention and make him look a little less isolated. (Oh, who knows, perhaps he was after a shag as well.) He asked the mandatory polite questions about my show, before pointing out a poster for his one-man comedy show and launching into a tirade about the review it had received, which, he informed me, was 'pure homophobia'. Having already seen his poster and mentally marked it as a 'show to avoid', I had my suspicions that a poor review might have been well-deserved, but I erred on the side of caution and cultivated a look of angry concern that such terribly outdated discrimination could possibly still be blighting us gay performers (I also felt it would be tactless to mention that my own show, which as an improvised show with an 80% male cast had, by default, started to involve a lot of onstage gay kisses, had generally received positive reviews).

After making my excuses and assuring him that I would certainly come and see his show if I was able to (he gave me the same assurance – we were both lying), I returned to my digs and found the review in question. It referred to the crassness of the ideas, the thinness on the ground of funny material, a cringe-worthy attempt at a grotesque character and the general redundancy of the whole thing, but nowhere, not once, could I find a single reference to homosexuality, or even what might have been a justifiable use of the phrase 'absurdly camp'.

I saw the same man several more times, both on the Royal Mile dressed as a cringe-worthily grotesquecharacter, as well as in the gay establishments which surrounded our lodgings, always standing on his own looking awkward (and often bitter). His problem was (and to be fair it was a problem that he shared with many people at the Fringe) that he thought he was something very special; that is why he had to assume that his review could only be the result of homophobia, and that is possibly why he was so unsuccessful engaging with other people.

of homophobic discrimination.

In any case, going into Edinburgh's gay bars hoping to impress the clientèle with your arty status as a performer is absolutely the wrong way to go about it, because the attitude of the Edinburgh locals generally towards Fringe performers is at best one of extreme indifference. Within the gay community in particular, they seem to take delight in their own normality. You won't dazzle them by being an actor even if your face is on a poster; in fact, you will probably make yourself ridiculous in their eyes.

So, it is useful to try and fit in with the locals as much as possible if you're not going to end up standing on your own looking awkward (and, depending on your frame of mind, possibly bitter). In fact, this is not as difficult as it may first appear; on the whole, the regulars are a friendly bunch – indeed, in some cases perhaps too friendly. There are no taboos in Edinburgh's gay bars about randomly starting conversations or, in some cases, randomly touching, examining and massaging people.

Ah, yes. One of us, trying to poster the first gay bar we'd been near, found ourselves within 10 minutes being massaged by a man who said he was a professional masseur. We're not sure what he wanted in return, but anyone taking part in the Fringe might want to take note of this free method of getting a massage after a long day's flyering. However, it was an unnerving experience and many people might feel that it is a dubious way of relaxing. They may feel equally unsure about the attentions of the keen admirers who keep trying to get their hands on you in a less professional sense.

So, you might not want to settle with the first group of gay Scots who attach themselves to you, but if you start enough random conversations you're sure to come across some friendly Celts you can actually bear to be with, and it's a fantastic way of learning about the area. And as a last resort you can always go and take part in the karaoke night at CC Bloom's. This is one place where a status as a performer, or just as somebody from further South, may come in handy: choose a suitably showy song (perhaps some Madonna or Bowie) and you will be received like a minor celebrity. (Just don't try anything ironic. If you attempt an impersonation of Louis Armstrong, say, they will just think you're taking the piss.)

CC Bloom's is a fairly typical Edinburghian gay bar: slightly seedy, the carpet could do with a clean, a mixture of people and camp cheese being played throughout the night. Habana is a favourite haunt of Edinburgh's younger gay folk and ever-so-slightly classier. If you wish to continue your evening in a club, our advice is simply to follow everyone else when it comes to closing time. Lists and details of all the possibilities are available everywhere and if you happen to be living around the Leith Walk area you can also use the widely-available gay map of Edinburgh to direct people to your house. The best source of information is the regularly published *ScotsGay*, which not only lists gay events and reviews shows with gay people or camp songs in, but also has a personals section full of adverts along the lines of '14 stone guy with protruding nipples would like to meet a big, hairy, well-hung daddy'. An essential read for everyone, really.

However, don't necessarily expect to find yourself a hot date. The Edinburgh gay community is not renowned for its beauty; as they will themselves happily inform you, 'the fet blooks are all in Glasgae', and for this reason they make regular journeys to go clubbing there for the purpose of bringing back fet blooks. If you ingratiate yourself with enough people you might even be asked to join one of their excursions, and we're sure it's a fine way of seeing Glasgow (or at least select bits of it).

Staying closer to the Fringe, the local gay press contain listings of other nights and, for those more shy, personal ads. Be warned, however, before you start browsing through searching for your perfect gay mate – you may find something like:

'Genuine sock fetish
Sock fetish guy – dark and clean – you know who you are. Non scene guy. 39, 5'9", hairy and masculine with good body. Seeking mature guys with similar interests.'

(In our copy, next to this advert there's a note with a line to 5'9' which just says 'that's one heck of a penis'. Neither of us remembers writing this, and we assume that it didn't come like that, but you never know – and it certainly would be one heck of a penis.)

Performers hoping to attract this wide and varied community to their shows will find that some of the gay bars have space for posters; on the other hand, be wary of bars that aren't displaying any. We once asked the bar staff at Planet Out to put up a poster for me. They graciously obliged, putting the poster up in a prominent position, then demanded free tickets. They justified this demand by saying that it would enable them to tell everyone how good our show was.

Later in the month, we discovered that our poster was no longer on display, and as far as we could tell the talk at the bar was not revolving around our show.

Finally, if you go to any of the gay bars and request a 'wee sherry light', you will get a vodka and diet coke. We have no idea whether this is equally true for the heterosexual bars.

Cash points

When they built Edinburgh, they forgot to put in any cash points. It's not simply a shortage, it's a complete absence. We would advise you to carry a lot of cash around with you, except that when you're in a city full of starving penniless artists that's a really bad idea. Although we said that crime is not a big problem in Edinburgh, there will always be people who might, in the friendliest possible way, clobber you and take your wallet. Scientologists, for example. In any case, if you're carrying a lot of cash you may be tempted to give some to a human statue, or a Peruvian Pan-pipe player, or a taxi driver… or a Scientologist.

Ultimately, you're probably going to end up buying a lot of useless chalk from the nearest newsagent with a debit card and getting cashback. Or you might choose to go hunting for a cash point – but people have gone hunting for cash points in Edinburgh and never returned… because there aren't any.

Internet access

If you're the kind of person who needs to check your email every 10 minutes, there are plenty of options: being a performer at a big venue usually has the perk of free computers with internet, although you have to share them with hundreds of other performers so a willingness to queue for hours then have several people behind you coughing impatiently while you're sending a long email to your aunt is essential. If you are the impatient type, the Fringe Office has cheap internet access and not so many people queuing. If you hunt around there are also plenty of internet cafés and the EasyInternetCafé on Rose Street provides a cheap and efficient service with about a million computers to choose from.

If you're fortunate enough to have a laptop with wireless internet connections then there are plenty of options. The Jolly Judge towards the top of the high street is happy for you to surf away to your heart's content as long as you occasionally buy a drink and, increasingly, the Fringe venues themselves have wireless access so you can sort out your web-business between shows.

Pelican crossings

An entertaining peculiarity of certain pelican crossings in Edinburgh is that they talk. Try the ones on Leith Walk.

In one direction of traffic flow you get an officious male voice, in the other you get a stern but oddly alluring female voice. It is impossible to tell what they are saying, because they speak with impenetrable accents and for all we know are using a weird dialect as well. It sounds like 'Passengers due on the road, have been seen on the rent'. Although parts of that statement may be true, especially in the Leith Walk area, it seems like odd advice to give people who are crossing the road.

Nevertheless, the voices are comforting, and well worth crossing the road for.

The pub that looks a bit like a house from an Enid Blyton book

We don't really know much about this, except that we passed it on a bus once and it looked interesting. It's sitting all on its own in the middle of the road that leads out of Edinburgh towards the airport, and while it's in quite a modern-looking built-up area it has a distinctly old look about it, with fogged-up tiny windows, smoking chimneys and a crooked door. We imagine that there may be an old gnome in there puffing on his pipe and selling magic furniture to unwitting children.

Is anybody who has been inside able to confirm our suspicions?

The Royal Museum

Finally, if you have any time to spare, you may find the Royal Museum on Chambers Street a bit interesting. Certainly if you find yourself needing to keep a couple of tiny cousins entertained there are sufficient amounts of stuffed animals to while away a few hours. But the main reason to go there is without a doubt to witness the scariest clock ever built.

Standing tall and proud at the end of the main hall is a wooden creation that looks like the result of a collaboration between the Brothers Grimm, Tim Burton and Alice Cooper, based on a blueprint by Francis Bacon and produced by Pete Waterman. Figures of starving pregnant women, skeletal dead soldiers and dying children stand among instruments of torture and the walking dead, while grinning skeleton clowns give the twisted suggestion that fun is somehow involved. Somewhere in the midst of it all there is a clock, but it is not the clock that grabs your attention; the passage of time is measured in the agony of the wooden, carved faces that stare at you, pleading for some kind of release.

Then, on the hour, that release comes; the skeletal clowns giggle as the huge visible cogs begin to turn, like in some terrifying expressionist propaganda film about industrialisation, and layer by layer the little figures come to life and start silently screaming; the dying children hit each other with sticks, figures of death start using the weapons of torture, a pair of prison guards begin sawing a man in half and a pregnant woman vomits up her own uterus.

That, at least, is the lasting impression it gives you.

The whole thing is accompanied by sinister tinkly music which implies that Danny Elfman got in on the creative act, and it all seems to last for several hours. It is as close to a glimpse of hell as we have ever come – and in the context of the Edinburgh Fringe, that's really saying something. You'd imagine that it would be wiser to keep the little cousins safely sheltered with the stuffed animals during this spectacle, but our experience shows that although the clock is enough to give grown adults nightmares for weeks on end, the under-5's will happily watch its macabre presentation without batting an eyelid. The current state of children's television probably has a lot to answer for.

Eating and drinking. And drinking.

Edinburgh is a city. Cities are full of places to eat and drink. If you're looking to go out for a drink, Edinburgh is pretty much as good as you're going to get for concentration of drinking establishments (except for most Irish towns). It may not quite compare to Italy for its cuisine, but it is nevertheless full of quality restaurants to suit all tastes. And should you wish to follow that with another drink, you're still laughing. To list all the options here would be a futile waste of space. For one thing, the information is all available in other Edinburgh guides and on the internet, the source of all wisdom and knowledge. For another, we never had enough money to visit all the restaurants and bars anyway.

We're assuming that, like us, a fair few people reading this book will be impoverished artists hoping to eat for as little money as possible, in order to have enough cash left over for a few (hopefully not too expensive) drinks afterwards. We will show you how. Even if you're on a decent salary and visiting for a few days, Edinburgh during the Fringe is frightfully expensive. Just paying for somewhere to stay will have set you back a significant few bob, so knowing about eating and drinking on a budget is always going to be useful.

If you're actually rich, this section may be of less interest, but we'd love to hear from you. We can both sew.

Eating

The first point to make about eating, obvious though it may sound, is that trying to live on one egg sandwich a day is stupid. We make this point because one of us was stupid enough to try it once and it didn't work out for the best.

On the other hand, it is entirely possible to live only on pies while in Edinburgh. Pies are pretty much everywhere you go – just as the Cornish have their pasties, the English have their tea and cakes and the Welsh have their leeks, the Scottish do an extremely good line in pies. Good, nutritious, tasty, succulent pies. The most obvious place to get them in Edinburgh is Piemaker on South Bridge (there are many other pie places, but often tucked away in corners that only the locals know about, and hunting them down probably uses more energy that you'd get from the pies once you get there). As is detailed on the paper bags they give you your pies in, Piemaker sits at the end of an ancient and honourable tradition of pie-making; the history of the pie is traced from Roman times through to the Cornish mining tradition (there we feel they get a little bit mixed up with the concept of pasties) and the subsequent downward turn in the quality of pies caused by the industrial revolution and the mechanisation of the pie-making process. Fortunately, it appears, Piemaker emerged in time to rescue the reputation of the pie with their quality pastry and fillings, making pies once again 'the food of Kings'.

That, at least, is what you can reassure yourself with as you tuck into the fifth pie you've eaten in two days.

With such impressive lineage, then, it is more than feasible to live off a mixture of meat and fruit pies. It just isn't advisable.

In the nature of getting a healthy, balanced diet, you should of course mix in some other food groups. So why not have a day off pies and have a nice burger at The Gourmet Burger on the Royal Mile? Once again, there is much comforting information about their products; all their beef is fully traceable Scotch beef (at least this is what they tell us, we didn't actually bother trying to trace it fully) and their buns are free from artificial flavourings. Reassuring indeed. You also get enough burger to fill you up for the rest of the day. It just may not be the best place to eat if you're planning on running all the way to the next show you've booked to go and see.

If you are trying to fit in several shows between meals, it may just be quicker to take what you can find near the venues themselves. The Pleasance Courtyard has a few options from sandwiches to solid meals – or, if you're really in a hurry, hotdogs. We suspect the latter might occasionally kill people, but we've been lucky so far. The Pleasance Dome also serves snacky bar-style food and since many other venues are built in or around buildings with food-serving capabilities there's never going to be a shortage of chips in Edinburgh. Failing that, look for the vans that hang around some of the venues, the Gilded Balloon in particular – you can always grab a waffle.

To round off your healthy diet of pies, burgers, chips and waffles, you would be foolish not to at least try something from Chocolate Soup on Hunter Square. As the name suggests, their specialities are chocolate and soup. They even do the ultimate combination of the two. You get some biscuity stuff to dip in it, but essentially this is just pure, soupified chocolate. For those not quite brave enough to attempt it, their range of coffees and chocolaty coffees makes it a good place to sit down during the day. But the chocolate soup makes a superb end to any meal.

Actual food

The more sensible Fringe-goer will perhaps make a more concerted effort to eat properly, although many don't. The cheapest way of doing this is naturally the communal eating option covered in the previous chapter, but that isn't always possible or desirable. It's worth knowing that it is possible to get decent, multi-course, non pie/burger/chocolate related fare for very reasonable prices. But as in any city the size of Edinburgh it is also possible that you end up re-mortgaging your house to pay for it. Shopping around to find the prices that suit the size of your wallet is essential.

Looking in the Leith Walk area is a good starting point, as the restaurants are mostly inexpensive and have an individual touch. You just have to bear in mind that this part of town has a rhythm and energy all of its own. Unless you can accept that, you may get upset.

We sat down for a bite to eat in the respectable-looking Giuliano's Bistro on Leith Walk, where the calm, Italian waiters and tinkle of jazz in the background inspired a degree of confidence. However, no sooner had we sat down when the background music stopped to be replaced by an intrusively loud techno beat; in walked a girl in a tartan skirt, who proceeded to lap dance on a bald gentleman at the table next to ours. After removing most of her clothes she directed him in various indecent tasks involving whipped cream and marshmallows, which he threw himself into with alarming zest. Enjoyable though he evidently found it, it was not really the kind of spectacle we were hoping to have to sit through over our salad. The salad itself, though, was rather good.

On the other side of town, we discovered Sardi's Ristorante Italiano on Forest Road. The exact Italian pedigree of this place is debatable – the waitress who served us took our orders with an impenetrable Italian accent but answered the phone in a broad cockney – but a sizeable two-course meal with drinks came to under £20 for the two of us. This is not to say that Sardi's is the only place where this is possible, but to point out that you can eat classy, pseudo-Italian meals at an affordable price.

Urinating

When you are out and about in Edinburgh, hopefully drinking a sensible amount of water and seeing as many things outdoors as possible, it is occasionally going to be necessary to take a leak. This is particularly an issue for flyerers, who may be doing a 2- or 3-hour shift and might quite reasonably hope to empty their bladders occasionally.

The Fringe organisers, brilliant though they are, have not thought to install toilets along the Royal Mile yet and, although it is Scotland, pissing in the street is not usually considered acceptable. The options are therefore quite limited.

The best option is to use toilets at one of the venues, ideally your own – most venues are fairly well-equipped and it is reasonable for you to expect to be able to use their facilities either as a potential audience-member or as one of their performers.

Unfortunately, this is practically quite difficult for most people as it is rare to be afforded the luxury of having a venue near to the best flyering grounds, and the Royal Mile itself is largely lacking in venues altogether. So, the only other thing for it (apart from cultivating a bladder of steel) is to sneakily use the facilities in one of the eating or drinking establishments that line the street. It's important to point out that this is very naughty, as almost all of them have notices up saying 'toilets are for the use of patrons only'. We often found The Filling Station a most convenient place to find relief, despite many, many notices telling us this wasn't allowed unless we patronised the place as well. Shamefully, I don't think we ever so much as bought a drink there. But the toilets are very nice.

If you want to be even more illicit, The Gourmet Burger just next door has a baby-changing toilet. Unless you actually see any babies in there eating burgers, this toilet is guaranteed to be free for use and surely one should feel no guilt about doing so when there are no babies whose convenience you might disturb.

The authors accept no responsibility for wrath incurred by the following of this advice, and suggest that it may be easier just to buy a drink somewhere and use the toilet as a patron – or settle for the empty bottle.

Eating and drinking

Often it's a good idea to find somewhere to eat where you can entrench yourself for the rest of the evening. A popular choice is biblos on Chambers Street, which plays good music and has a touch of class about it. It's a little pricey, particularly for a place that doesn't use capital letters at all, but it's open until 3 a.m. throughout the Fringe, so if you can get a seat it's a good place to stay.

One of the classiest joints we discovered is Centraal on West Nicolson street, which has an exciting range of Belgian beers and leather sofas. It's a bit like drinking on the set of a sophisticated film noir; there's also a range of good food and it's all very reasonably priced. If you're less worried about class, and would prefer to watch a football match or a pop video with your pint and plate of chips, try

The Tron on Hunter Square.

An entertaining option is to seek out the loony Fringe performers who make everything that little bit more unpredictable in August. We once found ourselves in a fairly run-of-the-mill chain pub as part of a group which had assembled for an impromptu Latin lesson from Perrier-nominee Alex Horne. Following a brief 'vocab test' we were all invited to take part in an educational reconstruction of the wooden horse at Troy, using tables, chairs and other customers.

We don't know what the other customers thought – most of them left too quickly for us to ask – but for our money it was better than any widescreen football match.

However, if you've had enough of wacky Fringe performers you could instead seek out one of the slightly out-of-the-way local pubs full of eccentric Scots, who can be every bit as entertaining. The Captains Bar on South College Street, for example, is the size of a large broom cupboard, has a barman you can't understand and an old tramp at the bar drinking two pints of ale and two different whiskies simultaneously, which he will tell you is 'tae get the contrast'. They're very friendly.

And drinking

If all you want to do is get sloshed, then your options are frankly endless. Increasingly, Fringe venues are equipped with alcoholic beverages so you can always combine your drinking with a bit of culture, or at least some substandard comedy. But don't be fooled into thinking that because they serve their lager in plastic 'glasses' these venue bars are nice and cheap like student bars; on the contrary, they see the venue trying to drum up more income to cover its spiralling overheads and you end up paying £2 for a plastic 'glass' of coke which has in fact been poured out of a can.

The cheapest option, should you wish to get drunk after, say, a particularly bad show (either one that you've sat through or one that you've performed in) is the off-licence, where you should pick up a four pack of Special Brew, find a nearby field and drink it all very quickly. If you then hammer on the door of a house being occupied by Fringe performers, you will usually find a bottle of gin to wash it down.

Unless you are unfortunate enough to choose the house of a group of nine-year-old nuns performing *Cabaret*.

Where do shows go?

To most people, the question of what happens to shows after the Fringe is one of theological uncertainty but only academic importance and, in honesty, frank indifference. Like the question of where people go after they die, there is a complex web of possibilities and questions, but sad as it is to see them go, in the end they're gone and many people stop wondering what's happened to them because there are so many living people to take an interest in instead.

Oh yes, a short-sighted way of dealing with death indeed because one day we're all going to die. Perhaps then we'll be wishing we had spent a little less time with the living and a little more time reflecting on where it's all going to end.

So it is with Edinburgh shows. It may be less bothersome to forget about the question of what exactly happened to the production of *Macbethany and the Girls of Edinburgh* that you really rather enjoyed and instead go to London to watch a shamelessly unsophisticated musical (we recommend *Mary Poppins*). But one day we're all going to be in an Edinburgh show that's just finished, wondering exactly what's going to happen to us and where it's going to end.

Okay, perhaps not all of us, but some of us, certainly. In that situation you'll need to know what the options and possibilities are, otherwise, you may wonder until you die, making the worst of both worlds. Either way, in this chapter we, like the church, explain what really happens. Like the church, we're not all that sure about some bits, we just have a lot of theories based on things we've done, things we've read, things we've heard from people who've been doing Edinburgh a little longer than us, and a stack of prejudices we're clinging on to. That really ought to be enough to go on with, until the day when we all discover the truth.

Let's make one thing clear

A lot of shows just die. We know, we know, it's sad. Perhaps it would be kinder to give children little pet Fringe shows when very young so that they learn in advance that even the most diligent producers and dedicated cast members see their babies quietly drop dead at the end of August. Metaphorical babies: as far as we know there isn't actually a connection between Fringe-going and infant deaths (although it wouldn't surprise us, mind). However, in case you're not already aware of the Fringe Facts of Life, we feel it would be cruel not to point out that the mortality rate of Fringe shows is higher than that of extras on *Star Trek* standing towards the back of the shot in an ill-fitting red sweater.

There just isn't any need for all those Fringe shows in real life. Edinburgh gives them their chance to live and breathe, to take their first few stumbling steps and learn the tiniest amount of vocabulary. Only rarely does a show actually grow wings and take flight as an independent and slightly mixed metaphor.

If you're taking a show to Edinburgh, you need to know that. Even if something is going to happen to your show beyond the Fringe, it will almost certainly require even more blood, sweat and toil, more frustration, and far fewer friendly people guiding you through the whole process. The Fringe is a playpen (going with the other metaphor: a nature reserve) compared with the big wide world. Even a degree of success at the Fringe – a few good reviews and/or famous person popping in and deciding they really like your show – guarantees nothing. People sell out at the best venues, people get fantastic reviews, people even win awards at the Fringe and are never heard of again.

The protective, creative atmosphere that allows all kinds of shows to have a stab at life is one of the great things about the Fringe, and a reason both to take shows there and see shows there. But you should have no expectations beyond that. In the circus of the arts, Edinburgh is a freak show, and outside the tent where they belong, freaks get laughed at and abused. (At least, they do in a Victorian society, which is what the arts world still is, on the whole.) It's far kinder to let them die with dignity.

If you understand this, you're far less likely to be distressed by what happens to your own show, the shows of those you love and the shows you feel should, in a fair world, have been the Next Big Thing in cultural history. Though you will still feel sick with envy when shows do actually achieve something after the Fringe.

What happens to the people?

Let's say that the average number of performers at the Fringe each year is about 10,000. This probably doesn't include the many people who run Fringe venues or indeed those who sell hot dogs in the Pleasance Courtyard, and probably leaves out a whole load of others, but it's a good round number and we'll stick to it. All those participants, often bereft of their shows, are left to go their separate ways when the Fringe ends – so where do they go? And how come you hardly ever see them anywhere else?

The following figures attempt to explain exactly what happens to the people who do the Fringe. They are mostly guesses. Well, they're all guesses. Even when the guesses have been based on some prior knowledge, percentages have been rounded up to the nearest whole number, which leaves rather a wide margin of error if we're assuming that 1% is 100 people. Never mind, trust the figures.

- 27% go back to school/university; after all, a large portion of the performers at the Fringe are in productions put on by the establishment at which they are being educated, be it a drama school, a sixth form college or a student drama society in some university.
- 19% become lawyers, the ultimate profession for people who really wanted to be actors, and spend the rest of their lives regretting the fact that they bottled out of performing so young in life, whilst being utterly dissatisfied with all the money they've earned and have no time to spend.
- 15% become bankers; see above, only without wigs.
- 11% return to the real world with no idea what to do at all, having just left their school/law firm/bank. They don't really fancy work, so go back to live with their parents, bathing in the glory of having done

an Edinburgh show that got three stars in *Fest*, because their relatives think that's pretty unique and are therefore prepared to put up with them living at home and sponging off them for the rest of the year.

- 9% continue to struggle to find acting/singing/dancing work in a competitive and small market, constantly taking on rubbish and unpaid productions to feed their addiction to performing, while less picky people do rubbish schools tours about issues such as drink, drugs and homosexuality for which they are well paid but wedded to Satan. A lucky minority get cast in adverts and earn a large amount of money for doing very little, but they too have sold their souls.

- 5% become journalists, having realised how much easier it is to criticise shows than to put them on; applying this principle to real life, they discover how easy it is to criticise everything, and indeed many end up writing for *The Evening Standard.*

- 4% never return. Nobody knows what has happened to them but it is assumed they have either decided to live in Edinburgh because the gay scene is so exciting, or that they have been accidentally locked up in a part of Underbelly that nobody else has yet discovered.

- 3% stay in Edinburgh because that is where they live.

- 3% go back to serious jobs in the creative arts: managing venues or acts, administrating for any number of creative projects or answering the phones for local radio stations.

- 2% get agents from the Fringe and continue to fail to get jobs as actors/singers/dancers; however, they now have somebody else to blame.

- 2% take their shows elsewhere so continue performing for a little while, but in a different environment, which highlights the urgency to come up with plans for something to do after they have finished. They begin planning an Edinburgh show for the next year.

- 1% marry one of their fellow performers.

- 1% are spotted by producers of low-budget straight-to-CD audio dramas and spend the rest of their lives playing a supporting character in a series and signing autographs at conventions for the cultish fan following it has gained.

- 1% become Scientologists.
- 1% die. This seems like quite a high number, but taking into account people who die from old age, those who die from overwork shortly after the Fringe experience, those who catch diseases from human statues and all the accidents there must be travelling back from Edinburgh by land, sea and sky, the figure doesn't seem quite so absurd.
- Kate Copstick goes back to being an actress*.

What these figures ought to highlight, apart from the fact that there are a lot of people out there who are pretty unhappy with what they're doing, is that there are some people at the Fringe who continue performing (or are trying to find ways of performing) in some capacity. (Of course, there are also those Fringe performers who have film, television and stage careers to go back to, but they are so few that the percentage was rounded down to Kate Copstick.) To some people the Fringe is a baptism of fire – if they get through the Fringe and still want to act then they possibly have what it takes. Other wannabe performers are put right off their chosen career by the Fringe and become lawyers. However, when so many people find that what they've gone back to lacks the excitement of the Fringe experience they thought they'd hated, it's maybe not surprising that so many people go back to do the Fringe again. Which suggests the terrifying possibility that the Edinburgh Fringe is actually about as exciting and fulfilling as life can ever get for a large proportion of the population. That's actually quite depressing.

On the bright side, not too many people get blown up by terrorists.

Awards

The Fringe has had many awards in its lifetime, but not all remain – The Perrier, and its moral alternative the Tapwater Awards, *The Scotsman* Fringe Firsts, *The Guardian* Student Drama Awards, The Total Theatre Awards – more will appear and some of these disappear

---

*We are aware that this makes 104%. (Or 104.01% if you count Kate Copstick, which many people do.) That is the problem with rounding up percentages.

in time. While it's awfully exciting to win an award, or even be nominated, it may not actually do that much for you. If you haven't got an agent, you might get one; if you have, you might get a TV show. These things do happen anyway, given enough time spent building up your ability and reputation, and some winners have had no greater visibility since than they had before.

At the end of the day, awards are a recognition of something that is already good enough to go further – and the chance for another party. The quality of the party sometimes leaves something to be desired – a recent Perrier one had karaoke. So be wise, and don't worry about them too much.

Transfers

When a show moves to somewhere else after the Fringe (perhaps even to another medium entirely, such as when Perrier winners sometimes get to rework their shows for TV), it's called a transfer. In many ways it's the best thing that can happen to a show – it keeps it alive, and while it's alive it can make back more of the money that was spent creating it.

Theatrical transfers can happen quickly (the New Ambassadors theatre in the West End does a post-Fringe season), but are usually dead slow (to give you an idea, *Amy Evans' Strike*, a 2001 Fringe First nominee, transferred to The Courtyard at Covent Garden – in 2005).

Transfers off the stage can be slightly faster – plays can move to Radio 4 very quickly and big Fringe successes can be put on TV within months. However even this isn't guaranteed – Garth Marenghi (Perrier winner 2001) didn't make it onto TV until 2004 (although that was a completely new show). To be considered for transfers, just tick the 'available for touring' box on the Fringe form; however, to actually be picked up you may have to spend time shmoozing with scouts, theatre directors, and so on. If this is your life rather than a very big hobby, you really want your show to be able to transfer and one way of making it more likely is if you have representation.

Agents

One reason to take a show up to Edinburgh is for the opportunity to be 'spotted'. Although, as already discussed, it's not the celebrity factory that many people assume it is, it's certainly one place where you might, if you're lucky, be seen by somebody who has the ability to further your career in some way.

Theatrical agents are what every unsigned actor dreams of having, and what every signed actor spends most of their time complaining about. There are many different types of agency, ranging from big companies who manage performers at the same time as producing theatre and television, to smaller, more personal management and cooperative agencies. Different agents specialise in different types of performer, too: some only manage comedians, others only manage certain types of actor and others manage only people who are already doing big Hollywood films.

There are various directories that list agents, who they represent and how to approach them. It's essential to check this out carefully because if you write to one of the agents who only deals in Hollywood celebrities they won't even finish reading your letter before handing it to the person who is employed solely to put things through the shredder. (Unless you happen to be Alan Rickman, in which case many thanks for reading this book, we're both admirers of your work and if you ever wish to employ us to write a film for you or in fact do any menial task we'd be more than willing to oblige – we can both sew.)

Writing to agents is the first thing to do – and you've got to write to them, they're not going to just turn up to your show – and you need to do it several weeks before the Fringe; if you're lucky, they'll at least be sending a representative up to Edinburgh for a few days so they may be able to fit you into their schedule, as long as they have enough advance warning. You should enclose as much information about yourself and the show as you think they'll read (i.e. not very much) and return postage. However, with any letter you send off, you ought to be prepared for one of the following three responses.

1   Nothing. It's very annoying, especially as you're probably wondering exactly what they're doing with your return postage. If it was us, we'd be sticking one of those 're-use envelopes' labels over your address and using them for all our admin post, saving us from ever having to buy stamps. But agents are more principled than we are. Surely?

2   Dear James,
Many thanks for your letter and the information you sent us about *Macbeth on Ice*. It looks very interesting. Unfortunately, Carris and Hunt are not currently taking on actors, as our books are full. We wish you all the best with your search for an agent and hope that your show is a success.
Yours sincerely,
Joanna Hunt

This letter, reproduced almost word for word by so many agents, is also very annoying. 'If my show looks so interesting,' you find yourself hissing at the walls of your bedsit, 'why aren't you at least coming to see it? *Clearly* you don't wish me all the best with my search for an agent because the other agents are your competitors, unless you actually think I'm shit so are wishing me onto another agent with malicious motives. You *obviously* don't hope that my show is a success, because if it is a success you'll be kicking yourself for having missed it.'

And what *does* this oft-repeated phrase 'not currently taking on actors as our books are full' really mean? Do agents only ever take on somebody new when one of their clients *dies*? In which case, how does *anyone* get an agent? Do they scour the obituaries column every day, and quick as a flash ring up saying, 'I notice you represented John Gielgud. I'm not old, blind or brilliant, but...'?

3   Dear James
Many thanks for your letter and the information you sent us about *The Sound of Music on Ice* (with little nuns). It looks unique. Unfortunately, we already have somebody with your skills and appearance on our books.

All the best with your production and future career.
Yours sincerely,
Rachael Hock

This is the most distressing letter of all. Just who is this person with your skills and appearance? Are your skills and appearance really so ordinary that another person could have exactly the same combination? What is his address so you can eliminate him, or at least change his appearance in some way?

Brace yourself for these responses, because nine out of ten agents you write to will use one of them. So do the maths – if you want to be seen by an agent, you need to write 10 letters. If you want to increase your chances of being seen by an agent who actually likes what you do, you probably need to write to 50, 60, perhaps even 80 or 90 agents. It's tedious, but the more letters you write off, the better your chances.

Even then, don't raise your hopes.

However, some people are successful, particularly those in relatively high-profile productions, and the post-Edinburgh period brings with it a world of new possibilities: the chance to have an agent, to get more auditions, possibly to make a living of sorts by doing acting.

If you're in that situation, hold your horses; don't rush into anything. Naturally, having an agent interested in signing you is a great situation and the temptation is to put your name on any bit of paper shoved in front of you. It is vital to make sure you've read the small print or, rather, since reading is often a bit of a challenge for theatrical types, that you've discussed thoroughly with your potential agent what your plans for the future are and what they are going to do about it. Make sure that you trust them and get on well with them. Make sure you know what they're expecting from you. There is nothing worse than getting stuck with an agent with whom you don't see eye to eye, who is going to continually send you to auditions for television costume dramas when you want to do musical theatre, and who doesn't really like you anyway. It sounds like an unlikely situation, but agents are only human and at the end of the day they sign people who they think will make them money, so you can't assume they'll be finding you the kind of work you're interested in.

Negotiations with agents can take months, but in the end it's worth it for the security of knowing what you're walking into. You are also far less likely to let them down – and if you're going to complain about somebody constantly it's well worth getting to know them first.

Talent scouts and casting directors

Talent scouts are not, as the name suggests, followers of Baden Powell dedicated not only to doing good turns and lighting fires, but to doing it really, really well because they're naturally good at it.

In fact, talent scouts are just scouts who are out to get their 'talent' badge by discovering somebody else who is naturally good at something and putting them into some sort of arena to show off their skill.

The nature of these arenas varies – some kind of variety show, a cruise liner or perhaps a TV show. In any case, it's doesn't hurt to get seen by them.

The problem is, you never really know where they're going to be or who they are, and they tend to visit shows that are doing quite well or that really interest them – so, just like any ordinary punter. You'll know who they are if they come to your show and like it, but that doesn't help you get them to your show in the first place.

Your best bet is to hang around a big venue to see if you can spot anyone with a clipboard or a special pass, then flyer them with your most charming pitch spending plenty of time explaining what's so good about your show. The only downside is that you may end up spending a long time flyering the boiler man. If you're very fortunate, you may spot somebody with a clipboard chatting to another performer and saying something like, 'I'm a talent scout'. In this case, they're almost certainly a talent scout. That, or a wily boiler man trying to get a free ticket.

A more likely option is to get a casting director to see you. Casting directors choose people to be in a variety of film, television and stage productions, and are obviously in a position to give your career a good kick up the backside. Unlike talent scouts, you can write to them in the same way as you might write to an agent. The same rules apply, however: write lots of letters and prepare for disappointment. Although casting directors are never going to tell you that their 'books are full', they are busy people and most won't have the time to come and see you.

It does happen, though – people do get spotted at the Fringe. There are people whose careers are launched by that one fortunate time when a casting director couldn't get a ticket for Paul Merton so went to see them in *Bacmeth – the Dyslexic Tyrant* instead, discovered their talent and cast them in a big television drama which propelled them into the limelight and won them a Golden Globe for the second series.

It just doesn't happen to very many people.

Doing the Fringe again

Practice with us: 'I will not do the Fringe again'. Nice. Repeat: 'I will not do the Fringe again'. Once more. Actually, write it out on a blackboard, like Bart Simpson: 'I will not do the Fringe again'.

Well done; you've got it. Now book your accommodation for next year. We'll see you there.

Appendix 1: 'Festival'

In 2004 a film entitled *Festival* was released. The first feature from director and writer Annie Griffin, it was promoted as a film which would finally reveal all about the laughter and tears behind the Edinburgh Fringe.

Having been commissioned at around the same time to write a book which would finally reveal all about the laughter and tears behind the Edinburgh Fringe, we were a bit pissed off. When you're telling friends and relatives that, oh, by the way, you've been commissioned to write a book about the Fringe which will hit the shelves next August, the last thing you want to hear is 'really? They've just made a film about that, haven't they?'

Nevertheless, we saw it as our duty to watch the film and comment on it. Not in the sense of telling you whether it's any good and would be worth your while to rent when you have a spare evening. Although it would be difficult to write anything about this film without at least hinting that not a single character behaves in a way that remotely resembles the way people act in real life (except perhaps the ditzy blond comedienne – one caricature that, alas, one really does meet occasionally). Or that if this were a Fringe show it would be worthy of a two, or at most a three star review, but since it purports to be a professional film, which clearly received funding from a number of sources, it is worthy only of contempt.

No, our purpose in writing about the film is this: how accurately does the film portray the one character that we are interested in - that of the Fringe itself?

To which the answer is very simply: about as accurately as Pearl Harbour manages to give an unbiased, unsensationalist, factual account of the events of 7th December 1941.

This film has as much to do with the Edinburgh Fringe as *Robin Hood, Prince of Thieves* has to do with archery. Although some of the scenes show an awareness of what happens at the Fringe, they are so far removed from the reality that it suggests Annie Griffin is somebody who has heard about the Fringe but not actually experienced it. She certainly hasn't read our book, and quite possibly writes for *Hollyoaks**.

In fact, you can learn more about the broad spectrum of material at the Fringe (and indeed see the most entertaining element of the film) by watching the deleted scenes of the jury deciding who should win the comedy award. One hopes that it is not an accurate portrayal of the way nominees for comedy awards are chosen, although one suspects it's closer to the truth than the rest of what we see. Certainly, the oblique references to the shows under consideration give a far better suggestion of a thriving, varied festival than anything we actually see of it.

The film itself explores alcoholism, paedophilia, fame, suicide and lots and lots of sex – such a bizarre collection of unrelated subjects that it begins to resemble a particularly gruesome piece of Fringe theatre, in fact – but of the festival itself we see very little. This is not to say that alcoholism, or at least alcohol in large quantities, doesn't feature in many people's experience of the Fringe. Paedophilia we would hope features less frequently. Fame, as we have already made clear, is experienced by so few people that it's best not to mention it. And the number of people who commit suicide is anybody's guess. And as for all the sex – that's surely an exaggeration? In this fictional Edinburgh it seems you can't walk into your rented living room without a horny actor desperately trying to seduce you. You can't walk past an innocent puppet shop without spying a comedian getting a good fisting. If any of this resembles a genuine experience of the Fringe, all we can say is that we've been living in the wrong houses and walking past the wrong puppet shops.

In any case, where on earth do they find the time? Perhaps there are people who do go up to the Fringe and enjoy a huge amount of sexual activity, but we find it difficult to believe that any of them find the time to do a show as well, least of all a successful one. As for the scene where a comedian shags a critic – well, that's just stretching credulity too far.

What we do see of the Fringe, apart from the few inserts of real life activity on the Royal Mile (a big cheer for the man with the hooters),

---

*Our research has not revealed any writing credits for *Hollyoaks* in her name, but then if you wrote for *Hollyoaks* you wouldn't necessarily use your real name, would you?

is hardly the most convincing set of scenes. The film starts with a young hopeful getting off a coach and touching the ground in gleeful excitement of being on Scottish soil. Actually, the roads in Edinburgh are pretty dirty – you wouldn't do that. Before she has even had a chance to drop her bags off at her accommodation, she is off along the road flyering people for her one-woman show. Again, you wouldn't do that. When you arrive in Edinburgh clutching half of your worldly possessions, you do not start handing out flyers, however keen you are. You are exhausted and clutching too many bags. The first thing you do is find the person with keys to whatever space you are renting and head for the place that you're going to be living.

Common sense aside, the more objectionable holes in her little plotlet are the ones relating to her show. When she turns up at her venue she discovers they've changed the time slot she was offered; no venue, however badly organised, would move a performer from an 11 p.m. slot to a 9 a.m. slot without telling them first and renegotiating prices. We then see her in a technical rehearsal with the theatre technicians, who are apparently doing the lighting for every show in the venue, doing a detailed (i.e. lengthy) rehearsal so they know exactly when to click on the yellow light to represent daffodils. So let's get this straight: this is somebody doing a one-woman show entirely without support from any kind of crew, relying on a venue whose techies light every show they have on and who have managed to schedule several hours of technical rehearsal for each of their performers.

Those wishing to see a film with a less fantastical style may wish to consider Jim Henson's masterpiece *Labyrinth*, or perhaps one of the Pokemon movies.

When we see this poor unrealistic character's show it turns out to be dreadful. That in itself is not necessarily a poor representation of what goes on in Edinburgh, but given the details already related, particularly the fact that she is entirely on her own, one wouldn't expect her to actually get audiences, or even survive Edinburgh for more than a week. (One-woman shows never do get audiences, anyway.)

A stronger element in the film is provided by the Canadian actors who spend most of their time lounging around their rented flat. Their behaviour in these scenes is pretty weird, but then they're Canadians – we don't know many Canadians, but we were convinced. What we see of their pretentious devised theatre, which involves slide projectors and a moment where the audience are invited to smell grass and reminisce about their childhood, is convincingly cringe-worthy and not far from some actual shows we have seen. What doesn't ring true (again) is the size of the audiences we see: there are actors who spend all day lounging about in their flats, but they don't get audiences. Theatre of that nature certainly doesn't get the rapturous response we see in this film. It gets people leaving halfway through, something that is notably lacking in the 102 minutes of *Festival* (except perhaps in the cinemas it was shown in).

Even less convincing are the audiences in the comedy shows glimpsed in the film. The comedians we see in these scenes are abysmal; this is not altogether unlike real life, because there are indeed many comedians in Edinburgh who do deliver earth-shatteringly awful material while drunk. But the audiences in this film, without fail, roar with laughter.

Since comedy is the main focus of this film, it is worth pointing out that stand-up comedy (not just at the Fringe, but in general) is nothing like what we see in *Festival*. Unless you are playing to your family, no audience will laugh and clap if you're not funny. Particularly at the Fringe, where there is always another comedy show just down the road, if you go onstage with material this poor you will not get laughs, you will get crucified. In the cosy fantasy world that the film occupies, a heckle put-down like, 'you're a cunt' gets whoops and cheers and applause. In real life, it would be greeted with a response along the lines of, 'you're a cunt too' and probably several pints of beer being chucked at the stage.

But then again, in the cosy fantasy world that the film occupies, these are the comedians who get nominated for big comedy awards. Again, not in real life, even if you do shag one of the judges. The comedy award leads to the film's climactic scene, the award ceremony itself, and without giving away what happens it is about as contrived as you can get in a film that apparently sets out to be realistic.

Of course, the film never claimed to be an accurate guide to the Fringe and everything in it, and for the sake of pure entertainment films have to take liberties with reality. However, it's a pity that this film is so far removed from the truth, because the real Fringe has far more interesting, touching and hilarious climactic moments than any of the contrived comedy and tragedy on show here. In fact, the Fringe itself is one damn fine drama, which suggests there is still a cracking film to be written about it – one in which the Fringe does not merely form the backdrop to an episode of *Hollyoaks*, but which shows something of the variety, the tears and the laughter of the actual Fringe. To be honest, it's all here in this book, so if anybody wants to adapt it for the big screen we're more than happy to negotiate.

Appendix 2: The Fit Scotsman Contest

It was found by some people in our last cast to be both a way of building up the anticipation for our trip to the Fringe and also a diverting challenge amidst the Fringe madness to have a competition to see who could pull 'a fit Scotsman'.

The authors would point out that not everybody in the cast took part in this contest, and the results were felt to be rather an anticlimax after the exciting build-up. Nevertheless, in case anybody else should wish to enjoy this challenge at their Fringe, we have included the rules that were devised below.

Happy pulling.

RULES

The aim of the contest is to pull a fit Scotsman, in line with the following definitions of the words 'pull', 'fit', 'Scot' and 'man':

PULL – some form of invasive bodily contact, either facial or above/below, but including at least one kiss of a perverted nature, implied or otherwise. 'Pulling' somebody in any other manner, for example up a hill in a cart, is not acceptable.

FIT – not necessarily as in well-toned and exercised; meaning attractive, in terms agreed on by no less than two fellow cast members, who shall take into account differences of taste but not necessarily make allowances for fetishes about things generally considered *not* to be fit, e.g. red hair, wrinkly eyes, protruding nipples.

SCOT – of direct Scottish lineage, either by one or more parents or a verifiable link with a significant Scottish personage (e.g. Sean Connery, Robert the Bruce); or in exceptional circumstances, somebody named Scott. A definite explanation and verification of this aspect of the pull is vital – it is not acceptable simply to pull an English person with a funny accent, or even a French person.

MAN – not a woman. An effeminate man is acceptable. A transsexual will need to be discussed by the cast, depending on how fit they are. Janet Street-Porter, although manly, is *not* acceptable.

Points will be awarded out of ten for each pull depending on the criteria of: the nature of the pull, the fitness of the pull, the Scottishness of the pull, and in extreme circumstances the manliness of the pull, although it is to be generally accepted that the pull is a man. The fitness of the pull is a prime aspect to be considered. If the pull is thoroughly revolting, however significant the pull, it must not be awarded more than two points.

Points will be accumulated per person for each *new* pull; pulling the same fit Scotsman more than once will not result in any further awardage of points.

Scottish people seem to be genuinely ugly all round. This should be taken into account when assessing their fitness.

Pulling somebody not Scottish *must not* in any way be included in this contest. I mean, well done! Hurrah! But *nul points.*

If 50 points are achieved by anybody before the end of the Fringe, they shall be labelled either a slut, or extremely fortunate.

Trousers may be employed.

The authors

James Aylett first appeared at the Edinburgh Fringe in 1995, wailing loudly and wearing a dress. As an undergraduate he performed and wrote regularly for the Cambridge Footlights, as well as taking roles in the usual swathes of Shakespeare, Shaffer and Ibsen, before squirreling himself away in the world of advertising where he has a tendency to invent things and give them really obscure names. Having developed an interest in film making and even spent a month in New York especially to learn about it, he has recently turned to the (somewhat affordable) medium of the short film, and was recently Director of Photography for *Hide and Seek*. A co-founder of improvisation group The Uncertainty Division, he has directed a number of the group's narrative shows, and performed in all of them, appearing across the country in a variety of guises, many of them wailing loudly and wearing a dress.

James Lark works sporadically as an actor, writer and musician, occasionally combining all three such as in his 2006 Edinburgh show *The Rise and Fall of Deon Vonniget*, a culmination of years of traipsing around venues all over the country singing comic songs about cheese. But he has done some serious plays as well, and when not acting in them he is usually directing the music for them. He has written for *Ealing Live!*, Focus Theatre Company and *The Friday Thing* and one of his monologues on BBC Radio won a Jerusalem Award in 2004. He has had music performed all over the world by the likes of English Voices, Girton College Choir and the organist Guy Bovet. He has co-written, directed and scored several short films, and written a couple of features which are now gathering dust. Although he co-founded the Uncertainty Division and has performed in all of their shows, he is a different person to James Aylett.

Although they are different people, as well as sharing the same name they share a blog which you can find at http://www.talktorex.co.uk/

They can both sew.

Index.